Artificial Intelligence and
Turbo Pascal

Artificial Intelligence and Turbo Pascal

Christopher F. Chabris

DOW JONES-IRWIN
HOMEWOOD, ILLINOIS 60430

This publication is designed to provide accurate and authoritative information in regard to the subject matter covered. It is sold with the understanding that the publisher is not engaged in rendering legal, accounting, or other professional service. If legal advice or other expert assistance is required, the services of a competent professional person should be sought.

From a Declaration of Principles jointly adopted by a Committee of the American Bar Association and a Committee of Publishers.

Library of Congress Catalog Card No. 87-61304

Printed in the United States of America

1 2 3 4 5 6 7 8 9 0 MT 0 9 8 7 6 5 4 3 2 1

ISBN 1-55623-074-5 [book]
ISBN 0-87094-963-2 [book/disk]

TRADEMARKS
ANSA is a registered trademark of Paradox, Inc.
Clout is a registered trademark of MicroRim, Inc.
Connection Machine is a registered trademark of Thinking Machines Corp.
Deskpro 386 is a registered trademark of Compaq Computer Corp.
HAL, 123 are registered trademarks of Lotus Development Corp.
INTELLECT is a registered trademark of Artificial Intelligence Corp.
Macintosh II is a registered trademark of Apple Computer, Inc.
MACSYMA is a registered trademark of Symbolics, Inc.
muMATH is a registered trademark of The Soft Ware House
Personal System/2 is a registered trademark of International Business Machines Corp.
Q&A is a registered trademark of Symantec, Inc.
VAX is a registered trademark of Digital Equipment Corp.

Figure 8-3 is reprinted with permission from *Vision*, by David Marr, W. H. Freeman and Company, 1982. Figure 8-4 is reprinted with permission from BBC *Horizon*.

To my parents

TABLE OF CONTENTS

PREFACE xiii

CHAPTER 1:   INTRODUCTION AND HISTORICAL BACKGROUND............. 1
    What is Artificial Intelligence? 1
    AI Applications 2
        Natural Language Processing 3
        Expert Systems.. 4
        Game Playing.. 5
    The History of Artificial Intelligence... 6
    The Computer and the Brain.. 14
    About this Book.. 16
        Organization and Topics Covered 17
        Programs and Exercises... 18
        Supplemental Material... 19
    References 19

CHAPTER 2:   GENERAL ISSUES 21
    Theories of Intelligence 21
    Detecting and Measuring Intelligence 23
    What Makes a Computer Program Intelligent?............................ 24
    A Knowledge Based Approach.. 26
        Knowledge Representation 27
        The Prepare/Deliberate Tradeoff...................................... 28
        Procedural and Declarative Knowledge 29
    Critics of Artificial Intelligence 30
        Hubert Dreyfus.. 30
        Joseph Weizenbaum 32
        John Searle... 33
    Human Beings and Machines... 35
    References 36

CHAPTER 3:   KNOWLEDGE REPRESENTATION......................................   **38**
   Representing Knowledge   39
   Semantic Networks   40
      Architecture of Semantic Networks....................................   40
      Design of Semantic Networks   43
      Manipulation of Semantic Networks   46
      Quillian's Semantic Networks...   49
      Problems with Semantic Networks   50
   Frame Systems   52
      Value Inheritance..   53
      Defaults and Cancellation...   56
      Procedure Attachment..   57
   Semantic Primitives and Episodic Memory..............................   57
      Conceptual Dependency...   58
      Scripts for Understanding   59
   Problems in Knowledge Representation   62
      The Type/Token Distinction...   62
      Intension versus Extension   65
      The Frame Problem   66
   A Frame Database in Pascal..   67
   Programming Exercises   68
   Summary...   69
   References   70

CHAPTER 4:   NATURAL LANGUAGE PROCESSING.............................   **72**
   What is a Language?...   73
   Syntax, Semantics, and Pragmatics   74
   Parsing Languages...   76
      Regular Languages..   77
      Context-free Languages   79
      Context-free Subsets of Natural Languages.........................   84
      Weak and Strong Context-free Languages   89
      General Grammars and Augmented Transition Networks.....   90
   Natural Language Interfaces to Software Systems......................   95
   A Natural Language Interface in Pascal....................................   98
   Programming Exercises   100
   Summary...   101
   References   102

CHAPTER 5:   EXPERT SYSTEMS AND KNOWLEDGE ENGINEERING **104**
What is an Expert System? 105
Applications of Expert Systems.. 105
Capabilities and Components of an Expert System 108
Case Study 1: Medical Diagnosis 109
    Production Rules 112
    Certainty Factors 114
    Goal-Oriented Reasoning.. 115
    Metalevel Knowledge 118
    Introspection and Learning 119
Case Study 2: Digital Electronics Troubleshooting 124
Knowledge Engineering 127
Performance of Expert Systems.. 130
A Production System in Pascal... 132
Programming Exercises 133
Summary.. 135
References 135

CHAPTER 6:   HEURISTIC SEARCH... **137**
What is Search? 137
Search Applications... 141
Basic Search Algorithms... 141
    The "British Museum" Procedure 141
    A General Search Strategy 142
    Depth-First Search... 143
    Breadth-First Search 147
    Comparing Depth-First and Breadth-First Search 151
    Operators May Not Have Equal Cost.................................. 152
    Uniform-Cost Search 155
Intelligent Searching 158
    Best-First Search 158
    The A* Algorithm 160
    The Behavior of A*.. 161
A New Search Example 162
    Measuring Search 163
    Design of Heuristics 166
    Choice of Search Algorithm 167
The A* Algorithm in Pascal 169

Programming Exercises 169
Summary 171
References 172

CHAPTER 7: GAME PLAYING **173**
MINIMAX and Game Trees 174
Refining MINIMAX 177
Cutting Off Search with Static Evaluations 177
Alpha-Beta Pruning 180
    Analysis of α–β Pruning 184
    Alternatives to α–β Pruning 185
Enhancements to the α–β Algorithm 186
    Quiescence Search 186
    Iterative Deepening 188
    Killer Move Heuristic 188
Game Playing in Pascal 189
Programming Exercises 192
Summary 193
References 194

CHAPTER 8: FUTURE DIRECTIONS **195**
Computer Vision 195
    The Vision Problem 196
    Representation in Vision 197
    Edge Detection 199
Machine Learning 203
    Rote Learning 204
    Concept Learning 207
    EPAM Models 207
    Version Space Models 211
Connectionism 214
    Applications to Speech Production 215
    Perceiving in Parallel 218
    The Problem of Sequential Processes 222
    Programming Connectionist Systems 224
References 225

APPENDIX 1: BIBLIOGRAPHY **227**
    AI Textbooks 227
    Monographs 229
    Articles, Papers, and Technical Reports 236
    Anthologies 255
    AI Languages 259
    Pascal and Programming 260

APPENDIX 2: SOURCES OF AI INFORMATION **261**
    Organizations 261
    Magazines 262
    Journals 263
    Industry Newsletters 265
    Online/Telecommunications Services 266
    Miscellaneous Resources 267

APPENDIX 3: AI PRODUCTS AND MANUFACTURERS **268**
    Programming Languages 268
    Software Tools and Applications 272
    Hardware Systems 276
    Consulting and Research Organizations 277

APPENDIX 4: GLOSSARY OF AI TERMINOLOGY **281**

APPENDIX 5: TURBO PASCAL SUMMARY **302**
    Compiler Directives 303
    Compiler Error Messages 303
    Editor Commands 305
    I/O Error Messages 307
    Runtime Error Messages 307
    Standard Identifiers 308

INDEX **310**

PREFACE

Writing *Artificial Intelligence and Turbo Pascal* has brought rewards far greater than the usual satisfaction that comes from producing a book manuscript. It has involved me in the exciting discoveries being made every day in areas like expert systems, natural language processing, game playing, and robotics. These are discoveries that will drive the development of a new generation of application software for the hardware of the 1990s and the next century. By making computers smarter and easier to use, AI technology will change business, education, government, and the way we work. Even today, the memory and processing needs of sophisticated AI programs are available from operating systems like Unix and computers like the Apple Macintosh II, Compaq Deskpro II, and IBM PS/2 Model 80.

I believe that *Artificial Intelligence and Turbo Pascal* is an authorative, readable guide to the key fields within artificial intelligence that will help you to do three things: write more interesting, easy-to-use, "intelligent" software; examine the flood of new products claiming to incorporate exotic "fifth generation AI technology" and make more informed decisions; and evaluate artificial intelligence as a science. And, the illustrative programs should demystify AI applications by demonstrating how simple algorithms can produce intelligent behavior.

Please report any corrections or additions you may note to the programs to me. I am especially interested in seeing your own improvements to or versions of the programs, even if they just follow the suggestions in the programming exercises. General comments are also welcomed, and while I cannot guarantee a personal response, I may be contacted in writing at this address:

Christopher F. Chabris
15 Sterling Road
Armonk, NY, 10504

I may also be contacted via electronic mail on Compuserve Information Service at PPN 73277,305. I look forward to your comments.

Finally, I would like to thank Alan Rose of Multiscience Press for his help, hard work, and reassurances, Richard L. Graves for introducing my father and me to Alan, Susan Glinert of Dow Jones-Irwin for taking a chance, and my parents for encouraging and supporting my efforts. Eric F. Bryan wrote the programs, Paul

King helped to port and debug them, and Shawn Wallace did the artwork and layout. Jonathan Amsterdam, Jack Chen, Brad Christie, Alec Crawford, Oren Etzioni, Jamie Hamilton, and many others made valuable comments and suggestions. Professor Harry R. Lewis taught me about computer science, Professors Mark Friedell and Jay Rueckl got me interested in artificial intelligence and cognitive psychology, and Bud Pollak, Robert Shapiro, and Alan Pryor taught me how to write. Jon Bell, James Caparell, Robert DeWitt, Nat Friedland, Matt Loveless, Jack Powell, Tay Vaughan, and Gary Yost, all of Antic Publishing at one time or another, have been kind enough over the years to publish the articles and manuals that enabled me to write this book.

Cambridge, Massachusetts
April, 1987

1. Introduction and Historical Background

Artificial Intelligence, or AI for short, looms large in the present and future of both computer science and industry. The applications emerging from university research laboratories are making their way to commercial products with increasing speed. Programs providing capabilities like English-language communication, expert reasoning and problem solving, and even master level chess skill are having a profound effect on how people use computers and what they use them for.

New developments in AI are often reported in the popular press as though they are the mysterious, unpredictable effects of some magical incantations devised by reclusive wizards in ivory towers, as though AI were a secret science practiced by a small sect that hides its knowledge from the rest of us. Far be it for microcomputer users and programmers to question the technology behind the arcane arts of Natural Language Processing or Chess Computers, let alone Expert Systems!

Of course, this vision is not a completely realistic picture of artificial intelligence. AI is a complex science, practiced by scientists and engineers in universities and corporations, but it is not magic. AI programs do not differ in any fundamental way from the programs you may be used to writing; in fact, they may be quite similar. The main objective of this book is to use *Turbo Pascal* to provide an introduction to AI from both the scientific/theory and engineering/application viewpoints, and to teach several basic algorithms and programming techniques that have been used in various AI applications. After reading the main chapters, you will be conversant in AI terminology and concepts, and should be able to use AI techniques to design and program your own "intelligent software."

What is Artificial Intelligence?

As an idea, artificial intelligence can provoke both fear and philosophical controversy. While many people possess an almost religious faith in AI, others will violently resist the very notion that a machine can be made to think like a human being

1

does. But though they may dispute its ultimate feasibility, defenders and detractors alike can usually agree that AI as a science is fascinating but misunderstood.

We will discuss some of the important issues AI raises in Chapter 2. But for our purposes here, we will make what I believe to be a reasonable assumption: that true AI is at least theoretically possible. After all, you wouldn't have read this far if you didn't have some belief in the *possibility* that a computer can, say, mimic the reasoning of human experts. But AI is much more than expert systems. As I see it, artificial intelligence is a highly interdisciplinary science composed of three closely related areas of investigation:

- **Robotics**: By this I mean not industrial automation, tactile sensing, or motion planning, but rather a general research program whose ultimate goal is the construction, by any available means, of a complete artificial simulation of a human being, presumably including both mental and physical attributes. It seems that many opponents of AI have chosen to target this goal of AI for criticism because it has serious philosophical and social implications and is still far from being achieved after decades of research.

- **Cognitive Science**: This is the study of cognition, or the thought processes, structures, and mechanisms used by human beings. Many psychologists working in this area use computer models of intelligence to help them learn more about the brain, and as we shall see later, more and more computer scientists are turning to cognitive models for insight into their own problems.

- **Intelligent Software**: We will concern ourselves primarily with making existing computer systems smarter—the engineering, applications-oriented side of the AI discipline, the art of writing experimental programs that display intelligent behavior. We will try to apply the theories and techniques of AI to make computers more useful to people and more fun to program.

AI Applications

Applied AI research concentrates on several different areas, most notably *natural language processing*, *expert systems*, and *game playing*, which will be covered in detail in later chapters. But before we move on to the historical development of artificial intelligence, we will get a brief preview of some of the real-world applications that motivate that basic research.

Natural Language Processing

Perhaps because of some old hyperinflated advertising claims about the BASIC programming language, this is something that many people think computers can already do, almost as though it were an inherent ability of the silicon wafer in the microprocessor chip. Natural language processing (NLP), the action being performed by a computer program that can accept some non-trivial inputs in a human language, is actually a difficult task that is far from being fully realized.

However, strong NLP capabilities will become essential to applications like database management and query in order to make them as easy to use as possible. Rudimentary front-end systems for microcomputer products can translate requests like "How many minority students took 20 or more units of credit last quarter?" into a database query language. Many database vendors, including Symantec, Ansa, and Microrim, are touting the AI capabilities of their products, and Lotus is selling HAL (Human Access Language) for its popular 1-2-3 spreadsheet package. The following sets of questions are representative of the kinds of inputs that current NLP systems are capable of understanding (of course, to answer the questions, an appropriate database is also necessary):

- How much does John F. Smith owe in his account? What was the date of the last purchase by Mary C. Jones? What did she buy? (*Clout*, Microrim)

- How many Spruance class ships are there? Who is the captain of the Kennedy? What is the length of Old Ironsides? (*LIFER*, SRI International)

- What are the sales of all products for February? Which sales region sold the most dishwashers? Which salesperson in the central region generated the most sales of refrigerators? (*INTELLECT*, Artificial Intelligence Corporation)

Clearly, applications software featuring the user-friendliness and convenience such NLP systems can offer will become increasingly prevalent as microcomputers spread throughout the business world.

No introduction to natural language processing would be complete without mention of the infamous *ELIZA* program by Joseph Weizenbaum of MIT. ELIZA could carry on a sort of stylized conversation with a user typing at a terminal. The program was designed to act like a psychologist, seemingly attempting to probe the thoughts and feelings of the user-patient. Amazingly enough, many people who encountered the program came away convinced that it understood and actually cared about their problems; one became so absorbed that she would only consult with ELIZA when no one else was in the room! Here is a sample conversation, with the program's output in italics:

> Men are all alike.
> > *In what ways?*
> They're always bugging us about something or other.
> > *Can you think of a specific example?*
> Well, my boyfriend made me come here.
> > *Your boyfriend made you come here.*
> He says I am depressed much of the time.
> > *I am sorry to hear that you are depressed.*
> It's true. I am unhappy.
> > *Do you think coming here will help you not to be unhappy?*
> I need some help, that much seems certain.
> > *What would it mean to you if you got some help?*
> Perhaps I could learn to get along with my mother.
> > *Tell me more about your family.*

We will not cover ELIZA or its derivatives in this book because it is quite far from the state of the NLP art. It relies on a primitive technique called *keyword analysis* to select certain words in the input sentence and insert them in precreated responses; for example, there is probably a rule specifying that whenever the user mentions "mother" the response should be "Tell me more about your family" or something similar. As we will see, modern NLP systems use sophisticated syntactic analyses and must integrate semantics, pragmatics, and real-world knowledge to do frontier applications like news digesting and story understanding.

Expert Systems

The most celebrated result of artificial intelligence research to date has been the *expert system* (ES), a computer program that purports to mimic the ability of a human expert in some narrow field of knowledge to reason about and solve difficult problems. In theory, by a process called *knowledge engineering*, a group of knowledge engineers corner the experts and torture their hard-won knowledge out of their minds and into the computer. In practice, it's not that violent, since the experts are usually either willing, ordered, or paid a sizable fee to comply peacefully.

Expert Systems can repay their costs very quickly if they enable automation of expensive reasoning processes like medical diagnosis or chemical structure discovery. Although many architectures for expert systems are being explored, the typical program uses a large number of IF-THEN *production rules* that specify conclusions that can be drawn whenever certain necessary preconditions are satisfied. The sequential application of these rules guides the user either forwards, from a set of observed facts to a solution, or backwards, from a hypothesis through a logical proof that it is consistent with the data.

Since they require sizable computational resources, both in memory and speed, expert systems are just now coming into their own for microcomputers with the widespread use of 16-bit and the advent of 32-bit processors. To spare users most of the complexities of ES programming, many vendors have released *shells* for ES development, tools that provide all the functionality of a complete system except for the domain-specific rules that constitute the knowledge of the system.

Game Playing

Traditionally, AI researchers have had good success when they confine their efforts to narrowly-defined problem domains, like those suitable for knowledge engineering, which can be modeled and understood completely within existing computers. Games, with their precise rules of play but virtually limitless complexity, were once thought to provide a complete but manageable microcosm of the key mechanisms of intelligence.

While the early optimism for chess as a testbed for AI may have died down, research into game playing certainly has not. From Alex Bernstein's first working chess program, which used a 6 x 6 board and barely made legal moves, through Richard Greenblatt's revolutionarily competent *MacHack*, to Hans Berliner's superfast, custom-VLSI *HiTech* that can beat over 99% of human chessplayers, game-playing has made more progress in terms of objective performance than has any other category of AI applications. And Berliner's backgammon system, admittedly the beneficiary of several lucky rolls, managed to defeat the world champion in a match. Other targets for game-playing research include Othello, Checkers, and Go.

Most game-playing programs operate on an idea central to AI programming called *heuristic search*, which casts problem-solving in terms of an abstract space of all possible solutions, together with operations that transform one state in that space into another, using heuristic "rules of thumb" to guide and constrain the process. Among the many other applications of search are *planning*, *symbolic mathematics*, and *automatic theorem-proving*, in which one spectacular result had a computer program prove a version of Gödel's First Incompleteness Theorem.

The History of Artificial Intelligence

As a science, artificial intelligence has matured over the past 50 years for the most part in the United States. And though the Japanese and Europeans are racing to catch up, most of the early discoveries, developments, and experiments, both theoretical and practical, occurred at American universities, research institutions, and corporations.

But while the intellectual and technological tools necessary to attempt AI, such as mathematical logic and the digital computer, only came into being in the twentieth century, the idea of mechanized intelligence already had been current in intellectual circles for some years. Homer may have been the first to hint at the possibility of AI, perhaps as early as 725 BC, in the *Iliad*. A well-known Greek myth has Aphrodite imbue with life a statue constructed by the Cypriot king Pygmalion; in medieval legend the Rabbi of Prague creates the first "golem," or robot. And the most familiar example of AI in literature is Mary Shelley's *Frankenstein*.

AI made an important jump from literature to philosophy in the seventeenth century with the work of the empiricists, whose numbers included Thomas Hobbes, David Hume, and John Locke. They believed that human cognition was divided into *sensations*, or external stimuli, and *conceptions*, or internal mental events; furthermore, they posited the existence of a finite set of *laws*, or rules, that associated conjunctions of sensations with conceptions. The natural consequence of this theory is that it must be possible to describe a computational process that duplicates the function of the laws. Right or wrong, empiricism was an important first step in the divorce of AI from mythology and mysticism.

Mathematicians carried the work of the empiricists into the early 20th century. Gottfried Leibnitz, in *De Arte Combinatorica* (1661), proposed "a general method in which all truths would be reduced to a kind of calculation." George Boole, whose name will be familiar to fans of Pascal's "boolean" data type, was also among the first to ponder artificial intelligence. In *An Investigation of the Laws of Thought, on which are Founded the Mathematical Theories of Logic and Probabilities* (1854) he wrote:

The design of the following treatise is to investigate the fundamental operations of the mind by which *reasoning* is performed ... The laws we have to examine are the laws of one of the most important of our mental faculties. The mathematics we have to construct are the mathematics of the human intellect.

In this pronouncement, and to an extent in those of the early empiricists, we can already see the seeds of the basic premise that underlies modern AI research:

There is some formalism through which we can view the behavior of the (human) brain as a form of computation.

The implication, of course, is that once we discover the precise nature of the brain's computations, we will be able to reproduce them with a computer, thus achieving "true artificial intelligence."

Bertrand Russell and Alfred North Whitehead began the awesome task of specifying a suitable formalism in their three-volume *Principia Mathematica* (1910-1913), which created a mechanically logical framework for all mathematical reasoning. Interestingly enough, one of the very first AI programs, the Logic Theorist of Newell, Shaw, and Simon, proved over 30 theorems in the Principia, and surprised its inventors by "discovering" an elegant proof of Theorem 2.85 that had been missed by the authors. Although the *Journal of Symbolic Logic* declined to publish the computer-generated result, Russell was reported to be "delighted" by the news.

FIGURE 1-1. IMPORTANT EVENTS IN THE MODERN HISTORY OF AI

1936 Turing formalizes the notion of a general-purpose computer.

1945 Von Neumann conceives "stored program" design for serial digital computers.
1946 *ENIAC*, the first implemented general-purpose digital computer, dedicated.

1950 Turing describes his test for machine intelligence.
Shannon speculates on the prospects for computer chess.
1955 Bernstein develops first working chess program.
1956 McCarthy organizes the Dartmouth Conference and coins the term *artificial intelligence.*
Newell, Shaw, and Simon develop the *Logic Theorist*, the first successful AI program.

1957   McCarthy invents Lisp (LISt Processor), the first popular AI programming language.
guage.
Newell, Shaw, and Simon begin the ambitious *General Problem Solver*.
Chomsky introduces transformational grammar to model the syntax of natural languages.

1965   Feigenbaum develops *Dendral*, the first expert system.
Dreyfus publishes "Alchemy and Artificial Intelligence" paper.
1966   Quillian invents the semantic network.
1967   Greenblatt develops *MacHack*, the first competent chess program.

1970   Winston's "Learning Structural Descriptions from Examples" pioneers machine learning.
Colmerauer invents Prolog AI programming language.
1972   *MYCIN*, first practical expert system to use production rules, developed.
Winograd completes *SHRDLU* natural language processing program.
1974   Minsky publishes "A Framework for Representing Knowledge" paper.
1975   The Lisp Machine, the first specialized AI computer, invented at MIT.
First personal computers are sold.

1982   Marr's revolutionary, comprehensive theory of vision published.
Japanese "Fifth Generation" AI research effort begins.
1986   Thinking Machines Corporation introduces the Connection Machine.
Berliner's *HiTech* is first chess computer to receive Senior Master title.
First 32-bit microcomputers become widely available.

Unfortunately, the philosophers and mathematicians were never able to verify or refute their theories about intelligence. The concrete intellectual groundwork for later AI research was laid in the 1940s and early 1950s, a century after Boole's speculations, by thinkers like Alan Turing.

Turing, who with his work on computable functions had already earned his place among the greatest computer scientists of all time, explicitly stated that machine intelligence was possible; furthermore, he devised a way to determine whether a given computer had the intelligence of a human being. In his famous and far-reaching 1950 essay *Computing Machinery and Intelligence*, Turing made specific recommendations for future research in artificial intelligence.

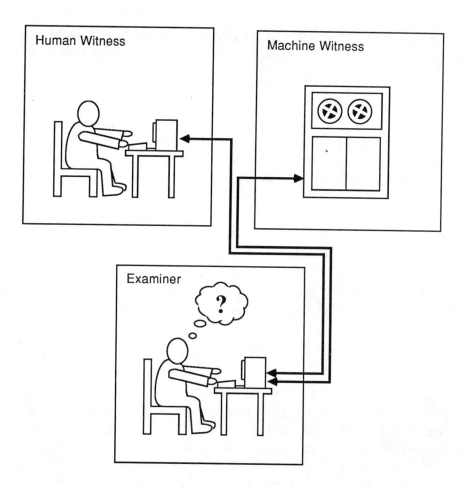

Figure 1–2. **The Turing Test**

In the *Turing Test*, a human examiner, another human being, and the computer are placed in separate chambers. There are teletype links between the examiner and the human being and between the examiner and the computer. The examiner most likely would pose a series of questions to both the human being and the computer, attempted to discriminate between them based on their responses. Here is a sample of the dialog that might ensue after a witness (either man or machine—we do not know which) has composed a poem at the request of the examiner:

EXAMINER: In the first line of your sonnet which reads "Shall I compare
                 thee to a summer's day" would not "a spring day" do as well
                 or better?

WITNESS: It wouldn't scan.

EXAMINER: How about a winter's day? That would scan all right.

WITNESS: Yes, but nobody wants to be compared to a winter's day.

EXAMINER: Wouldn't you say Mr. Pickwick reminded you of Christmas?

WITNESS: In a way.

EXAMINER: Yet Christmas is a winter's day, and I do not think Mr.
                 Pickwick would mind the comparison.

WITNESS: I don't think you're serious. By winter's day one means a
                 typical winter's day, rather than a special one like Christmas.

The computer passes the test, and presumably is considered intelligent, if the
examiner cannot determine with certainty that it is not the human being (and vice-
versa). Having as evidence only the excerpt above, for example, most people would
not conclude that the witness is not a human being.

Suffice it to say here that, although it immortalized his name, the Turing Test is
a flawed measure of intelligence. We will take it up again in Chapter 2, when we try
to decide what special criteria qualify a program as "intelligent" and make it a good
example of AI.

In the same year that Turing proposed his test, Claude Shannon, the father of
information theory, speculated on the game of chess as a vehicle for the study of
machine intelligence in "Programming a Digital Computer for Playing Chess,"
which appeared in *Philosophical Magazine*. Surely a computer that was able to
master such a complex game would be considered intelligent. In 1958, Newell,
Shaw, and Simon presented the reasons for studying computer chess in "Chess-
Playing Programs and the Problem of Complexity":

Chess is the intellectual game *par excellence*. Without a chance device to
obscure the contest, it pits two intellects against each other in a situation so
complex that neither can hope to understand it completely, but sufficiently
amenable to analysis that each can hope to outthink his opponent. The game is

sufficiently deep and subtle in its implications to have supported the rise of professional players, and to have allowed a deepening analysis through 200 years of intensive study and play without becoming exhausted or barren. Such characteristics mark chess as a natural area for attempts at mechanization. If one could devise a successful chess machine, one would seem to have penetrated to the core of human intellectual endeavor.

Making the most in-depth investigation in his time of two fundamentally different approaches to the problem, Shannon began the process and tradition of studying AI through a particular example of intelligent behavior, rather than as an abstract issue.

Turing also recognized the basic choice of methodology that AI researchers would have to make. In *Computing Machinery and Intelligence*, he speculated:

We may hope that machines will eventually compete [in terms of performance, not economics] with men in all purely intellectual fields. But which are the best ones to start with? Even this is a difficult decision. Many people think that a very abstract activity, like the playing of chess, would be best. It can also be maintained that it is best to provide the machine with the best sense organs that money can buy, and then to teach it to understand and speak English. This process could follow the normal teaching of a child. Things would be pointed out and named, etc. Again I do not know what the right answer is, but I think both approaches should be tried.

As we shall see later, Turing's prophetic article anticipated the subsequent general course of AI research to this day.

The term *artificial intelligence* was coined in 1956 by John McCarthy, a math professor who was to become one of the world's leading AI researchers. He organized a "two-month, ten-man study of artificial intelligence" at Dartmouth College "to proceed on the basis of the conjecture that every aspect of learning or any other feature of intelligence can in principle be so precisely described that a machine can be made to simulate it." Although most of its participants agreed that little of substance was accomplished at the conference, four of them went on to form AI research centers that became the leading such operations in the world: McCarthy at Stanford University, Marvin Minsky at the Massachusetts Institute of Technology, and Herbert Simon and Allen Newell at Carnegie-Mellon University.

For the first decade or so of AI research, through the mid-1960s, scientists concentrated their efforts on discovering the "secret of intelligence," presumably some general-purpose algorithm or data structure that was the key to all human behavior. These activities, along with other projects to duplicate the structure or function of the brain, parallel Turing's second recommended approach.

Gradually, it became apparent that they would not succeed. *GPS*, the General Problem Solver algorithm developed by Newell, Shaw, and Simon, was simply too general to function adequately on problems that were not trivial or already effectively solved by the way in which they were posed. Attempts to let computers "evolve" into intelligent machines failed dismally, as did many efforts to get them to "learn" the rules of general intelligent behavior.

It was at this time that the rise of so-called applications-oriented AI research began, with large-scale projects concentrating on the development of expert systems. *DENDRAL* predicted molecular structures, *MACSYMA* solved difficult problems in symbolic mathematics, and *MYCIN* could diagnose bacterial blood infections.

Such programs, which seek not to completely simulate a human being and/or his mind, can be viewed as examples of Turing's first suggestion: that we study an abstract activity, presumably attempting to endow machines with skills for that activity and only that activity. In the case of an expert system, we are creating behavior that is "so intelligent" that only a few human experts are capable of it.

Another example is the study of computer chess, as originally proposed by Shannon in 1950. In the late 1960s, the first program not to utterly disgrace itself against human opposition, MacHack, was developed by Greenblatt at MIT. Now, in 1987, chess-playing machines have improved to the point where only a tiny handful of the top players are expected to defeat the best computer, Berliner's HiTech, in a tournament game.

Finally, an example from the field of natural language processing. In 1972 at MIT, Terry Winograd completed for his doctoral dissertation a program called *SHRDLU*. In a style reminiscent of that of ELIZA, SHRDLU could converse with a human being on the subject of the *blocks world*. Here is a sample dialog:

Pick up a big red block.
   OK.
Grasp the pyramid.
   I don't understand which pyramid you mean.
Find a block that is taller than the one you are holding and put it into the box.
   By "it" I assume you mean the block that is taller than the one I am holding. OK.
Can the table pick up blocks?
   No.

Had you touched any pyramid before you put the green one on the little cube?
> *Yes, the green one.*

Does a steeple—
> *Sorry. I don't know the word* "steeple."

A steeple is a stack that contains two green cubes and a pyramid.
> *I understand.*

During the interaction, a video screen displayed the blocks world and an animated robot arm executing the user's instructions while the dialog continued as subtitles. But however clever the atmospherics of the simulation, the key innovation for AI in SHRDLU was that it actually *understood* what it was hearing and saying, by building and maintaining an internal model of the external blocks world. To answer a question, it did not simply massage its syntax, make some clever substitutions, and spit out the result. Instead, it examined and modified its data structures, using its knowledge to make deductions and execute procedures. Notably absent from the sample dialog is ELIZA's tendency to randomly change the subject—SHRDLU keeps up with the user.

Naturally, these and other achievements of the early 1970s, including Waltz's work on vision and Winston's on learning, were hailed by most of the AI community as great successes. But their unifying theme was that each of program literally performed so well in its own domain that it was lost outside of it. Looking at the conversation with SHRDLU above, you might imagine that it could pass a sort of Turing Test restricted to blocks. Ask SHRDLU about automobiles, DENDRAL about wine, or HITECH to play blackjack, and you invariably get a negative response.

All are confined to a *microworld*, a well-defined domain that can be dissected, studied, and understood in isolation from the rest of the real world. The explosion of microworlds and applications-oriented AI research soon led to the development of an entire subscience of *knowledge representation*, which is concerned with the synthesis of machine-ready data structures that encode real-world knowledge. Expert systems need knowledge about solving problems, chess programs need knowledge about strategy and tactics, and natural language processors need knowledge about syntax and vocabulary.

Now although many results with implications for psychology and AI in general came out of the microworld projects, the development of practical applications is their greatest byproduct. We will study several of these applications later, but it is becoming increasingly apparent that making the jump from a microworld to the real world is a difficult task. Simple, straightforward ways of generalizing programs like SHRDLU have proved elusive. Consequently, the great expectations for AI caused by the success of the microworld programs have not been satisfied. In essence, the microworld concepts work well for applications, but are difficult to adapt for larger systems.

The Computer and the Brain

All of the research discussed above follows the *information processing* paradigm first used by Newell, Shaw, and Simon in their mid-1950s work. Simon had approached AI from the background of an economist who studied human organizational behavior (for which work he eventually won the Nobel Prize), and with the view that the job of a computer was to compute—to compute mathematical functions, that is. The differences between machine and mind were all too apparent, but as he worked on the Logic Theorist, Simon came to see that information processing was a focal idea that brought "thinking" and "computing" together as activities common to digital computers and human brains:

> When I first began to sense that one could look at a computer as a device for processing information, not just numbers, then the metaphor I'd been using, of a mind as something that took some premises and ground them up and processed them into conclusions, began to transform itself into a notion that a mind was something which took some program inputs and data and had some processes which operated on the data and produced output. There's quite a direct bridge, in some respects a very simple bridge, between this earlier view of the mind as logic machine, ad the later view of it as a computer.

So the information processing model is essentially an abstraction of the features of brain and computer to a sufficiently high level that we can view them as identical. But the problem remains to implement the model in real computer systems, and for this purpose evolved the idea of the *physical symbol system*, which Newell and Simon championed in their Turing Award Lecture as having "the necessary and sufficient means for general intelligent action." In such a system, information is processed by manipulating, according to well-defined rules, symbols that represent real world concepts. A digital computer, with its unerring accuracy, can obviously be the basis for an excellent system.

The sequential symbol manipulation program quickly came to dominate AI because it proved to be the only practical method of creating intelligent behavior, defeating several other early research projects. One failed attempt sought to harness the speed advantage of the computer over the neuron, which can "only" transmit messages at millisecond speeds, compared to the nanosecond propagation delays of transistor gates. The group tried to simulate the process of evolution with computers, reasoning that they should need little time to make the progress that the slow human brain had taken millennia to achieve. Another weak idea had the computer generate random bit strings, one after the other. The experimenter would somehow "reward" the machine for creating meaningful patterns, such as machine instructions or complete programs, and penalize it for spitting out garbage. Actually, given infinite time, both these projects might have come to fruition; to their detriment, information processing beat them to the punch with both interesting results and practical applications.

Information Processing:

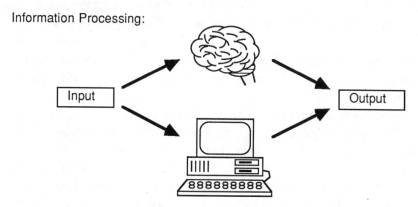

Cognitive Modeling:

Figure 1–3. **Information Processing and Cognitive Modeling**

But the one alternative line of research that predates information processing has continued to this day despite many setbacks and a lack of spectacular results, and recently has been gaining momentum in the wake of increasing disappointment with microworlds. *Cognitive modeling* approaches the problem of AI by asking not "How can the machine best perform a particular task?" but rather "How can we

model the way the brain performs that task?" One way to model the brain's performance is to model its structure, especially its fundamental unit, the neuron.
However, with the enormous complexity of the brain and the limitations of early
digital computers, most early efforts foundered; when the model was made simple
enough for efficient implementation, as with the *perceptron*, it was proved too simple to produce interesting behavior.

But theoreticians forged ahead, undaunted by the difficulty of practically
implementing larger systems, and in the 1980s the new science of *connectionism* is
offering a mathematical formalism with which we can make a computational analysis of so-called *neural networks*. Connectionism, by melding cognition and computation in a framework that relies not on individual symbols but the connections
among many tiny processing units, allows models that are at once biologically plausible, computationally sound, and perhaps most importantly, within the reaches of
today's technology.

So in the 1980s, the pendulum of research is swinging back towards Turing's
"second method" of AI. The "generalist school" has revived itself, emerging with a
much more sophisticated view than its naive optimism of the 1950s. And whereas
the 1960s were dominated by general problem solving and the 1970s were definitely the decade of expert systems, the 1980s might come to be considered the era
of machine learning. Promising research is underway in learning—a central
attribute of higher intelligence—within both the symbolic and connectionist computing paradigms. While it is always possible that future generations will look back
on current work as just a new incarnation of a persistent old folly, it seems increasingly likely that AI has found the right direction to go even if it cannot yet glimpse
its destination.

So AI research is rapidly diverging into an applications field, which tends to
keep the microworlds approach, and a more theoretical field, which is adopting a
global posture that centers onlogic, learning, and simulating the operation of the
human brain. Turing's indecision about methodology is reflected by this current
divorce of theory and applications, a split which has even been institutionalized by
the recent division of the National Conference on Artificial Intelligence into separate "science" and "engineering" tracks, the latter to presumably study practical
systems while the former worries about weighty theoretical issues.

About This Book

I cannot hope in this single volume to acquaint the reader with even a fraction of the
huge body of AI research that has gone on over the past forty or so years. However,

we can explore several interesting AI theories and applications that are by now well understood. Using Turbo Pascal, we can develop small demonstration programs that share many characteristics with their larger minicomputer and mainframe versions.

Organization and Topics Covered

Chapter One, which you are reading, provides an introduction to artificial intelligence, sketches the field's history, and discusses the contents of the rest of the book.

Chapter Two explores certain philosophical and psychological issues surrounding AI, concentrating on the question of what characteristics distinguish a program we might consider intelligent, such as an expert system, from an ordinary application, like a database management system. We will also consider some of the many critics and criticisms of artificial intellegence.

Chapter Three will consider various schemes for knowledge representation, especially semantic networks and frame systems, as well as the inheritance mechanism. After examining some advanced issues, including semantic primitives, episodic memory, and the so-called "frame problem," we will develop our first Pascal example: a program to manage a simple frame-based database.

Chapter Four makes a brief excursion into natural language processing, introducing the key concepts of syntax, semantics, and pragmatics. We will consider various methods of specifying and parsing languages, including finite automata, context-free grammars, and augmented transition networks. To illustrate the use of semantic grammars for database interfaces, we will discuss a Pascal program to convert English-like sentences into commands to the frame system developed in Chapter 3.

Chapter Five covers expert systems. After looking at several problems to which knowledge engineering has been applied successfully, we will use two case studies of working programs to understand the basic principles of expert systems. For a practical illustration, we will build a small production system interpreter in Turbo Pascal and sample knowledge bases to which we can apply it.

Chapter Six discusses heuristic search, one of the fundamental ideas underlying many AI algorithms. After formulating a sample problem that can be solved with a variety of search algorithms, we will examine the depth-first, breadth-first, uniform-cost, best-first, and A* searches. Of course, we will implement an algorithm in Turbo Pascal and discuss other search-related issues.

Chapter Seven builds on the search concepts introduced in Chapter Six to discuss computer game-playing. Using chess as our main example throughout, we will examine the MINIMAX algorithm, the alpha-beta pruning enhancement, and other techniques. Before developing a complete checkers program in Turbo Pascal, we will explore the techniques being used on the frontier of computer chess research.

Chapter Eight is a look to the future of AI research. We will briefly cover three important topics: computer vision, machine learning, and connectionism. Algorithms for edge detection and concept learning and applications to problem solving, speech production, and word recognition will be explored.

Programs and Exercises

Five Turbo Pascal programs form the set of core examples that are associated with Chapters 3 through 7. They are intended to be easy-to-understand demonstrations of AI algorithms and techniques, not examples of large-scale or commercial-quality software. The programs were first developed using the "standard Pascal" features of Turbo Pascal in order to make them compatible with as many Pascal implementations as possible. They will compile and run with no problems under Borland International's Turbo Pascal 3.0 for MS-DOS, which is reviewed in Appendix 5.

Each chapter in which programs are discussed includes a summary and several programming exercises of varying difficulty and time requirements at its end. As the book is not intended primarily for use as a textbook, no solutions or specific hints are offered aside from what information can be found in the chapters themselves. Readers are encouraged to use the exercises to guide their further study and experimentation, as most suggest specific modifications or extensions to the programs.

Supplemental Material

One function of this book is to provide a total resource for the Turbo Pascal programmer who is interested in learning about artificial intelligence. I urge you to take full advantage of the remaining appendices, which are organized as follows: Appendix 2 lists many sources of AI information like periodicals and professional associations, Appendix 3 lists vendors of AI software and their products, and Appendix 4 provides a glossary of some AI terminology used in this book and elsewhere.

Each chapter concludes with a discussion of the sources used in its preparation, and Appendix 1 organizes those and many other references in bibliographic form for your convenience. It has been my experience that the most important product of one's initial exposure to a scientific topic, such as this book is intended to provide for artificial intelligence, is an understanding of that terminology and nomenclature which is peculiar to the field. Concepts, algorithms, and data structures that are unclear at first will crystalize later as you continue your study, and the best place to do that is in the vast research literature produced by AI workers. Where appropriate I will refer to specific papers that I have found particularly illuminating or interesting; after reading this book you should be able to read them as well.

References

An entertaining history of the quest for artificial intelligence is McCorduck's *Machines Who Think*, but it covers only the period through 1979. Gardner's *The Mind's New Science* (1986) traces the development of cognitive science as an interdisciplinary field with roots in AI, psychology, neuroscience, linguistics, philosophy, and anthropology. Ladd's *The Computer and the Brain* discusses very recent events, emphasizing biological information processing.

There are now several excellent textbooks on AI; I recommend those on the advanced undergraduate level. My own favorite is Charniak and McDermott's *Introduction to Artificial Intelligence*, which emphasizes an exploration of the detailed principles and theories underlying AI research at the expense of material on applications. However, it uses a unified approach of first-order logic as a representation language and Lisp as a programming language to cover topics like memory organization and language understanding to unusual depth. Winston's *Artificial*

Intelligence, 2nd edition, the most popular AI text, is less rigorous and easier to read, but it achieves this quality by glossing over many of the implementation details discussed at length in Charniak and McDermott. Other good textbooks include Rich's *Artificial Intelligence* and Tanimoto's *The Elements of Artificial Intelligence: An Introduction Using Lisp*.

   The Handbook of Artificial Intelligence, though not a textbook, makes an excellent companion to one. It is three volumes of short (5-10 page) articles on key AI concepts and programs, providing sketches of the most important achievements in AI through the 1970s. *The Handbook of Human Intelligence* (not a companion to the *Handbook of AI*) gives an interesting psychological perspective on AI. The two-volume AAAI-86 Proceedings form a snapshot of current AI research.

2. GENERAL ISSUES

We saw in Chapter 1 that artificial intelligence has its intellectual origins in the work of the empiricist philosophers of the 17th century, who debated the possibility that cognitive phenomena were explainable within a consistent framework of laws. With the development of computers in the 20th century, AI researchers began to consider the feasibility of "automating" the processes of intelligent behavior that produced those laws.

But before we can even think about designing intelligent software that makes computers smarter, we must lay down some ground rules for our enterprise. To do this, we should attempt to answer such questions as:

- What is intelligence?

- How would we know intelligence it if we saw it?

- Why should we believe that artificial intelligence is possible?

- What is the best approach to producing intelligent behavior?

- What are the main criticisms of artificial intelligence?

Theories of Intelligence

In the universe of concepts in common use, perhaps none is as nebulously defined as *intelligence*. When asked to define intelligence, many people might paraphrase Supreme Court Justice Potter Stewart and say something like "I can't say what intelligence is, but I know it when I see it." Now although Stewart was actually talking about pornography, his comment captures the essential vagueness of words like intelligence—words that get their definition from their context instead of an established model or set of criteria. Just as society has struggled (with questionable success) to produce an acceptable definition of pornography, cognitive science has struggled to clarify what it means by intelligence.

FIGURE 2-1. SOME ATTEMPTED DEFINITIONS OF INTELLIGENCE

Intelligence is a state grasping the truth, involving reason, concerned with action about what is good or bad for a human being ... it seems proper, then, to an intelligent person, to be able to deliberate finely about what is good and beneficial for himself, not about some restricted area (e.g., about what promotes health or strength) but about what promotes living well in general.

Aristotle

Intelligence.... is the faculty of making artificial objects, especially tools to make tools.

Henri Bergson

We expect an intelligent agent to be able to have mental attitudes, learn, solve problems, understand, plan and predict, know its limits, draw distinctions, be original, generalize, perceive, and use language.

Martin A. Fischler & Oscar Firschein

The test of a first-rate intelligence is the ability to hold two opposed ideas in the mind at the same time, and still retain the ability to function.

F. Scott Fitzgerald

Intelligence is a term frequently used to express the myth that some single entity or element is responsible for the quality of a person's ability to reason. I prefer to think of this as representing not any particular power or phenomenon, but simply all the mental skills that,at any particular moment, we admire but don't yet understand.

Marvin Minsky

The intelligence of a system is the degree to which it approximates the knowledge level, or the extent to which it uses its knowledge; we cannot fault a system that has little knowledge but uses it well.

Allen Newell

Intelligence is the one quality common to all activities that people at any given time perform better than computers.

After Elaine Rich

An intelligent agent is one that exhibits goal-directed adaptive behavior.

Robert Sternberg

The ability to learn or understand from experience; ability to acquire and retain knowledge; mental ability; the ability to respond quickly and successfully to a new situation; use of the faculty of reason in solving problems, directing conduct, etc. effectively.

Webster's Dictionary

Figure 2-1 lists a small sample of the many definitions of intelligence that have been proposed over the years. If anything, their only unifying themes are diversity, imprecision, and vagueness. For these reasons, despite it figuring prominently in the name of their scientific pursuit, AI researchers tend to avoid making explicit use of the term *intelligence* (much as philosophers and psychologists eschew *conscious* and similar words). Instead, they talk of interpreting, manipulating, modeling, and even understanding.

Detecting and Measuring Intelligence

But shifting the discussion to these grounds gains us little, since we can define these new terms only slightly more precisely than we could intelligence. But this was realized early by Turing, who tried to shift the question from "what is intelligence" to "how can intelligence be identified"—an eminently more practical and achievable goal. As a first approximation to the answer, he proposed the Turing Test (TT), diagrammed in Figure 1-2, a sort of trial in which a human examiner attempts to discriminate between a computer system and another human being on the basis of anonymous natural language dialogues with the two.

While attractive at the time and seemingly a useful goal for AI research, the TT has several drawbacks. For one, although the examiner has free rein to require any task of the witnesses, he can communicate only in written language. The TT cannot test perceptual abilities like speech and vision, social performance like an interaction between the witnesses, or motor skills; whereas none of these may be necessarily required for intelligence to exist, all are probably strong correlates.

However, even if we admit that the TT only tests the ability to communicate intelligently, we cannot escape its basic shortcoming as a psychological experiment. Since it is essentially a free-response task, demanding no uniformly *measurable* performance from its subjects (computers), its results tell us little about the processes underlying their behavior. As Ned Block has pointed out, one could theoretically create a giant table listing all possible conversations between man and machine, including the most recent utterance by the human being, and associate with each entry an appropriate response for the computer. A simple program would scan the list until it found the text that matched the previous conversation, and simply print out the indicated sentence. Steven Harnad has proposed the *Total Turing Test* (TTT) to get around this limitation, by insisting the complete behavior of an agent to be considered intelligent must be indistinguishable from that of a human mind. In principle, though, even the TTT can be fooled by a clever enough programmer who amasses enough data to create a facade of intelligence.

But in practice, of course, it is virtually impossible to create the huge lookup tables necessary to defeat either the TT or the TTT. Kenneth Colby created a program called *PARRY*, patterned after ELIZA, to simulate the conversation of a paranoid schizophrenic that apparently fooled several clinical psychiatrists. However, in the general case, for just a few minutes of conversation, the staggering combinatorial explosion of possible dialogues would overwhelm the capacity of any computer currently envisioned. Nevertheless, the point remains well-taken that a strictly performance-based test, whether the TT, the TTT, or any of the standardized IQ tests used on children, can only measure how closely the external behavior of a system resembles that of a benchmark. It cannot directly determine the nature of the internal methods the system is using to manufacture that behavior, let alone whether those methods are truly "intelligent."

What Makes A Computer Program Intelligent?

It is apparent that a simple comparison with human performance levels on various tasks will not suffice to determine whether AI has been achieved. Today's computers, just like all machines, have areas of strength (such as numerical analysis) in which they outperform their human counterparts, and areas of weakness in which they have difficulty with even the most basic tasks (such as playing Go or interacting with several other agents in a conversation). Whereas the former set of tasks is always increasing as computers gain in speed and memory, the latter set is being slowly reduced by the progress of AI techniques. But what is the real difference between the domains in which computers seem naturally superior and those in which human beings tend to excel?

FIGURE 2-2. QUICKSORT PROGRAM

Quicksort (QS): Given an array *A*, sort it into ascending order so that each $A_i < A_{i+1}$.

(When QS is first called, Let i=1, j=size of A)
1. If A[i] through A[j] contains at least two distinct values then do the following:
    a. Let v be the larger of the first two distinct keys found
    b. Permute A[i], ..., A[j] so that for some k between i+1 and j, the following are true:
        i. A[i], ..., A[k-1] all have keys less than v
        ii. A[k], ..., A[j] all have keys greater than or equal to v
2. QS(A[i..k-1])
3. QS(A[k..j])
4. Return A

Consider the programs outlined in Figures 2-2 and 2-3: a quicksort algorithm that might be found in a bank's account-management software system, and a set of rules for symbolic differentiation that could be used by an expert system in calculus.* Both are recursive—they break larger problems up into smaller ones, call themselves to solve them, and recombine the results—but there is an important distinction.

FIGURE 2-3. **DIFFERENTIATION PROGRAM**

Differentiate (DIFF): Given a function *f(x)*, return its derivative with respect to x, $\partial f / \partial x$.

1. If f(x) is of the form: *u(x) + v(x)*
    Then return: DIFF(u(x)) + DIFF(v(x))
2. If f(x) is of the form: *u(x) - v(x)*
    Then return: DIFF(u(x)) - DIFF(v(x))
3. If f(x) is of the form: *u(x) * v(x)*
    Then return: (v(x) * DIFF(u(x)) + u(x) * DIFF(v(x)))
4. If f(x) is of the form: *u(x) ÷ v(x)*
    Then return: (v(x) * DIFF(u(x)) - u(x) * DIFF(v(x))) ÷ v(x)2
5. If f(x) is of the form: $u(x)^c$
    Then return: c * $u(x)^{c-1}$ * DIFF(u(x))
6. If f(x) is of the form: *x*
    Then return: 1
7. If f(x) is of the form: *c*
    Then return: 0

It should be apparent that the fundamental structures of the two programs are different. QS follows a traditional step-by-step algorithm, and although some of the steps are left vague in Figure 2-2, we can see that the design of the program almost predicts in advance the sequence of operations it will carry out. In short, QS performs a very *general task* on a very *wide variety* of input data. By contrast, DIFF consists of seven rules which match patterns in the format of the input with transformations that will produce the desired output. Therefore, DIFF performs very *specific tasks* on very *few inputs*. QS can sort any list of data elements, but DIFF can only differentiate mathematical functions.

Underlying this key difference in performance between the two programs is a difference in the nature of the task involved. Sorting a list of numbers or words requires only that the program be able to compare two elements and decide which should appear first in the sorted order. Differentiating functions demands much more extensive *knowledge* of the methods used, which depend on the structure of

---

* The general format in which these algorithms are described in Figures 2-2 and 2-3 will be used throughout the book for all AI algorithms. Each major step is given an Arabic numeral, with substeps denoted by lowercase letters or Roman numerals. We hope that this conceptual format, sometimes called structured english, will be easier to understand and follow than either Pascal code itself or a Pascal-like psuedolanguage.

the input. If we agree that DIFF is a more intelligent program than QS, an assumption which is certainly compatible with intelligence tests and common understanding of human learning, we are forced to make this key observation:

Intelligent programs are knowledge-based programs!

As we saw in Chapter 1, this crucial realization came somewhat late to the early AI researchers. Joel Moses, who developed the gigantic MACSYMA symbolic mathematics system, recounts the criticisms from Allen Newell and Marvin Minsky of his work and sums up what was then the "new view" of intelligence in AI:

> The word you look for and hardly ever see in the early AI literature is the word *knowledge*. They didn't believe that you have to know anything, you could always rework it all ... it took a long time for [this view] to wither away ... I came up with an argument for what I call the primacy of expertise, and at the time I called the other guys generalists ... Minsky's view of my thesis was that it wasn't AI. He came to my exam and said, this isn't AI. Papert and he had had a five-hour argument the day before. But the old ideas were dying ... [Newell] called my position the "big-switch" theory, the idea being that you have all these experts working for you and when you have a problem, you decide which expert to call in to solve the problem. That's not AI, you see, but he didn't say that ... Essentially I think Newell is doing some very good work right now, but it took almost fifteen years. And it took Minsky nearly as long. (Quoted in *Machines Who Think*, pp. 228-229.)

A Knowledge-Based Approach

This modern, knowledge-based approach to building intelligent software will be ours throughout the rest of this book. Apart from the connectionists, whose ideas are covered in some detail in Chapter 8, most AI researchers today are scrutinizing their problems and systems with an eye towards finding more places to apply focused, domain-specific knowledge. But information is not knowledge, and throwing more and more data into an AI program may only slow it down and reduce its performance. So before we can fully adopt the "knowledge is power" thesis, we must briefly examine the nature of the knowledge we want to use and what we must do to use it.

Knowledge Representation

To become knowledge, information and data must be encoded in a form suitable for direct use. Note that this does not preclude a piece of data from simultaneously being information with respect to one application and knowledge with respect to another. For example, a tabulation of physical constants and equations like the speed of light c and $e=mc^2$ is just more information when presented in a listing of great scientific discoveries. However, it is important knowledge to an experimenter in astrophysics who is analyzing his observational data. And that data might in turn be synthesized into knowledge by extracting its regularities and deducing a useful qualitative law from them.

In a computer, everything might seem like data at first, since it is just bit patterns of 1s and 0s. To an alien scientist, the brain might appear to have the same property, being just a tangled-up bundle of nerve fibers with various chemical concentrations. But in each case, there is a dynamic process at work on the data; for the serial computer, it is the central processing unit executing a program represented by some of the data; in the brain, it is the changing pattern of interactive message-passing between neurons. Both systems have dynamic components that *interpret* their static components, implicitly treating some as knowledge, some as data, and some as irrelevant to their current state of affairs (as in a microprocessor during an interrupt or the brain when the eyes are closed).

Brian Smith has formulated the fundamental axiom of AI that connects the structures of an intelligent agent with its processes as the *Knowledge Representation Hypothesis*, which states:

> Any mechanically embodied intelligent process will be comprised of structural ingredients that (a) we as external observers naturally take to represent a propositional account of the knowledge that the overall process exhibits, and (b) independent of such external semantical attribution, play a formal but causal and essential role in engendering the behavior that manifests that knowledge.

If we accept this principle, as a knowledge-based approach must, we are led to a functional division of an intelligent computer system into a dynamic, process-oriented component, and a static, knowledge/data-oriented component. Structurally, they may be combined into one homogeneous unit, as in the brain, but functionally, they are distinct. In stating the *Reflection Hypothesis*, Smith took this conclusion one step further:

In as much as a computational process can be constructed to reason about an external world in virtue of comprising an ingredient process (interpreter) formally manipulating representations of that world, so too a computational process could be made to reason about itself by virtue of comprising an ingredient process (interpreter) formally manipulating representations of its own operations and structures.

In later chapters, we shall rely implicitly on both of these hypotheses as we consider systems that integrate highly domain-specific knowledge and powerful interpretive algorithms.

The Prepare/Deliberate Tradeoff

With these hypotheses in hand, we can begin to explore Moses's "primacy of knowledge" in intelligent systems. But just as your program cannot deduce all necessary knowledge from first principles, your programmer cannot encode in advance every piece of knowledge you will need. Unforeseen circumstances or the sheer size of most program databases preclude this solution, so all applications will require the reasoning component or interpreter to conduct some sort of search at runtime to regenerate unstored knowledge or explore new areas of the problem domain. An example would be a chess program that had a "book" of opening move sequences—prestored knowledge—which would expire after ten moves, forcing the interpreter component of the system to do more of the work.

There is a definite tradeoff at work here between *preparation*, in the form of prestored knowledge, and *deliberation*, in the form of on-the-spot reasoning and search. Figure 2-4 displays this graphically with a series of isobars representing lines of equivalent performance along the knowledge and search axes. As we would intuitively imagine, by having more prestored knowledge, one program can display intelligence equivalent to that of another program which conducts a larger amount of search.

Whereas the emphasis has shifted from the early AI programs like the Logic Theorist and General Problem Solver, with few rules but more search, to expert systems with more rules and less search, human-like behavior points undoubtedly lie on the outer isobars. The chess computer HiTech has taken the search-based route to the human performance level; as you can see, the side benefit of its position at the far end of the search axis is its ability to increase performance rapidly with the addition of relatively little knowledge.

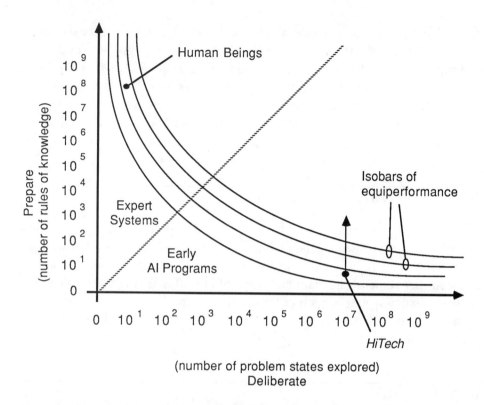

Figure 2–4. The Prepare vs. Deliberate Tradeoff

Similarly, it is assumed that human intelligence results from a vast knowledge base coupled with a small amount of selective deliberation; the limited capacity of human memory seems to be the primary factor limiting human movement towards higher performance (through either more preparation, with little payoff, or more deliberation, with a great payoff). The prepare/deliberate tradeoff is ubiquitous in AI, often travelling as the store/compute or the representation/reasoning tradeoff. Keep it in mind as you study various AI applications.

Procedural and Declarative Knowledge

Finally, we should take note of the early controversy in AI between the proceduralists and the declarativists over the nature of knowledge that is useful for solving problems. *Procedural* knowledge, a sort of "knowing how," encodes knowledge as process, asserting that a procedure for solving a problem is the knowledge of how to solve it. *Declarative* knowledge, "knowing what," describes the information necessary to solve the problem in a general way, without providing a direct method for its solution. For example, the knowledge to solve a mechanics problem in physics could be represented declaratively as a set of differential equations. These represent all the necessary information, and imply that the value(s) which satisfy all the constraints simultaneously are the solutions. A procedural representation might specify a series of steps the problem solver should take, one after the other, to arrive at the solution from the initial description of the problem.

Critics of Artificial Intelligence

As a science, AI is still in its infancy, and just like other fields in their youth, it has its share of critics, disbelievers, and heretics. Having concluded that a knowledge-based approach is the right one for our study of AI and its applications, we should pause to consider some of the main criticisms of our efforts. Apart from a healthy "loyal opposition" who intend their criticisms to be purely constructive, three individuals have taken it upon themselves to expose AI as a fraud, an illegitimate science, or a potential social ill.

Hubert Dreyfus

Hubert Dreyfus was the first to gain notoriety for his anti-AI writings, which began when he was hired by the Rand Corporation in the summer of 1965 to conduct a reasonably impartial study of current AI research. His long-unpublished evaluation, a paper provocatively entitled *Alchemy and Artificial Intelligence*, was a sweeping indictment of AI whose principal charges were voodoo results, outrageous predictions, and a fundamental misunderstanding of the differences between human and machine intelligence (if the latter were even possible). Unfortunately, Dreyfus's perceptive comments have never been taken at face value by the AI community (supporters of AI research efforts) because of their vitriolic tone and Dreyfus's own defensive tendency towards personal attacks and criticisms. Nevertheless, it is instructive to consider some of his main points.

Basing his arguments on the classical view of the computer as a monolithic number-crunching device that deals only in "isolable, atomic, alternative choices," Dreyfus places AI in a historical perspective of rationalist philosophy. Claiming that human behavior and intelligence cannot yield to the sort of reductionist analysis that works well in disciplines like physics, he charges that AI is fraught with confusion over its intellectual roots. Psychologically, he finds information processing an inadequate level of detail to describe what is essential about human cognition, since it takes into account neither the role of the entire body nor that of the current social situation or context in organizing our behavior.

That behavior may *appear* logical and rule-like, Dreyfus says, but that is an illusion that leads to an incorrect epistemological assumption in AI: the confusion of a model that simply *describes* observed performance with one which *explains* how it is created. Since observed behavior only appears orderly to us because of our expectations and existence within the same global system we are trying to understand, it is natural to make the "mistake" of attributing it to rules. Dreyfus also points out the computer's "intrinsic" inability to weed out useless alternatives in the way the human mind can immediately settle on a decision. Finally, he turns the words of the early AI experimenters against them, noting that their systems are just toy programs that can perform well on some problems but will never reach the status of full intelligence, and ridiculing their unfulfilled predictions of that the achievement of AI was imminent.

It is the last of Dreyfus's attacks that really stung the research community. Had he confined himself to a philosophical statement on the possibility of AI, and an exposition of his alternative *phenomenological* theory of intelligence, his writings might have been taken at face value, though, by comparing AI to alchemy and its early successes to climbing trees in order to reach the moon, he aroused the wrath of AI giants like Herbert Simon and Seymour Papert, who fought fire with fire by making Dreyfus look as foolish as the straw men of AI he had set up in his own paper. One of his strongest claims was that computers simply could not play chess well enough to beat a human being. This was true until the late 1960s, when a challenge match between Dreyfus and MacHack was arranged, in which the computer triumphantly checkmated the philosopher. Of course, this embarrassment only increased the ill will on both sides of the issue, but it perhaps served to moderate Dreyfus's initially absolute positions. Since being demonstrated the power of computers to perform seemingly intellectual tasks, Dreyfus has become more constructive and less vitriolic in his criticisms.

Among other things, he has recently relaxed his early claim that the biological assumption of AI, that a human being is a walking instantiation of a computer program and his neurons are equivalent to on/off circuits in the brain, is invalid. Of course, a one-to-one mapping between neurons and transistors is not necessary for computer simulation of thought processes; but moreover, Dreyfus now believes that a machine that models the neurobiological structure of the brain sufficiently closely could surmount the obstacles he sees to traditional, information-processing AI. This tacit concession to connectionism will be examined more closely in Chapter 8, but for now we should recognize the enormity of the admission: if a large Connection Machine, which is manifestly a programmable computer, can be intelligent, cannot any computer that simulates the operation of massively parallel processor do the same?

As he slides down this slippery slope he has created for himself, Dreyfus may find his strong claims losing their force. However, his specific criticisms of microworlds and knowledge representation are likely to endure. He was one of the first to see that programs like SHRDLU were not readily generalizable out of the toy blocks worlds in which they functioned well. But this time, he also offered an explanation of why this is so: knowledge representation is impossible in the fullest sense, because any piece of knowledge is incomplete without all its connections to other concepts. Since the computer cannot yet automatically weed out the irrelevant meanings of a concept like the mind can, it must encode them all and consider them all; therefore, any knowledge representation system is incomplete unless it represents literally *all* knowledge, and since this too is impossible, AI systems can never break out of their toy problem domains. This claim, made during the 1970s and more perceptive than his 1965 tirade, has proved difficult to refute. No simple chess match will do here. Douglas Lenat's CYC project is attempting to construct a giant knowledge network of encyclopaedic proportions, but how such a structure could be efficiently used in a practical system remains unclear.

Joseph Weizenbaum

Some of the newer critics of AI are computer scientists themselves, including Dreyfus's brother and collaborator Stuart, Terry Winograd of SHRDLU fame, and ELIZA creator Joseph Weizenbaum. In his *Computer Power and Human Reason* and subsequent presentations, Weizenbaum describes being profoundly disturbed at the reactions to ELIZA. Psychiatrists believed it really embodied therapeutic knowledge and could help patients, users would spend hours with it as though it were either their analyst or a lifelong friend, and some of his colleagues made exaggerated claims for its insight into natural language processing problems. But Weizenbaum only intended the program as a quick hack to demonstrate the ease with which a computer could *mimic* human behavior without any real component of understanding.

Starting with these observations, Weizenbaum concluded that since individuals were easily duped by computers, placed too much trust in inhuman machines, and could not objectively evaluate their performance, computers ought to be restricted from certain areas of human society. He viewed these problems of symptomatic of a larger invasion of computers into human life, one which is causing us more and more to view the world in mechanistic terms. He has decried the willingness of science to subordinate itself to military interests (in the United States, the Department of Defense currently supplies much of the funding for basic AI and computer science research) and the apparent lack of moral reflection on the part of scientists.

Although he repeats some of the traditional arguments against AI as a science, Weizenbaum tries to confine himself to moral questions. His first point, about excluding computers from certain areas of human life, is well illustrated with the example of an artificial intelligence program being used as judge and jury in criminal trials. Appropriately programmed, a computer could conceivably understand and generate legal arguments, have instant access to a huge database of precedents and laws, and be a fair and impartial critic of the evidence. It would not be biased bigoted, racist, predisposed, or swayed by extralegal factors. The prospect sounds ideal to many, but Weizenbaum sees a danger in placing authority and power in the "hands" of what is essentially an alien life form.

Like other aliens, the computer-judge would not share in the total history of human experience in which every member of society has been reared since birth. Presumably, it could understand concepts like genocide only in terms of numbers killed and the like, and not in the historical and emotional contexts of human suffering. And even if a computer were raised from "birth" as a robot to have the same experiences as its human "brothers," it could still never have our genetic memories, our parent-child relationships, or our sexual feelings; naturally, the prospect of biological computers surmounting these problems might be even more frightening. By elaborating on Dreyfus's phenomenological ideas and surveying the possibilities for the future of computer power, Weizenbaum has produced a convincing argument against a computer society without making unreasonable claims about the immediate applications of intelligent software like chessplaying programs. Of course, much of the technology Weizenbaum foresees is not yet available, but when it is, we will have to reckon with the important problems he has set forth.

John Searle

John Searle, like Dreyfus a Berkeley philosopher, has attempted to provide a positive justification of the impossibility of artificial intelligence. In a provocative article entitled "Minds, Brains, and Programs," he drew a distinction between the research programs of *strong AI* and *weak AI*, the latter being concerned as we are with elucidating the processes of human behavior and developing computer applications based on those principles. Strong AI, though, is the "robotics" branch which contemplates the creation of a complete artificial intelligence whose mind actually does *understand* and *think* in the same sense that a human being does. Conceding that weak AI is a legitimate pursuit, Searle proposed that strong AI cannot be achieved, as long as the computer is the medium for its creation.

The feature of Searle's argument that has gained the most notoriety (and satire) is the so-called *Chinese Room*. To make a concrete analogy to a programmable computer, Searle imagines himself locked in a room in China with no way out. He is handed Chinese writings, but since he speaks only English, he cannot understand them; however, when he is also given a second set of Chinese writings and a set of rules in English to correlate the two batches, he can make associations between sets of what are, for him, meaningless formal symbols. If this process is repeated for a long time with more and more Chinese writings and English rules, Searle will become so proficient that he can do things that *seem* like expert problem solving, story understanding, and Chinese-language communication. In short, though he has absolutely no idea what he is doing, Searle is interacting in the Chinese language just as a native Chinese speaker would. If the room is a computer and Searle is its program, then the people handing him the writings and rules—the programmers—have created an instantiation of a computer program, remarkably similar to that described by Dreyfus as the AI conception of the human being.

Searle's point is that a computer can, in principle, simulate the overt behavior of a human mind. But like the Chinese Room, it cannot *understand* in the same way the mind can. The reason for this is that the computer lacks *intentionality*, that quality of mental states and thoughts which directs them at objects and concepts in the real world. Intentionality is the underlying explanation of beliefs, desires, emotions, fears, and other concepts that actually do seem alien to the formal world of the computer. Searle even goes so far in his exposition to criticize the present states of neurobiology and psychology for ignoring this essential component of human cognition.

When the original paper was published, it generated perhaps more criticism than Dreyfus's first attack. This could be because there were more AI researchers in 1980 than in 1965, or that Searle's arguments were perceived as more reasonable and worthy of counterattack than Dreyfus's apparently *ad hominem* rantings, or it could be because the Chinese Room was a frightfully convincing analogy. Searle was able to field some of the less robust rebuttals, but he seemed to be tripped up by the same cognitive modelling arguments to which Dreyfus has partially yielded.

Zenon Pylyshyn provided a biting commentary in "The 'Causal Power' of Machines," where he proposed that Searle must think that intentionality is caused by the human brain and only the human brain, as though it were a secreted hormone. He continued with a small story in the style of the Chinese Room itself:

> If more and more of the cells in your brain were to be replaced by integrated circuit chips, programmed in such a way as to keep the input-out *function* of each unit identical to that of the unit being replaced, you would in all likelihood just keep right on speaking exactly as you are doing now except that you

would eventually stop *meaning* anything by it. What we outside observers might take to be words would become for you just certain noises that circuits caused you to make.

The obvious implication is that there is no fundamental architectural/structural difference between the units of the brain and the units of the computer, or at least none that cannot be overcome. But Searle was not convinced, and his obstinance on the issue led an angry Douglas Hofstadter to suspect that what lies at the root of most disagreements over the feasibility of AI are religiously held convictions:

> This religious diatribe against AI, masquerading as a serious scientific argument, is one of the wrongest, most infuriating articles I have every read in my life ... it seems to me that what Searle and I have is, at the deepest level, a religious disagreement and I doubt that anything I say could ever change his mind. He insists on these things he calls "causal intentional properties" which seem to vanish as soon as you analyze them, find rules for them, or simulate them.

If Hofstadter is right about Searle's motivations, dark clouds may lie on the horizon for AI. Few researchers are still disturbed by the Chinese Room, but many must fear the reactions to their work from people who, like Searle, simply do not "believe in AI" and will never accept it no matter how convincing the proof.

Fortunately, though strong AI may be in for a rough ride, such conflicts are not yet appearing in the field of weak AI. Intelligent software like natural language interfaces, expert systems, and game-playing programs will be accepted by computer users as long as they are truly useful applications and not just toy demonstrations. We can proceed with reasonable confidence of success without worrying about intentionality, militarism, or phenomenology, but we must keep those concerns in mind if we are ever to actually design an artificial mind.

Human Being and Machines

John von Neumann, the father of the modern digital computer, was preparing to deliver a series of lectures on "The Computer and the Brain" just before his death in the 1950s. Like Shannon and Turing, he had been seriously pondering the possibility of AI several years before the first experimental programs were constructed. But he took a different approach, actually comparing the computer and brain as physical devices (a philosophically bold step in itself) to see if their differences could be reconciled. His notes, though limited by the current state of neurobiology, concluded essentially that the enormous dissimilarities in number of processors, processing speed, interconnections, method of data representation, and so on demand an approach to AI that plays to the strengths and away from the weaknesses of the computer.

AI researchers recognize this necessity, and have become very cautious over the years in their claims of intelligence for their systems. In the rest of this book, we will be considering individually many problems whose solutions can be either *components* of a total intelligent system or standalone applications. But though they are difficult and interesting, they are amenable to implementation on the serial symbol-processing computers of today. The programs presented to illustrate these solutions are not claimed to be intelligent in themselves in the fullest sense, but they are knowledge-based and they do solve problems that we would have expected only an intelligent human being to be able to solve just a few decades ago.

References

Fischler and Firschein's *Intelligence: The Eye, the Brain, and the Computer* introduces just what it claims to quite well in a style the authors describe as intended for "the *Scientific American* level reader." The authors' article on the central role of representation that appeared in *AI Expert* magazine is equally illuminating. Pylyshyn's dense *Computation and Cognition* explains why some form of computation must underly intelligent behavior, and how one should go about studying its mechanisms.

Minsky's absorbing *The Society of Mind* is one of the most fascinating books to appear in recent years, unifying his profound thoughts on intelligence in a truly novel approach. Newell's knowledge-intensive SOAR project is described in "SOAR: An Architecture for General Intelligence;" for a more detailed explanation of a similar theory, see Anderson's *The Architecture of Cognition*. The Knowledge Representation and Reflection hypotheses originated in the prologue to Smith's *Reflection and Semantics in a Procedural Language*, reprinted in Brachman and Levesque's *Readings in Knowledge Representation.*. Figure 2-4 is based on a presentation by Newell in *Unified Theories of Cognition*, the 1987 William James Lectures at Harvard University.

For an overview collection of papers on the issues and problems of AI, Haugeland's *Mind Design* cannot be beat. It includes authors like Newell, Simon, Marr, and Minsky on one side, with Dreyfus and Searle among the opposition. Weizenbaum spells out his position extensively in *Computer Power and Human Reason* (1976), Dreyfus explains his philosophy in *What Computers Can't Do*, 2nd edition

(1979), and Searle defends himself in *Intentionality: An Essay in the Philosophy of Mind* (1983).

More recently, Winograd and Flores have written *Understanding Computers and Cognition: A New Foundation for Design*, which was reviewed by five AI researchers in *Artificial Intelligence*, vol. 31, no. 2, with a response by the authors. Lenat describes his massive knowledge representation endeavor in *CYC: Using Commonsense Knowledge to Overcome Brittleness and Knowledge Acquisition Bottlenecks*. And Von Neumann's book is still in print as *The Computer and the Brain*.

3. KNOWLEDGE REPRESENTATION

The central problem of modern artificial intelligence is *knowledge representation* (KR), which means encoding real-world, "commonsense" knowledge in a format both readable and understandable by the computer. In Chapter 2 we considered some general theoretical problems of artificial intelligence; here we will concentrate on the practice of representing diverse forms of knowledge, working from the assumption that a way to do so actually does exist.

Having adopted the Knowledge Representation and Reflection Hypotheses, we will assume that any quantum of real-world or introspective knowledge can be encoded into some particular configuration of bits in a sufficiently large computer memory. Similarly, the relationships among objects and concepts can also be recorded. But furthermore, we must also stipulate that our representations be such that we can manipulate them to perform what is commonly termed *reasoning*. There is no advantage to having a representation of the world if it cannot be used to advantage.

The main goals of this chapter are to:

- Understand what knowledge representation is, why it is important, and how it underlies all aspects of artificial intelligence.

- Explore the semantic network, one of the first serious attempts to develop a unified KR formalism.

- Move from our semantic network to a frame-based system with property inheritance, the basic mechanism of modern declarative knowledge representation.

- Discuss some more advanced KR concepts within the frame paradigm, including defaults, cancellation, and demons, semantic primitives, and the representation of events and stories.

- Examine some vexing problems for all KR schemes, including the type/token distinction, intension versus extension, and the so-called frame problem.

- Implement and see how to extend a simple frame knowledge base in Turbo Pascal.

Representing Knowledge

In this chapter we will be concerned with *symbolic* knowledge representation, whereby symbols in memory are mapped directly onto the concepts they represent. For example, we could represent the concept of a dog by the string "DOG", a symbol that is taken to stand for the concept it names. Note that symbols are general enough to be used for both concrete and abstract concepts, but specific enough to name individual instances of such concepts. This property is an asset, for it enables us to encompass all the knowledge we need with a single representation method, thus obviating any need to convert back and forth between representations.

Of course, within the broad class of symbolic representations, there are several competing subclasses with distinctive features. as enumerated by Patrick Winston, the key characteristics of good knowledge representation schemata are listed in Figure 3-1.

FIGURE 3-1. **DESIRABLE FEATURES OF KNOWLEDGE REPRESENTATIONS**

---

1. They make the important things explicit.
2. They expose natural constraints, facilitating some class of computations.
3. They are complete (we can say all that needs to be said).
4. They are concise (we can say things efficiently).
5. They are transparent to us (we can understand what has been said).
6. They facilitate computation (we can store and retrieve information rapidly).
7. They suppress detail, but keep it available in case it should be needed.
8. They are computable by an existing procedure (computers can manipulate them).

While these desiderata are generally agreed upon within the artificial intelligence community, the question of which representation scheme embodies the most of them is very much in dispute, as is the question of which are and are not most appropriate for certain problems.

Winston makes another fundamental point about representations: their equivalence. Reductionists will be quick to argue that the question of which representation to use is really moot, since at lower and lower levels to the computer, all representations decompose to data structures, which decompose to words, bytes, and eventually patterns of bits. So we are just using different bit patterns to stand for different concepts.

In a narrow and ultimately inconsequential sense, this is true. It is as true as saying all modern programming languages are equivalent because they are all sufficiently powerful to compute any computable function. However, we recognize that each language has its special advantages and disadvantages, and that each is suited to certain classes of programs. The exact same is true of knowledge representation formalisms: while they are fundamentally equal, their high-level features can aid our thinking about problems and their solutions.

Semantic Networks

One of the first AI researchers to realize that knowledge representation had to be addressed as a problem in itself was Ross Quillian. Prior to his pioneering work, many "representations" had been *ad hoc*, spur-of-the-moment programming hacks cooked up to keep a project on schedule. The central importance of the choice of representation to any AI effort had yet to be realized, and there existed neither a theory of knowledge representation nor a generally known catalog of representation techniques.

Quillian's thesis introduced the *semantic network* formalism for representing commonsense knowledge—information about objects, people, concepts, and the specific relationships between them. His program was intended to model the thought processes one uses when asked to "compare and contrast" two words in a lexicon. By accessing a semantic network through well-defined procedures, it could piece together an answer to such a question on any words represented in the network. A typical modern semantic network (somewhat different from Quillian' models) is shown in Figure 3-2.

Architecture of Semantic Networks

A semantic network consists of a network of labelled *nodes* and *links*, and a system of semantics that gives meaning to the patterns of nodes and links in that network. One reason for the appeal of semantic networks is readily apparent in their highly intuitive, visual nature. Without any prior knowledge of semantic networks, you

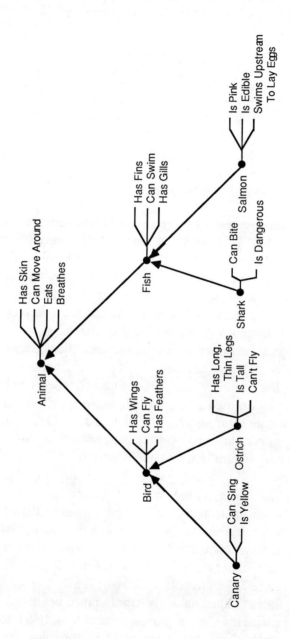

Figure 3–2. A Typical Semantic Network

can probably discern that the sample network in Figure 3-3 represents the knowledge embodied in the English sentence "Victor is a penguin."

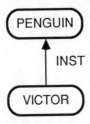

Figure 3–3. **Simple Semantic Network**

In the network, each node represents a physical or mental concept, such as VICTOR (an individual) and PENGUIN (a class, or type of individual). For there to exist a data structure for a node in the computer's memory is for the machine to "have knowledge" that the concept it represents exists. But just having a node in memory does not confer any knowledge *about* a concept other than of its existence: all of the content and features of a concept known to the machine are derived from the relationships between that concept and other concepts in memory.

Those relationships are denoted by links in the semantic network, which always run between two nodes. A link is basically just a pointer from one node to another, much as in a linked list or binary tree, but with an attached label that gives it a meaning. The only relation used in our sample network, INST, might be understood to mean that the concept from which it points is an *INSTance* of the concept to which it points. If you couldn't interpret the network before, you should now be able to read "Victor is a penguin" without much trouble.

Most semantic networks in use today share the basic network structure described above; where they differ is in their semantics. It is important to understand that in itself, a semantic network is meaningless. The meanings of the nodes, links, and labels are completely determined by the procedures that manipulate the network. No matter what the informal conventions of our language and society, the network means what its user wants it to mean. For example, you will probably agree that our sample network in Figure 3-3 represents the knowledge that Victor is a penguin, or more precisely, that the individual named Victor is a member of the set of all things that are called penguins. However, a procedure that took INST to mean "hates" could interpret the sample network as stating that Victor hates penguins. Remember, the semantics of a network are relative to the network's interpreter.

Of course, it would be foolish to write a network-manipulating procedure that represented the relationship of hatred with a link labelled INST. To make networks easier to work with, we normally use labels whose natural meanings are equivalent to the meanings we intend our procedures to ascribe to them. Therefore, it makes sense to use INST to represent the class membership relation as long as the programs that use the network will do the same.

Design of Semantic Networks

So how can we use a semantic network? Really, what kinds of procedures can we create to manipulate such a data structure, or knowledge base? What should the semantics of a network be? We have already seen one of the most common applications of semantic networks: taxonomic classification. When a group of individuals and sets can be organized into a hierarchical structure, such as the animal kingdom, that structure can easily be mapped onto the semantic network formalism.

FIGURE 3-4. **FACTS ABOUT THE ANIMAL KINGDOM**

---

1. Victor is a penguin.
2. All penguins are birds.
3. All birds are animals.
4. All mammals are animals.

5. All dogs are mammals.
6. Charley is a poodle.
7. All poodles are dogs.
8. All terriers are dogs.

We already know that Victor is a penguin; if we add the facts listed in Figure 3-4 to our knowledge base, we get the new network shown in Figure 3-5. It is considerably more complex, and represents more knowledge than the original. You may have noticed a nice feature of semantic networks. Since the information they represent is effectively context-free, or independently defined, they can be augmented incrementally without modifying any existing knowledge. It was a simple matter to add the facts in Figure 3-4 to the network in Figure 3-3, producing the one in Figure 3-5, since adding each new fact was as easy as adding the previous fact.

It is easy to see how we can extend our taxonomic semantic network to cover the entire animal kingdom, or adapt it to cover society's classification of job occupations (a professor is an educator, an educator is a professional, a professional is a salaried employee, a blue-collar worker is ...) or any other suitable domain. We can also add non-taxonomic relationships: suppose that Victor likes Charley, since the dog chases away Victor's natural enemies. Adding a LIKES link pointing from the

VICTOR node to the CHARLEY node inserts this knowledge into our network. If Charley happens to enjoy Victor's company, we could also put a LIKES link in the opposite direction. The resulting network fragment is shown in Figure 3-6.

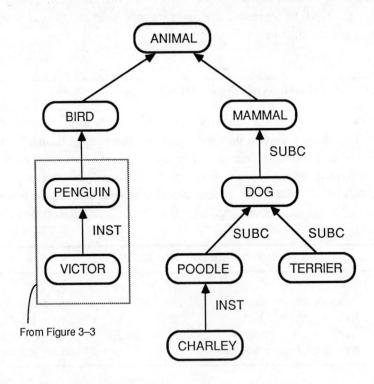

Figure 3–5. **A Larger Semantic Network**

Here we are describing a relationship between two objects, or individuals. To represent the features, or *properties* of an individual or class, we will need new nodes for certain abstract concepts. Suppose we want to represent the sentence "A bird can fly." We need a node for the concept of the ability to fly, plus a link to draw to it from the BIRD node. That link will be labelled PROP, for "has property". Adding some more properties to our network, we get Figure 3-7.

Extending the network from here is easy. We can add a PART link type to allow for objects having separate parts attached to them, an EATS link to show what different species and individuals prefer to eat, and so on. Unfortunately, losing control of the network is even easier. Adding new links like EATS and LIKES may seem fine to those of us who intuitively understand their meaning, but what about the poor program that must interpret the network to give it a semantics for the computer? Each link makes the interpreter that much more complex, and *the real knowledge begins to be transferred from the network to the procedures that control it*. While we recognize that an interpreter gives meaning to the network by using it in a certain way, we must not allow knowledge that should be represented in the network to accumulate in the interpreter. The program will not only slow down but also grow more complex, obscure, and difficult to maintain, and consequently become less and less capable and useful.

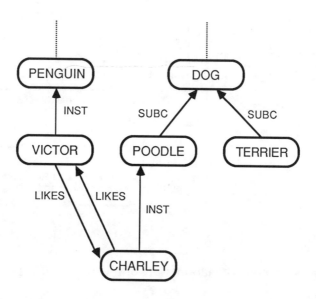

Figure 3–6. **Semantic Network with Property Relations**

A procedure that interprets a semantic network will normally do so by starting at a given node and following pointers to various other nodes, deciding which paths to choose along the way with certain rules about the labels of the links. The more different labels in the network, the more complex the procedure. It is clear that we must limit the semantics of our networks.

Doing so requires that before we create a semantic network, we select a relatively small set of link types that we will stick to. It may also be a good idea to design the programs that will access the network beforehand as well, in order to get a firmer grip on the precise semantics of the network in question. This will help to constrain our work in designing the network itself.

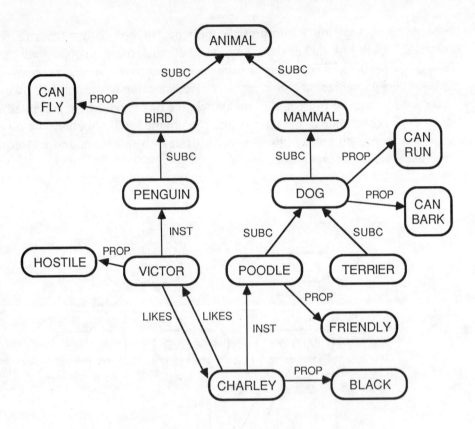

Figure 3–7. **Complex Semantic Network with Properties**

Manipulation of Semantic Networks

Suppose we are asked to develop a knowledge base of facts about the animal world, similar to the example we have been loosely following so far this chapter. The database must hold both taxonomic and property information, and be able to be continually updated and expanded, so at this point, a semantic network design seems an ideal choice. Presumably, we will have to encode an initial amount of information and then design general-purpose procedures for adding new facts and extracting existing knowledge later.

What programs will we have to design? This is the same as asking what questions we will want to ask of the knowledge base. Certainly, will need to find out whether a named animal is an instance of a class of animals ("Is Victor a dog?"), whether one class of animals is a subclass of another class ("Is a dog a bird?"), and whether a given object or class possesses a certain property ("Can a penguin fly? Is Charley nocturnal?"). For now, we will stick with this set of likely queries; but since other good ones, such as "Do dogs prey on birds?" (an inter-class relationship) are possible, we will try to leave our system as open-ended as we can.

The first thing to note is that we *must* have access to each and every object about which the system has knowledge. Since we cannot begin to determine Victor's properties if we can't locate his node, the network must be oriented around the nodes rather than the links. Therefore, it makes good sense to start with a data structure to represent a bare list of nodes, and then build the link/label structure on top of that base. This is known as a *content-addressable memory* (or *associative memory*) because we can access a node in the network by name rather than searching every node until we find the one we need.

Many data structures suggest themselves for this task, among them linked lists, arrays, and balanced search trees. However, none of these fully offer the immediate access to objects that our application demands. A hash table, however does feature a relatively constant lookup time for any key that is in the table. Using one, we can refer to an object by name and quickly access all of the links emanating out of its node. Hash tables are at their weakest when elements must be deleted, but this situation should not come up in our application of representing unchanging, real-world knowledge. Since this is an illustration, to keep things simple we will use the linear search method of resolving collisions in the table.

Each entry in the hash table will correspond to a single node in the semantic network, and will be a record consisting of the object's name (a string) and a list of its links to other objects (a pointer). The node's links will be contained in a simple linked list, with each element a record specifying the link's label, the object to which it points (an index into the hash table), and a pointer to the next element. Figure 3-8 lists the Pascal declarations for this simple semantic network data structure.

We can already design an easy procedure to look at the network and determine if it contains any knowledge of a given object: simply compute the hash function on the object's name, go to that position in the table, and start a linear search for that name in the key field. If we find a match, we have a handle on the object; if we reach an object record with an empty key field, we know that the object does not have a node in the network. Viewing the collection of procedures we are creating as an intelligent system, we can say that it now has the ability to decide whether or not it knows about any given object.

Next we can tackle the problem of determining whether a given object is an instance or subclass of another object. Referring to the objects as Object-1 and Object-2 respectively, we see that there are two positive cases: either Object-1 has an INSTANCE or SUBCLASS link directly to Object-2, or Object-1 has an INSTANCE or SUBCLASS link to a third object, Object-3, which itself is an instance or subclass of Object-2. To answer negatively, we must determine that neither of these cases apply. Essentially, we must develop a procedure that will find any path that exists through the network's INSTANCE and SUBCLASS links from Object-1 to Object-2.

FIGURE 3-8. DECLARATIONS FOR SEMANTIC NETWORK DATA STRUCTURE

```
const
  MAXNODES=101; {Arbitrary maximum number of nodes and size of hash table}
  NAMESIZE=32; {Maximum length of an object name, in characters}

type
  NodeIndex=1..MAXNODES; {Index range for nodes in hash table}
  ObjectName=string[NAMESIZE]; {Object names are short strings}
  LinkLabel=(INST, SUBC, PROP); {Only three types of links allowed}
  LinkRecPtr=^LinkRec; {For linking the list of links}
  LinkRec=record {Link is a label, an object it points to, and a pointer to the next link}
          labelname : LinkLabel;
          pointsto : NodeIndex;
          next : LinkRecPtr;
      end;
  NodeRec=record {Node includes an object and a set of links to other objects}
          object : ObjectName;
          links : LinkRecPtr;
          end;
  Network=array[NodeIndex] of NodeRec; {A network is just one of these tables}

var
  theNetwork : Network; {This variable will actually contain our knowledge base}
```

To do this, we must search the semantic network, starting at node Object-1, for node Object-2. An algorithm called the *Value Inheritance Procedure* (VIP), so named for reasons that will be revealed later, performs this task. As sketched in Figure 3-9, it is based on the *breadth-first search* algorithms, which itself is discussed more fully in Chapter 6. While examining this algorithm (and the others in this chapter), remember that since we have declared the entire semantic network to be a global variable, we are not actually taking nodes out and putting them into queues and the like. Rather, we are storing references to the nodes, in this case indices into the array *theNetwork*.

Quillian's Semantic Networks

At this point you should be comfortable with the basic concepts of semantic network representations. We are now equipped to take a short digression and examine some details of Quillian's pioneering research. Interested primarily in cognitive modeling, as were many AI researchers of his day, Quillian wanted to simulate the data structures and algorithms that human beings use to store and manipulate *semantic memory*, or memory for concepts and the relationships between them, rather than for episodes and their causes and consequences. In retrospect, it is not surprising that he should have coined the phrase *semantic network*.

FIGURE 3-9. SIMPLIFIED VALUE INHERITANCE PROCEDURE (NETWORKS)

INPUT: Two nodes in the network, **Object-1** and **Object-2**.
TO COMPUTE: Is **Object-1** an instance or subclass of **Object-2**?
OUTPUT: YES or NO answer.

1. Form a queue consisting of **Object-1** followed by all the other nodes to which **Object-1** has a direct INSTANCE link.
2. If the queue is empty (no more objects), terminate and return NO.
3. Otherwise, remove the first node from the queue and call it **Object-X**.
   a. If **Object-X** is equal to **Object-2**, terminate and return YES.
   b. Otherwise, add all the nodes to which **Object-X** has a direct SUBClass link to the end of the queue and go back to step 2 above.

Actually, Quillian's networks were considerably more complicated than ours, but the basic structure of nodes/concepts and links/relationships is the same. (Figure 3-10 shows a representative fragment of Quillian's network. Note the explicit partition of the network into separate planes, which gather related concepts.) His first program modeled a hypothesized procedure for answering the standard "compare and contrast" question for any two concepts in human semantic memory. The procedure, called *Intersection Search*, relied on a process called *spreading activation* to model the human memory access activity.

As the question is asked, for example "Compare and contrast the concepts CRY and COMFORT," the search begins at the nodes for CRY and COMFORT. Each is *marked* with a tag of some sort that indicates that it has been visited on the path from either CRY or COMFORT during the search. On the next iteration of the search, all the nodes connected to CRY and COMFORT are similarly marked, after that all their neighbors, and so on. If a node ever acquires two marks, it lies on the intersection of two paths of links, and is said to denote a concept that belongs to the intersection of the two given concepts. By retracing and analyzing the paths to the intersection, the program can generate sentences in a pidgin English to answer the compare-and-contrast question. Figure 3-11 shows some answers so produced that illustrate the sophisticated results of this deceptively simple procedure.

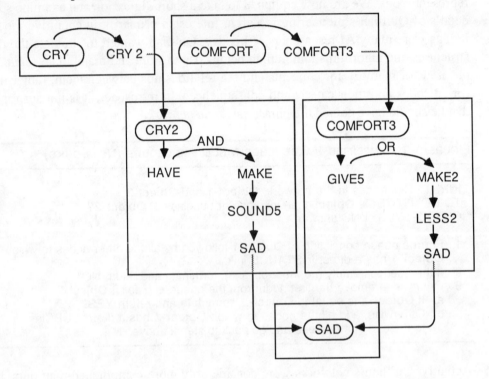

Figure 3–10. **A Fragment from Quillian's Dictionary Network**

Quillian's spreading activation paradigm, while powerful and psychologically profound, is not the principal way in which semantic networks are used today. In the interest of efficiency, modern networks are not designed to model human memory as closely as Quillian's did, since his search procedures were horribly slow. Instead, they usually seek to encode domain-specific knowledge about a limited class of relationships among the members of a relatively small class of concepts.

Problems with Semantic Networks

It turns out that our simple network definition is sufficient to represent many kinds of taxonomic and property information. Assuming that an object can represent quite a large concept, we could build a knowledge base as complex as that shown in Figure 3-2, in which vertical links are SUBClass relations and horizontal ones are PROPerties. At first glance, that network seems perfectly acceptable, but in fact it is very difficult to make serious use of such a structure, since *its semantics are ill-defined.*

FIGURE 3-11. SAMPLE INTERACTION WITH QUILLIAN'S PROGRAM

---

1. *Compare: CRY, COMFORT*
   A. Intersect: SAD
       (1) CRY2 IS AMONG OTHER THINGS TO MAKE A SAD SOUND.
       (2) TO COMFORT3 CAN BE TO MAKE2 SOMETHING LESS2 SAD.
2. *Compare: PLANT, LIVE*
   A. 1st Intersect: LIVE [Note that concepts can intersect in each other]
       (1) PLANT IS A LIVE STRUCTURE.
   B. 2nd Intersect: LIVE
       (2) PLANT IS STRUCTURE WHICH GET3 FOOD FROM AIR. THIS FOOD
            IS THING WHICH BEING2 HAS-TO TAKE INTO ITSELF
            TO7 KEEP LIVE.
3. *Compare: PLANT, MAN*
   A. 1st Intersect: ANIMAL
       (1) PLANT IS NOT A ANIMAL STRUCTURE.
       (2) MAN IS ANIMAL.
   B. 2nd Intersect: PERSON
       (1) TO PLANT3 IS FOR A PERSON SOMEONE TO PUT SOMETHING
            INTO EARTH ["person" is an adjective modifying "someone"].
       (2) MAN3 IS PERSON.
4. *Compare: PLANT, INDUSTRY*
   A. Intersect: INDUSTRY
       (1) PLANT2 IS APPARATUS WHICH PERSON USE FOR5 PROCESS IN
            INDUSTRY.

As William Woods pointed out, semantic networks are only as valuable as their semantics are well-defined. Simply hanging a bunch of sentences off nodes in the network does not give those objects properties with which we can reason later. For example, consider the network fragment shown in Figure 3-12, which can be constructed using the declarations given in Figure 3-8 above.

Can we write a procedure to determine if Charley's color is black, or to print out the name of Charley's color, or to decide whether Susie and Charley are the same color? The answer is no, since the network shown has absolutely no knowledge of the concept of *color*. It no more knows that Charley's color is black than that his automobile or leash is black, or perhaps that his personality is "black" in a figurative sense. It just knows that some property of Charley is black—no more, no less. Precisely, its shortcoming is that violates Rules 1 and 3 of good knowledge representations from Figure 3-1: it fails to make the important thing, the nature of the relationship between Charley and his property black, explicit, and it is in fact incomplete, since there is no way to represent this knowledge *purely within the network*.

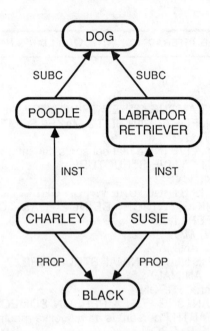

Figure 3–12. **What Can We Do With This Network?**

Frame Systems

In practice, the informality of these network links can be severely limiting. For a semantic network to work well, each concept it uses must have an explicit representation within the network. But the simple architecture we have introduced here cannot represent all the concepts it needs. To remedy the problem, we will turn the network into a simple *frame system* by replacing the weak PROP link with a new SLOT field. An object may have any number of SLOTs, each of which must have a *name* and a *filler*, which are simply pointers to other objects in the network. Figure 3-13 below shows the changes to our original declarations that are necessary to implement the new system.

With these changes, the expressive power of the network increases dramatically, as does the collective capacity of our programs to reason with it. Figure 3-14 shows the structure of a frame system—note that each object, or frame, is structured like a database record (slots & fillers, fields & values), and the whole system can be thought of as a database with inheritance properties.

Indeed, a modern frame system can often be thought of as an hierarchical relational database. An object's properties, as defined by SLOT/FILLER pairs, can originate with itself or with its superclasses in the hierarchy (which is typically taxonomic in some sense, as with the animal kingdom). For example, suppose all dogs were predatory. To represent the fact that Charley, an INSTance of the class DOG, is predatory, we should not have to add a new slot and filler to the CHARLEY node. Instead, we want Charley to *inherit* the property of being predatory from his superclass of dogs.

FIGURE 3-13. **MAKING THE SEMANTIC NETWORK INTO A FRAME SYSTEM**

```
type
  LinkLabel=(INST, SUBC, SLOT); {Only three types of links allowed}
  LinkRec= record
          labelname : LinkLabel; {The type of the link}
          slotname : NodeIndex;
              {For INST and SUBC, this is what the link points to}
          fillername : NodeIndex;
              {Make this a 0 (dummy value) for INST and SUBC links}
          next : LinkRecPtr; {Pointer to next link in list}
      end;
```

Value Inheritance

We can now undertake a full explanation of value inheritance, a procedure to which we alluded before. Inheritance is one of the most powerful knowledge representation mechanisms for enforcing the principle of *cognitive economy* from Rule 4, which states that no concept should be overrepresented (by more nodes or links than necessary). With inheritance, an object can automatically take on all the properties of all its superclasses without adding a single node or link. Figure 3-15 shows a sample frame system with inherited properties.

Inheritance is an inference process that allows us to deduce implicit information that is not explicitly represented in the network. Therefore, we can divide the knowledge represented by the network in Figure 3-15 into explicit and implicit categories as follows:

EXPLICIT: Charley is a dog, Charley's color is black, Charley's owner is
Chris, Black is a color, Chris is an owner, Chris is an animal, Chris's dog
is Charley, A dog is an animal, An animal's home is earth.

IMPLICIT: Charley is an animal, Charley's home is earth, Chris's home is
earth.

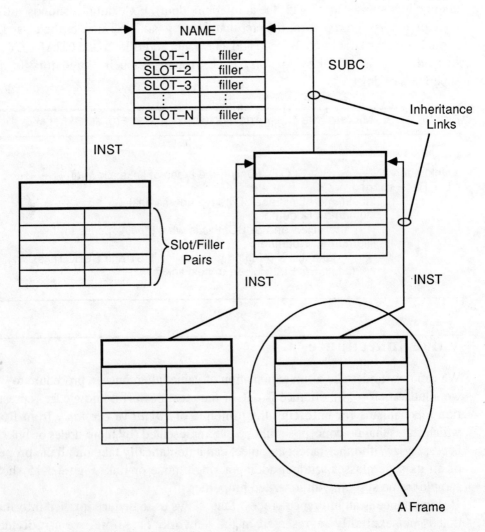

Figure 3–14. **The Structure of a Frame System**

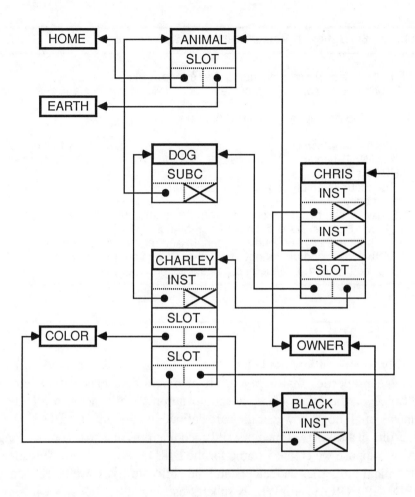

Figure 3–15. **Inheritance in a Simple Frame System**

Obviously there is great economy of storage in the creation of implicit knowledge, but we pay for it in the increased cost of extracting that knowledge. To get at each piece of explicit information listed above, we just look up a node in the network and go through its list of links. But to compute each piece of implicit information, we must run the Value Inheritance Procedure, which in turn must use several pieces of explicit information, making for an obviously more expensive process. Figure 3-16 shows a new VIP that works with the slots and fillers in a frame system.

FIGURE 3-16. GENERAL VALUE INHERITANCE PROCEDURE (FRAME SYSTEMS)

INPUT: An object **N** and a slotname **S** in the network.
TO COMPUTE: Assuming **N** represents an individual or class and **S** a property, what
　　　　　　 is the value of **N**'s **S** property?
OUTPUT: The appropriate slot filler(s), or an error if none exist.

1. Form a queue consisting of **N** followed by all the other nodes to which **N** has a
   direct INSTance link, followed by all the other nodes to which **N** has a direct
   SUBClass link.
2. If the queue is empty (no more objects), terminate and return a "no value"
   error code.
3. Otherwise, remove the first node from the queue and call it **X**.
   a. Find all of **X**'s SLOT links with slotname **S** (if any).
   b. If there are any such slots, terminate and return a list of their fillers.
   c. Otherwise, add all the nodes to which **X** has a direct SUBClass link
      to the end of the queue and go back to step 2 above.

Defaults and Cancellation

One way to look at inherited slot fillers in frame systems is as *default values*, or
prototype properties that apply to all members of a class. If we create a new
INSTance of the DOG class, it should automatically acquire all the standard
attributes of all dogs, however they are defined in the frame for DOG. As we know,
this results in a savings of memory and encoding time at a cost of processing speed.

　　Now suppose we create a frame for the BIRD class, giving it slot/filler pairs for
such typical properties as feathers and the ability to fly. If we make frames for the
ROBIN, SPARROW, and WREN subclasses, simple SUBC links will serve to give
those kinds of birds all the default properties of normal birds. However, what if we
put the PENGUIN class into our taxonomy? A penguin has no feathers and cannot
fly, so we do not want it to inherit all the properties of a BIRD. We may want it to
inherit properties like being cold-blooded or small in size, though.

　　As specified in Figure 3-16, our general VIP already implements the *cancellation* mechanism for avoiding this problem. Basically, cancellation occurs when an
object has its own filler value for a slot that one or more of its superclasses already
possesses. In our example, the PENGUIN can keep all the default BIRD properties
it wants and replace those that do not apply (feathers and flying) by adding appropriate slot/filler pairs to its own frame. When the VIP comes to the PENGUIN
frame, it will look at its slots for appropriate values before adding its superclasses
to the queue; therefore, any relevant fillers will be found at the lowest possible level
of the network, thereby cancelling out any further inheritance.

Procedure Attachment

Often, the value of a slot's filler depends on other information in the database, as with a frame for a RECTANGLE whose AREA value is equal to the product of its LENGTH and WIDTH values. At first, we could insert the LENGTH and WIDTH, calculate the AREA by hand, and insert it too. However, if the LENGTH and/or WIDTH should change, the AREA value will become inconsistent, and must be recalculated. But the system has no way of knowing that it is invalid. A better solution is to use an *if-needed demon*, a procedure that sits in the AREA filler field until someone asks for the AREA, at which point it automatically computes and returns the appropriate value.

In the value inheritance procedure from Figure 3-16, the application of if-needed demons would take place in step 3b. Having retrieved all the slots with the given name for the current object, we would obtain their values by either looking at a filler (the standard case) or a pointer of some sort to the if-needed procedure, which we would execute to compute the final filler value.

Such *procedure attachment*, one of the key features of Minsky's original frame proposal, gives a frame database virtually limitless flexibility. Anything that cannot be expressed with the internal language of the system objects, slots, and fillers can be accomplished via an external procedure. If-needed demons are an obviously useful application of procedural attachment. In a total system, certain slots could have special procedures to calculate their values based on factors both inside (as with if-needed demons) and outside (such as perceptual input or user prompting) of the database.

Unfortunately, there is no reasonable way to mix data and program code in Pascal, as required for procedure attachment. Nor is there a facility for adding code to a running program, as when an if-needed demon is created for a new frame. But even when implemented conveniently, procedure attachment can easily become a slippery slope, its unrestricted use creating a tangled mess of undecipherable code and data. Confining it to if-needed demons and other well-defined, essential features is necessary to preserve the relatively clean semantics of frame systems.

Semantic Primitives and Episodic Memory

Frame systems with inheritance provide a basic framework for investigating declarative knowledge representations. But the concept that knowledge can be represented in the computer would not be useful if it were not always possible to decide whether two such representations in fact encoded the same piece of knowledge. Within the same framework, then, any concept ought to be represented always in the same way. This is the theory underlying research into *semantic primitives*, or systems of elementary conceptual units into which any piece of knowledge can be decomposed for representational purposes.

Several proposals for a comprehensive system of semantic primitives exist. *Roget's Thesaurus* includes a "synopsis of categories" that attempts to organize the 1040 basic concepts. Yorick Wilks has proposed a system of about 70 elements, divided into entities, actions, type indicators, sorts, and cases. Combining these elements into a class hierarchy, he creates a microlanguage in which concepts of any complexity can be expressed by constructing formulas. For example, the concept of liquidity, *[FLOW STUFF]*, is a formula using the action of flowing and the entity of stuff; likewise, *[THRU PART]* expresses the idea of an aperture. However, the most successful system of semantic primitives to date has been conceptual dependency theory.

Conceptual Dependency

Roger Schank has been the most forceful advocate of semantic primitives, and he has developed over a 20-year period a comprehensive theory of knowledge representation and system of primitives called *conceptual dependency* theory (CD). CD is normally applied to natural language understanding tasks, like story comprehension and news digesting, but its basic function is as a model of *episodic memory* or knowledge of sequential events.

The primitives of CD are eleven *acts*, or types of event, which are summarized in Figure 3-17; an additional DO act is sometimes added to indicate an unknown event. Any event can be represented as a simple record with the following fields:

FIGURE 3-17. THE PRIMITIVES OF CONCEPTUAL DEPENDENCY

ATRANS	Transfer of an abstract relationship, such as possession or ownership
ATTEND	Action of directing a sense organ towards an object
EXPEL	Expulsion from the body of an animal into the world
GRASP	Grasping of an object by an actor
INGEST	Taking in of an object by an animal
MBUILD	Construction of new information from old information
MOVE	Movement of a body part by an animal
MTRANS	Transfer of mental information between actors or within an actor
PROPEL	Application of physical force to an object
PTRANS	Transfer of physical location of an object
SPEAK	Action of producing sounds from the mouth

Name	(An identifier for this particular event.)
Location	Where did the event occur?
Time	When did the event occur?
Actor	Who (or what) performed the act?
Action	What act occurred?
Object	What was the act done to?
[Direction]	
From	Where did the act start?
To	Where did the act end?
Instrumental	How was the act performed? (A link to another concept.)

It is important to remember that only events can be represented by the CD primitives; to fill in the slots in this frame, we must rely on standard semantic information such as names and times. Such concepts cannot be reduced to simpler symbols, but are themselves elementary units of knowledge. In a practical system, episodic and semantic knowledge can be mixed in a single frame database, as shown in Figure 3-18.

With a unified representation for events in hand, we can look at applications. A common account of human reasoning holds that the process of comprehension is based substantially on the matching of *events* to *expectations*. Upon encountering a new situation (in real life, reading, on television, etc.), we summon up a stored representation of a stereotyped, almost caricatured, version of the events. By matching the variables in such *schemata* with the actors and objects we encounter, we construct a mental model of the proceedings that we can later manipulate and modify as events continue.

Scripts for Understanding

As we saw in Chapter 1, the use of structural models of the real world was one of SHRDLU's important advances in getting computers to actually understand the symbols their programs were juggling. Schank has built upon this idea to produce a more formal theory of understanding based on conceptual dependency and centered on the *script*. A script is just that: a description of how events should be acted out in a real-world scene. Each time we instantiate a particular script in memory, we create a model of the real-world situation that we can use to make predictions about future events and answer questions about past ones.

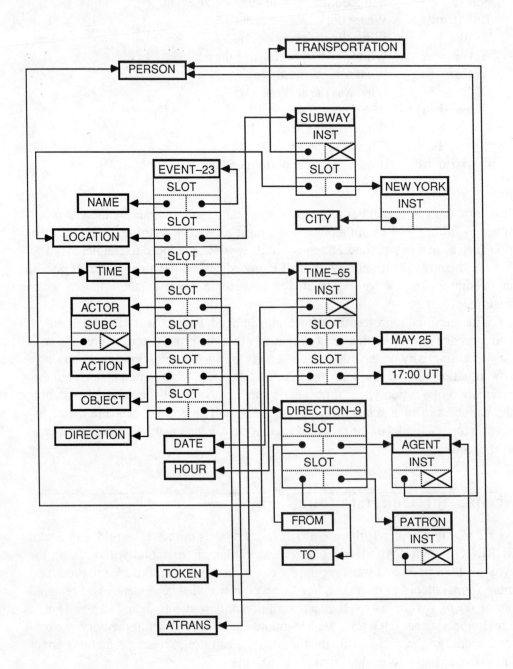

Figure 3–18. **Representing Events in Conceptual Dependency Theory**

Figure 3-19 diagrams a typical script: the subway ride. Actors are identified with boldface type, CD events with capital letters. Note the availability of an alternative scenario in episodes 2-3 for reaching the platform—it is possible to include both alternatives because their ultimate result will be the same: the ride will be completed. The interplay between the episode descriptions and the maincons, or goals, is what gives the system its power of explanation.

FIGURE 3-19. THE "SUBWAY SCRIPT" IN OUTLINE FORM

E=Episode/event, M=Maincon (goal of episode), patgrp="group of patrons"

E1: Patron enters station
M1: **patgrp** PTRANS to inside station
E2: Patron goes directly to turnstile   [E3: Patron gets a token, then goes to turnstile]
M2: **patgrp** PTRANS to turnstile   [M3: **agent** ATRANS token to **patgrp**]
E4: Patron goes through turnstile, goes to platform
M4: **patgrp** WAIT at platform
E5: Subway arrives
M5: **trainman** PTRANS subway to platform
E6: Patron enters subway and sits down
M6: **patgrp** MOVE to seat
E7: Subway goes to a new destination
M7: **trainman** PTRANS subway to new destination
E8: Patron leaves the station
M8: **patgrp** PTRANS from station

Minsky's original frame proposal contained many similarities to Schank's scripts, and indeed we can represent scripts quite simply within our frame database. The events in a script are normally organized in simple chronological order. Therefore, if an event is represented as a frame whose slots are its location, action, direction, and so on, a script can be a frame whose slotnames are the names of its individual subevents and whose fillers are the event frames themselves. In essence, as shown in Figure 3-20, we are imposing a new "event hierarchy" on our frame system, complementing the inheritance hierarchy already in place. Indeed, there is no reason why the tree cannot have even more levels to represent scripts of scripts, or more detailed "microscripts" for events.

Scripts are powerful reasoning tools because of their ability to make predictions and fill in missing details about sequences of events. If you are in your dentist's office and instantiate the proper script, once you sit down in the chair you will anticipate having your teeth examined. Similarly, if you read a news item about the president signing a new law, your "how a bill becomes a law" script will let you infer that both houses of Congress have already passed the measure. Figure 3-21 shows Schank's *SAM* (Script Applier Mechanism) program using a restaurant script to understand and answer questions about a short story.

Script systems today are considerably more complex than simple frames of events. They include alternatives, multiple levels of detail, and elaborations. Other key aspects of the understanding process, such as plans, goals, and themes, are incorporated into systems that can analyze political arguments, digest and summarize newspaper articles, and interpret more complex narratives with respect to the intentions of the actors. Practice has shown that conceptual dependency and script theory can be integrated with frame systems to produce a viable model for practical knowledge representation systems.

Problems in Knowledge Representation

Just as astrophysicists struggle with the neutrino and missing mass problems, AI researchers have identified their share of qualitative sticking points. These difficult problems, such as the combinatorial explosion in search and the assignment of credit in learning, are fundamental to the artificial intelligence enterprise. To conclude our study of knowledge representation, we will survey three such problems for KR formalisms: the type/token distinction, intensional versus extensional concepts, and the "frame problem" itself. All three problems considered here are thorny ones for knowledge representation. Still, progress has been made, and the existence of working systems proves that they need not be immovable obstacles in the paths of commonsense reasoning and representation.

The Type/Token Distinction

Sometimes inheritance can be too powerful, as in the example of Figure 3-22. Does this semantic network represent the knowledge that Victor is an endangered species? According to our standard inheritance procedures, it does. But is that piece of knowledge one that we intended to represent when we put the SUBC link between the PENGUIN and ENDANGERED-SPECIES nodes? Probably not, since it is unusual to think of individuals as being themselves in danger of extinction; rather, we understand that they are members of a species that is endangered.

This example demonstrates the need for a *type/token distinction*. Ordinary semantic networks and frame systems have fuzzy notions of the class and the individual. It is perfectly clear that Victor is an individual and Penguin is a class, but it

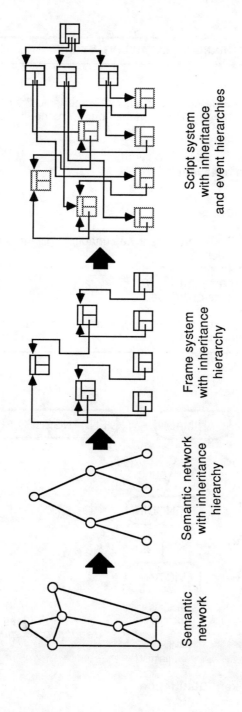

Figure 3–20. Increasing Hierarchy from Semantic Networks to Scripts

FIGURE 3-21. **SAM UNDERSTANDING A RESTAURANT STORY**

Input text:

John went to a restaurant. He ordered a hot dog. The waiter said they didn't have any. He asked for a hamburger. When the hamburger came, it was burnt. He left the restaurant.

Question answering output:

Q1: Did John sit down in the restaurant?
A1: Probably.
Q2: Did John order a hot dog?
A2: Yes.
Q3: Did John eat a hot dog?
A3: No, the waiter told John the management was unable to give it to him.
Q4: What did the waiter serve John?
A4: The waiter served John a hamburger.
Q5: Why didn't John eat the hamburger?
A5: Because the hamburger was overdone.
Q6: Did John pay the check?
A6: No, John was angry because the hamburger was overdone and so he left the restaurant.

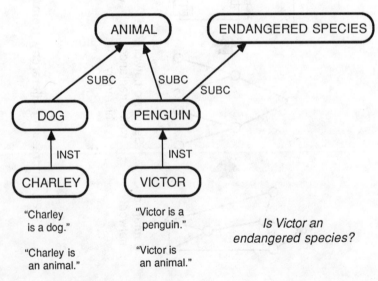

Figure 3–22. **The Type/Token Distinction**

is also obvious that some properties of the class should be inherited (no feathers, subclass of animal, cannot fly) and some should not (endangered species). The latter property applies to the class itself (the *type*), as though it were an individual in a hierarchy of classes, whereas the former properties apply to the prototype member (the *token*) of the class. This distinction, though essential, can be difficult to implement.

One solution would create two nodes for each concept, one for its type and one for its token (for actual individuals, like Victor, the type node would be superfluous). Properties of the type would be inheritable only by SUBClasses, whereas properties of the token would extend also to individual INSTances of the object. But although this kludge will solve our sample problem, it might not be general enough to account for all the type/token ambiguities that come up in knowledge representation. A true solution may have to address the fundamental distinction between intensional and extensional concepts.

Intension versus Extension

Beyond the type/token problem, the meaning of a represented concept may be unclear. Consider the following sentence:

The morning star is the evening star.

Is it true? Yes and no. In fact, the real-world astronomical entities referred to as "the morning star" and "the evening star" are in fact the same object. But the two concepts are quite different; after all, if they were really nothing more than the same object, there would never have evolved two different names. Clearly, the concept "morning star" has some attributes that do not apply to the concept "evening star" and vice-versa.

The *extensional* meaning of a concept is the set of real-world objects it describes, whereas the *intensional* meaning of that concept is its intrinsic meaning, as defined apart from the present state of the world. We might think of extensions as denotations or references, and intensions as connotations or senses. For example, the concept "dog" can be defined extensionally as the set of all dogs in the world, or intensionally according to the features unique to "dogness" and the ideas associated with dogs.

Unfortunately, knowledge representation schemes like our semantic network and frame systems often fail to distinguish between intensional and extensional concepts. How could we properly represent all that is conveyed by the sample sentence above? Anthony Maida and Stuart Shapiro have suggested that semantic networks should strive to model intensions in preference to extensions whenever possible. In their view, a program constrained to represent only extensional concepts is ill-equipped to believe and disbelieve or reason hypothetically, let alone creatively. Consider this sentence:

The president of the United States is a woman.

As of this writing, the sentence is factually false. However, we can readily contemplate it and its consequences, just as we can answer questions like this:

How many horns would a two-headed unicorn have?

Clearly, both intensional and extensional concepts must be representable within a system that is to be truly capable of "commonsense" reasoning.

The Frame Problem

The infamous "frame problem" (which has little to do with frame theory as we have been studying it) is that of describing, computationally, what properties persist and what properties change as actions are performed or simulated. In other words, how can a system that receives new knowledge know which pieces of its existing knowledge are rendered invalid or inconsistent by the new information?

The following concrete example is commonly used: suppose you are a robot programmed to wander throughout an unfamiliar building and gather enough information to draw a floorplan of that building. Your knowledge at any point in time, represented as a semantic network or frame database in memory, includes information about the time, your location, the surrounding furniture, etc. As you move out of a room and into a corridor, the part of your knowledge that said you were in that room is no longer correct. But how do you "know" that it is incorrect, and how do you find and excise that fact and others that may depend upon its validity, such as the fact that there were two chairs behind you, and so on?

The frame problem results from the logical nature of the representation schemes used by a reasoning system. Although we have tried to avoid murky discussions of formal logic in knowledge representation, it is undeniable that both semantic networks and simple frame systems have their roots in basic *first-order logic*, or the *predicate calculus*. Each fact in the knowledge base can be thought of as a true logical proposition—an axiom—and each fact we can deduce from those explicitly present corresponds to a theorem. Therefore, the system's knowledge at any point is the set of axioms it knows and theorems it can prove from those axioms and already proven theorems.

However, it should be apparent that the size of this set can only increase as time goes on, and situations change, unless we allow the removal of axioms. But if we remove an axiom, we must also remove or rejustify all the theorems in whose proof we used the no longer valid axiom. And even if this is easily done, it is hard to know which axioms to remove in the first place! We therefore say that first-order logic is *monotonic* in that it provides no mechanism for reducing the number of true propositions should an axiom become invalid. By extension, all representations based on first-order logic will suffer from the frame problem unless extraordinary non-logical reasoning procedures are used.

A clean solution to the frame problem is an elusive goal for research into reasoning with knowledge bases. The main line of attack involves the development of alternative logics with special operators such as "it is provable that" or "it is believed that" in addition to the normal AND, OR, and NOT. Such formal systems, with names like circumscription, default logic, modal logic, non-monotonic logic, persistence logic, temporal logic, and the exotic S4, S5, and Z, all attempt to build in avoidance of the frame problem. However, they have proven difficult to apply in practical systems, since the clarity and computational tractability of inference procedures for first-order logic often vanishes with the introduction of the complex mechanisms of belief and similar concepts.

A Frame Database in Pascal

The listing SEMANTIC.PAS contains Turbo Pascal source code for the data structures and basic procedures of a simple frame database of the type we have been discussing throughout this chapter. *NETMENU* is a complete program, based on the code in SEMANTIC.PAS, that implements a menu-driven interface to the various procedures for manipulating the system.

When you run the program you get a simple menu of operations to perform on the database, which are explained below:

Hash (object)	Compute the hash function on an object
Find (object)	Find the index of an object in the table
AddNode (object)	Insert a new object into the network
AddLink (node,linktype,slot,filler)	Give a node a new link
DescribeNode (node)	Print out the links of a node
GetLink (node,linktype)	Find a node's links of a certain type
GetSlot (node,slot)	Find a node's fillers for a certain slot
ValueInherit (node,slot)	Find a node's (inherited) filler for a slot

Each of these is a Pascal procedure that should be self-explanatory. Manipulating a semantic network or frame system involves little more than simply walking through the data structures outlined in Figures 3.8 and 3.13; although the details of pointer dereferencing and array indexing can get messy, the basic concepts are remarkably simple.

Programming Exercises

1. NETMENU's output is annoying because it likes to identify an object by a number—its index into the network hash table—rather than by its name. Eliminate this inconvenience and improve the user interface of NETMENU, trying whenever possible to shield the user from the details of the frame system data structures.

2. Our current frame system data structure is messy and inconsistent in at least two ways. First, it separates INST and SUBC links from SLOTs, using a "dummy value" for the filler in the latter two cases. Second, it requires an entire slot/filler pair for each filler—you cannot specify a list of fillers for a single slot, such as "favorite foods". This creates ambiguities with inheritance. Try to fix these problems by making INST and SUBC slotnames with equal status, and by converting the filler field into a linked list of object indices. What new problems do these changes introduce, and how can you fix them?

3. (After completing exercise 2.) Rewrite the value inheritance procedure in SEMANTIC.PAS to operate on the new frame system data structure. It should work as before, but with the added capability of inheriting both superclasses and ordinary slot fillers. If Charley is a dog, and a dog is an animal, the new procedure should be able to determine that Charley is an animal, not just that he inherits the ordinary properties of an animal.

4. A frame or semantic network knowledge base is not useful if we must rebuild it at the keyboard each time we want to use it. Create a format for storing a database on disk; remember that since the data structures are dynamic, it is not good enough just to try to write out the hash table in order. Write procedures to load and save these files.

5. After reading one of Quillian's papers, design a data structure to implement his original form of semantic network. How can different planes of memory be represented? Implement a version of his intersection search algorithm, and use it to find concepts commonly related to various different word pairs.

6. Working from our basic frame database structures, create a unified representation for events and scripts. What types of programs can be created to reason with such structures? Look into the Schank's work described in *Inside Computer Understanding*, and try to implement some of his algorithms. Do the type/token distinction, intension and extension, or the frame problem play a role in your efforts?

7. Maida and Shapiro described methods for representing intensional concepts in semantic networks. After reading "Intensional Concepts in Propositional Semantic Networks," implement their network in Pascal. What parts of our data structures can be retained, and which must be changed or discarded? Try to write inference procedures to answer question like McCarthy's telephone number problem. Is the integration of intensional representations into the network necessary for all applications, or can it be a burden?

Summary

Since the discovery in the 1960s that knowledge is fundamental to intelligent behavior, the development of better ways to represent knowledge has become a central enterprise of artificial intelligence. A good representation scheme has several characteristics, including explicitness, constraints, parsimony, and computability. Commonsense knowledge is ordinary information about real-world objects and the relationships between those objects.

The semantic network is a useful representation formalism for such knowledge, allowing the easy expression of taxonomies and properties. Intersection search can find extended relationships between concepts. Inheritance allows an individual or class in a hierarchy to automatically acquire the properties of its superclasses, producing economy of memory at the expense of retrieval time—the store/compute tradeoff revisited. Frame systems improve upon semantic networks by adding slots and fillers, as well as advanced capabilities like defaults, cancellation, and procedure attachment.

Episodic memory can be modelled with conceptual dependency theory, which decomposes events into a small set of elementary actions. The use of such semantic primitives and their combination in scripts facilitates understanding and reasoning about real-world knowledge and stories. Three difficulties with reasoning knowledge representation are the type/token distinction, intension versus extension, and the frame problem.

References

AI textbooks must necessarily cover knowledge representation. Winston, from whom Figure 3-1 is taken, offers an approach similar to ours, emphasizing semantic networks and frame systems, whereas Charniak and McDermott concentrate on logic-based formalisms. The general issues of knowledge based systems are reviewed from a personal perspective by Levesque in his 1985 Computers and Thought Award Lecture, "Making Believers out of Computers." Data structures like hash tables are covered in Aho, Hopcroft, and Ullman's *Data Structures and Algorithms* and Reingold and Hansen's *Data Structures*.

The best starting point for an investigation of the literature is Brachman and Levesque's *Readings in Knowledge Representation*. Among the 31 classic papers reprinted in its pages are McCarthy's "Epistemological Problems of Artificial Intelligence," Quillian's pioneering description of semantic networks, "Word Concepts: A Theory and Simulation of Some Basic Semantic Capabilities," Maida and Shapiro's "Intensional Concepts in Propositional Semantic Networks," Brachman's "On the Epistemological Status of Semantic Networks," Woods's penetrating "What's in a Link: Foundations for Semantic Networks," and Minsky's groundbreaking "A Framework for Representing Knowledge." (Figure 3-2 appeared in Brachman; Figures 3-10 and 3-11 are from Quillian.)

Schank's work on conceptual dependency is illustrated in *Inside Computer Understanding*, the source of Figures 3-19 and 3-21, which presents Lisp "micro-versions" of SAM and other well-known CD programs. The frame problem is the exclusive subject of Brown's *The Frame Problem in Artificial Intelligence: Proceedings of the 1987 Workshop*. The use of knowledge is explored in Halpern's *Theoretical Aspects of Reasoning About Knowledge: Proceedings of the 1986 Workshop*.

Touretzky's *The Mathematics of Inheritance Systems* provides a complete formal analysis of value inheritance in networks, as well as its computation by special-purpose hardware of the type described by Fahlman in *NETL: A System for Representing and Using Real-World Knowledge*. Fahlman also argues for a "knowledge substrate" and a fast set-intersection operation as fundamental tools for intelligence. And as usual, *The Handbook of AI* provides a comprehensive survey of representation techniques.

4. NATURAL LANGUAGE PROCESSING

As we saw in Chapter 1, *natural language processing* (NLP) is a characteristic application that has been a prominent goal in both academic and commercial AI research circles for several decade; indeed getting the artificial to understand the natural is the emblematic problem of all AI. The dreams of easy and efficient natural language communication with software and computer interpretation of various texts are closer to reality today than when AI was born, but there are still many problems to be solved. Nevertheless, much ground has been covered from ELIZA's psychological mimicry to Q&A's "Intelligent Assistant," and we will try to retrace some of the progress that has been made to date in NLP.

Ironically, the very first experiments with natural languages and computers were rather spectacular failures in the field of *machine translation*. In the mid-1950s, scientists demonstrated that the new devices could automatically translate sentences like these from Russian or any other foreign language to English:

> *The quality of crude oil is determined by calorie content.*
> *The quality of saltpeter is determined by chemical methods.*
> *TNT is produced from coal.*
> *They obtain dynamite from nitroglycerine.*

Such impressive results generated considerable enthusiasm for translation research, which received substantial funding for about ten years until progress simply stopped occurring. When faced with texts larger than single sentences, even when restricted to technical domains, the translators could not produce output that was comprehensible without much post-editing by human assistants.

But whatever its follies, machine translation research did have the beneficial effect of illuminating many important problems in the broader field of natural language processing, including syntax versus semantics and pragmatics, referential ambiguity, word-sense disambiguation, and the role of context. Throughout our exploration of modern NLP techniques, we will be forever re-examining these problems and their possible solution.

The main goals of this chapter are to:

- Introduce the problem of language processing and understanding.

- Understand the central concepts of syntax, semantics, and pragmatics.

- Investigate various formalisms for representing and parsing languages, including regular expressions, context-free grammars, and augmented transition networks.

- Consider semantic grammars and the application of natural-language interfaces to database management systems and other software.

- Implement such an interface, by means of a recursive-descent parser, to the simple frame system from Chapter 3.

What is a Language?

In order to process languages, we must have a rather precise definition of what they are. Classically, a formal language is simply a *set of sentences*. A sentence is just a string, and any sentence that is in the established set is a proper sentence of the language. Any sentence that is not a member of the set does not belong to the language. For example, the "sentence" AND is in the language {AND, OR, NOT}, but IMPLIES is not. As you can see, when a language is *finite*, a simple table lookup procedure suffices to decide whether a given string is in that language.

If English, which we will assume to be a reasonably typical example of a natural language, were finite (which it is manifestly not), we could conceivably enumerate all the sentences that were in it. However, it is virtually certain that natural languages are *infinite*, so we can never hope to list out all their member sentences. To work with an infinite language, natural or otherwise, we must create a finite specification of the language, or a description of the *general structure* of its member sentences. (One way to think of finite and infinite languages is that the former are defined extensionally, whereas the latter are defined intensionally.)

The structure of an infinite language can be finitely delineated by a *decision procedure*, which takes as input a sentence and outputs "yes" if the sentence is a legal one for the language or "no" if it is not. For example, consider the language whose

sentences are all the strings that consist only of zero or more uppercase letter **A**s.*
Since there are an infinite number of such strings, the language is infinite.
Therefore, we create this pseudo-Pascal decision procedure to model it:

1. Let i=1
2. If string[i]=NIL then return YES.
3. If string[i]="A" then do the following:
   a. Let i=i+1
   b. Go back to step 2
4. Otherwise, return NO

Given a string whose last element is NIL as input, this algorithm will return YES
only if the string is either empty or consists entirely of **A**s. It will halt and return
NO as soon as it finds a non-**A** element in the string.

As you can imagine, creating a decision procedure for a natural language will be
a difficult chore, if it is in fact possible to accomplish. We will build up to the task
by considering some well-defined classes of simpler languages that are still important to explore. But even if we had such a procedure, would it be useful in actually
understanding natural language? It would be interesting, but not very practical, for
a program to just decide whether an utterance were a valid English sentence. To be
considered intelligent, the program should know what the sentence *means*, at least
in as much sophistication as is necessary to properly utilize and respond to the sentence.

Syntax, Semantics, and Pragmatics

Determining that meaning requires an analysis of the sentence on several different
levels: the *syntactic*, the *semantic*, and the *pragmatic*. Syntax is a tool for describing
the structure of sentences in the language (as discussed above), semantics denotes
the "literal" meaning we ascribe to a sentence, and pragmatics refers to the
"intended" meaning of a sentence. And although the sentence has classically been the
basic unit of linguistic analysis, AI often demands yet a higher level, that of the *discourse*, or conversation, between two or more individuals.

A concrete example may illuminate the distinction between the levels. Consider
the following short conversation:

---

* Henceforth we will follow the convention of writing all symbols in strings of formal languages
  in boldface type.

Elizabeth:	*Did you know that Victor used to smoke just like you?*
Jack:	*No. What happened to him?*
Elizabeth:	*Lung cancer. He kicked the bucket.*
Jack:	*I'm sorry to hear that.*

Focus on Elizabeth's statement "He kicked the bucket." Syntactically, we understand that a male individual did an action (verb) to a noun object. We could discover this by diagramming the sentence as we were probably taught in school. Semantically, we see that he used his foot to propel some sort of container, but pragmatically we realize that "Victor died" is what is really meant. Finally, we realize that the main role of this sentence in the discourse is as Elizabeth's warning to Jack not to smoke too heavily.

What is really going on at each level of analysis? At the syntactic level, we are dividing the sentence up into functional parts and assigning a part of speech, or role, to each word. The successful conclusion of this *parsing* process also indicates that the sentence is a member of the language as far as formal structure is concerned. With semantic analysis, we retrieve some description of the meaning of each word and combine those meanings (according to the sentence's syntax) to form a meaning for the whole utterance. In pragmatics, the surrounding sentences start to creep into our analysis, as we try to determine the referents of pronouns and other ambiguous syntactic objects, as well as to discover whether our semantic analysis was correct or whether the sentence has a deeper meaning. Finally, discourse analysis places the sentence in the overall context of an interaction by modelling the beliefs, goals, intentions, and plans of the speakers.

Our analysis of a sentence can fail at any one of these levels. "Kicked bucket him the," for example, does not even make it past the syntactic test. And while "The bucket kicked him" is certainly a well-formed sentence, the meanings of its words do not combine to form a plausible semantic image. If Elizabeth had said *"She kicked the bucket,"* instead of *He*, an undefined pronoun reference would damage the pragmatics of the sentence. Likewise, her saying "He kicked the *ball*," rather than *bucket*, would be an incongruous statement in the overall discourse about smoking and lung cancer.

One of the errors of machine translation research was its failure to account for all the relevant levels of language analysis. By keeping within the bounds of syntax, perhaps making a few semantic excursions, the programs were able to do quite literal translations. But as the following sample output passage shows, weighty considerations of semantics and pragmatics, not to mention discourse structure, were eschewed:

Biological experiments, conducted on *various/different* cosmic air-craft, astrophysical researches of the cosmic space and flights of Soviet and American astronauts with *sufficient/rather* persuasiveness *showed/indicated/pointed*, that *momentary/transitory/short* orbital flights of *lower/below* than radiation *belts/regions/flanges* of *earth/land/soil* in the absence of the *raised/increased/heightened sun/sunny/solar* activity with respect to radiation *are/appear/arrive* report *safe/not-dangerous/secure*.

(When this program could not choose between two or more translations of a word, it gave all the possibilities in italics, separated by slashes.) Consequently, it was often impossible to determine the correct "sense" of a word without an analysis of its intended meaning and its larger role in the passage being translated.

Two key points should now be clear. First, there are several levels of analysis on which we can process natural languages, and each level has its distinguishing features. Second, a system must analyze at all those levels in order to synthesize any true "understanding" of natural language inputs; consequently, we must be familiar with syntax, semantics, pragmatics, and discourse analysis to construct comprehensive systems.

Parsing Languages

We will begin with syntax, which is normally analyzed through the process of *parsing* a language. Since all interesting languages are infinite, to parse a language is to execute the decision procedure for that language, which defines the language and accepts or rejects sentences if they are or are not members of the language.

Languages vary in complexity, which measures the difficulty of parsing them. Normally, we divide languages into the classes of *regular*, *context-free*, and, for want of a better term, *general*. For each class, there exists a shorthand notation for describing the structure of the language, as well as a model of a computational device that is just sophisticated enough to "accept" the language by executing its decision procedure.

Regular languages (which include all finite languages) can be described by *regular expressions* or *regular grammars*, and are accepted by simple machines called *finite-state automata*.

> **Context-free languages** can be described by *context-free grammars* or *recursive transition networks*, and are accepted by machines called *push-down automata*.

> **General languages** can be described by *context-sensitive grammars* or *augmented transition networks*, and are accepted by machines called *Turing machines*.

There is currently some debate about the class in which natural languages belong. While no one believes they are regular, it is not clear whether we can construct a strictly context-free grammar for English. And even if we could, it might prove too large and unwieldy to be of practical use, in which case the greater expressive power of an augmented transition network might be more convenient. On the other hand detailed studies by Mitchell Marcus of human language use suggest that augmented transition networks are too powerful. We will examine this issue in more detail soon, after looking at regular languages to get a more concrete understanding of the parsing process.

Regular Languages

The simplest infinite languages are the regular languages, which can be represented by regular expressions. A regular expression is a string consisting of any combination of the symbols in the alphabet of the language, as well as the empty string *e*, parentheses *( )*, star *, and the union (logical OR) operator ∪. Therefore, the following are all regular expressions: A^*, A^*B^*, $(A \cup B)$, $(A \cup B)^*$, $A(A \cup B^*)^*A^*$.

Regular expressions are interpreted as a condensed pattern for all the sentences in the particular regular language. The parentheses denote a subunit of the expression, the star operator indicates one or more occurrences of its operand, and the union operator indicates that either of its operands may be used. Union allows the representation of finite languages by listing each possible sentence and separating them with ∪, as in $(A \cup B \cup C)$, the language whose sentences are either "A", "B", or "C".

Armed with this information, we can characterize the example regular expressions listed above as follows:

1. A^* Any number of **A**s (we have already developed a decision procedure for this language).
2. A^*B^* Any number of **A**s followed by any number of **B**s.
3. $(A \cup B)$ Either an **A** or a **B** (one character only).

4. $(A \cup B)^*$ Any length combination of **A**s and **B**s.

5. $A(A \cup B^*)^* A^*$ Any combination of **A**s and **B**s that starts with an **A** (note
that this regular expression is somewhat redundant).

While it can be tricky to create a correct regular expression from a qualitative description of the regular language (and to figure out such a description for a given regular expression), it is apparent that regular languages can only follow simple repeating patterns. Consequently, it should be no surprise that an extremely unsophisticated machine, a finite-state automaton, can be created to accept any regular language. Figure 4-1 shows such a device for language 5 above.

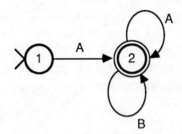

Figure 4-1. A Finite Automaton that Accepts the Language A(A $\cup$ B)*

Finite automata consist of a finite set of *states* and a list of *transition rules* that describe from which state to which new state the machine should move depending on the next input symbol. They operate sequentially, scanning their input symbol by symbol until there is none left. Each symbol causes the machine to change state or remain in its current state; at the end of the process the machine is either in one of a predefined set of accepting states, indicating that the input was accepted as a member of the language, or not, indicating that the input was not in the language.

Pictorially, the states are the nodes and transition rules are the edges in a directed graph. Operation begins in the start state (marked with a >). Therefore, the automaton in Figure 4-1 would behave as follows when confronted with the sentence "ABB": state 1, state 2, state 2, state 2. Since the node for state 2 is double-circled, indicating that 2 is an accepting state, we know that "ABB" is in the language $A(A \cup B^*)^* A^*$. Figure 4-2 shows a more complicated finite automata and its regular expression; can you describe the language it accepts?

The key limitation of finite automata is their lack of memory outside of their current state. Although the language $(III)^*$, whose sentences are all the unary notation natural numbers divisible by three, is perfectly regular (see Figure 4-3), there is no regular expression for the language whose sentences contain some number of

As followed by the same number of **B**s. $A^n B^n$, as this language is denoted, cannot be regular because to parse it sequentially requires that we remember the number of **A**s we saw while we are engaged in counting up the **B**s. (This intuitive argument is formalized in the famous *Pumping Theorems*, which exist for both regular and context-free languages.)

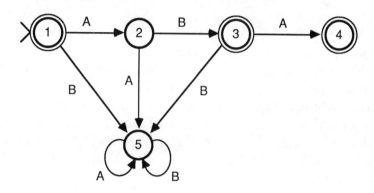

Figure 4–2. **A Finite Automaton that Accepts the Language (AB ∪ ABA)***

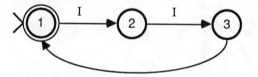

Figure 4–3. **A Finite Automaton that Accepts the Language (III)***

Context-free Languages

To handle tasks that require a stack-organized memory, which gives us access to one stored symbol at a time, and to represent languages with recursive structures (as opposed to the linearity of regular languages), we must turn to context-free languages (CFLs). These languages are described by context-free grammars (CFGs), such as this simple example for the language $A^n B^n$:

(1) S → e   [An S consists of either an empty string]

(2) S → S′   [Or an S′]
(3) S′ → ASB [An S′ consists of an A followed by an S followed by a B]

This grammar consists of three *rewrite rules*, numbered 1 through 3, each of which has a *non-terminal symbol* on the left hand side of the arrow and one or more symbols on the right hand side. Any symbols which can actually appear in the sentences of the language (as usual indicated by boldface type) are called *terminal symbols*, and can only appear on right hand sides of rules.

The sequences of terminal and non-terminal symbols appearing on right hand sides specify patterns of structures appearing in the sentences of the language that may be abbreviated by the non-terminal symbol on the left hand side. Since the non-terminal S conventionally stands for "sentence," it is the top level symbol of the grammar. Right hand sides of S-rules therefore specify the alternative structural patterns for sentences in the language; in our example, a sentence is either an empty string or an S′ structure. In turn, an S′ is an **A**, followed by an S structure, followed by a **B**. It is useful to model this property of (mutual) recursion with a tree structure, as shown in Figure 4-4.

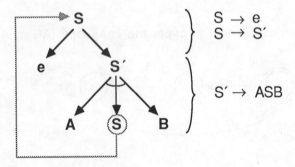

Figure 4–4. **A Context-free Grammar for $A^n B^n$**

Before proceeding, you should convince yourself that the CFLs are a superset of the regular languages. If we restrict the rules in a CFG to patterns of the forms X → **A** and X → **AY**, so that the right-hand sides contain either terminal symbols only or terminal symbols followed by a single nonterminal symbol, we have a *regular grammar*. Such grammars generate exactly the same languages as regular expressions; for example, the two-rule regular grammar {S → AS, S → e} represents the same language as **A***. Therefore, regular languages are a subset of context-free languages, which are fundamentally more complex.

A *derivation* is a demonstration that a given sentence is in the language, and it shows in order the rewrites that must be performed to *generate* that sentence from scratch. Figure 4-5 gives a derivation showing that "AABB" is a sentence in our A^nB^n language.

If we rearrange this derivation into a tree structure, we get a *parse tree*, as shown in Figure 4-6; you may note its similarity to the grammar tree in Figure 4-4. The parse tree is a sort of special case of the overall grammar tree, with the unused branches pruned off and the recursively explored ones extended accordingly. It describes exactly how a particular sentence was determined to be in the language by showing where its grammatical structure matched the overall structure of the language.

FIGURE 4-5. **A DERIVATION WITH A CONTEXT-FREE GRAMMAR**

At each step, the rewritten portion of the string is underlined

S → S´	Rule 2: S → S´
S → ASB	Rule 3: S´ → ASB
S → AS´B	Rule 2: S → S´
S → AASBB	Rule 3: S´ → ASB
S → AABB	Rule 1: S → e

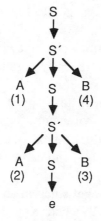

Numbers of terminal symbols indicate their position in the parsed sentence

Figure 4-6. **A Parse Tree for the Derivation of Figure 4-5**

When we parse a sentence with a context-free grammar, we would ideally like to discover not only whether the sentence is in the language defined by that grammar but also how it fits into the language. Therefore, we need a general algorithm to create a parse tree given a grammar and a sentence. The two principal alternatives, *bottom-up* and *top-down*, differ in approach by the direction in which they go about building the tree.

In bottom-up parsing, we only create a new node N in the parse tree when we have found a rule of the form N → XYZ and we have the symbols XYZ in order in the sentence being processed. This method makes the parsing problem into one of *matching* the right-hand sides of rules against substrings of the input sentence and *replacing* those substrings with left-hand side (always nonterminal) symbols when matches are made (for convenience, the input sentence can be modified as replacements are made). Of course, problems can arise when the same substring is found in more than one right-hand side; in such cases, the parser has no choice but to try each alternative one-by-one until the entire sentence is processed. The parser knows it is finished when sufficient replacements have been made successfully so that the sentence has been transformed into simply *S*, the root symbol of the grammar, and there are no more unparsed symbols in the input stream.

Top-down parsing, by contrast, starts at the root of the grammar and recursively builds the tree until it reaches the leaves. Again, when two or more rewrites are possible for a nonterminal symbol, each must be tried. Costly *backtracking* can then result when trying one rule causes an inconsistency later in the parse, such as a completion with input still remaining, or exhausting the input without constructing a full tree. In this case, the parser returns to its state before the last *choice-point*, at the same point in the input string as it was then, and tries the next available rewrite. If the entire input string is not in the language, the top level of the parsing process will run out of "S → ..." rules to try without finding one that works.

These parsing algorithms share a serious efficiency problem. Depending on the grammar and the input string, it is theoretically possible for either procedure to repeatedly reach the end of the sentence before realizing that an incorrect choice was made earlier, forcing backtracking; if this happens at every symbol on every pass through the string, the time to parse will increase exponentially (as the function 2^n) with the length n of the input. Better context-free parsers run in better than cubic (n^3) time, a significant improvement, and can be faster (quadratic, or sometimes linear) with restricted grammars.

Furthermore, a top-down parser can get stuck in an infinite loop. Suppose the grammar has a rule of the form X → XY, where X is a nonterminal symbol and Y is any combination of terminal and nonterminal symbols. This is called *left recursion*. If the parser has a goal to "parse an X" in the input, and it unwittingly applies this rule, it will only generate another identical goal, and there is nothing in the grammar or the input to stop this from continuing *ad infinitum*. Although left recursion can always be eliminated by adding more rules, the best parsing algorithms should work with all grammars regardless of their rule structures.

One way to attack the inefficiency of these parsers is to recast the grammar as a *recursive transition network*, a structure similar to the finite automaton. Recall that a labelled arc from one state node to another is traversed just in case the symbol in the label is found next in the input string. An RTN is a machine that, in addition to simply scanning for symbols, can also make a recursive jump to the start of another network to parse some of its input. Each network in an RTN parser embodies the right hand sides of all the rules for a nonterminal symbol in the corresponding grammar. Figure 4-7 shows an RTN for the language A^nB^n derived from the grammar discussed earlier.

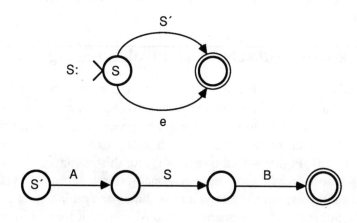

Figure 4–7. **A Recursive Transition Network for the Context-free Grammar in Figure 4–4**

With grammars containing groups of rules like {X → UVW, X → UVZ}, only RTNs avoid repeating the U and V parses. If an ordinary top-down parser, for example, could not parse a W under the first rule after successfully parsing the U and V symbols, it would blindly start again with the second rule, forgetting that U and V had already been processed. As shown in Figure 4-8, RTNs capture the similarities between rules like these and encode them as consecutive states, postponing the choice of rules until after the U and V have been parsed. If a W cannot be parsed, a Z is immediately tried, avoiding some of the wasted effort of top-down parsing.

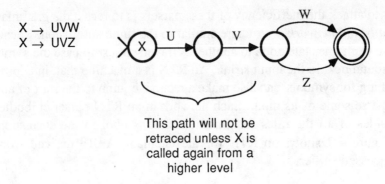

$$X \rightarrow UVW$$
$$X \rightarrow UVZ$$

This path will not be
retraced unless X is
called again from a
higher level

Figure 4–8. **An RTN Can Manage Alternatives Efficiently**

Context-free Subsets of Natural Languages

Throughout our discussion of language parsing, we have been dealing exclusively
with such "unnatural" languages as $A^n B^n$. To see how context-free grammar techniques can be applied to natural language processing, consider the grammar in
Figure 4-9, which represents a very rough approximation to the surface level of
English syntax. Figure 4-10 shows an RTN for this grammar.

This grammar will generate a reasonably large subset of syntactically valid
English sentences; unfortunately, it also allows several incorrect constructs to slip
through. Subject-verb agreement, notoriously difficult for CFGs, is waived, as are
non-present tense verb forms, auxiliary verbs, and morphological analysis. And of
course, the terminal symbols listed for the various syntactic categories are only a
tiny fraction of the total number available.

Nevertheless, we can use this grammar to analyze sentences like "Colorless
green ideas sleep furiously," a famous example of Noam Chomsky. Figure 4-11
shows the parse tree generated for this sentence; the numbers next to the nodes
indicate the order in which a top-down parser would add them. (If you have read
Chapter 6 or are familiar with basic graph theory, you will recognize the order as a
depth-first numbering of the tree.) Figure 4-12 shows the stages of processing
through which bottom-up parsing would pass. Note that both diagrams assume that
the parsers decide correctly at all choice-points, resulting in no backtracking, an
unlikely coincidence in practice.

FIGURE 4-9.   **A CONTEXT-FREE GRAMMAR FOR A SUBSET OF ENGLISH**

Rewrite Rules:

1.1	S	→	NP VP	NP=Noun Phrase
2.1	NP	→	DET ANP	VP=Verb Phrase
2.2	NP	→	ANP	DET=Determiner
2.3	VP	→	*TV* NP AVL PPL	ANP=Adjectival Noun Phrase
2.4	VP	→	*IV* AVL PPL	TV=Transitive Verb
3.1	DET	→	*ART*	AVL=Adverb List
3.2	DET	→	*POS*	PPL=Prepositional Phrase List
3.3	ANP	→	*ADJ* ANP	IV=Intransitive Verb
3.4	ANP	→	NT	ART=Article
3.5	AVL	→	*ADV* AVL	POS=Possessive
3.6	AVL	→	**e**	ADJ=Adjective
3.7	PPL	→	PP PPL	NT=Noun Type
3.8	PPL	→	**e**	ADV=Adverb
4.1	NT	→	NON	PP=Prepositional Phrase
4.2	NT	→	PN	NON=Numbered Ordinary Noun
4.3	PP	→	*PREP* NP	PN=Proper Noun
5.1	NON	→	*SON*	PREP=Preposition
5.2	NON	→	PON	SON=Singular Ordinary Noun
5.3	PN	→	*NAME*	PON=Plural Ordinary Noun
5.4	PN	→	*PRONOUN*	
6.1	PON	→	*SON* **S**	

Syntactic Categories:

TV	[HIT GIVE WATCH CHASE IGNORE TAKE ASK WRITE]
IV	[SLEEP LIVE DIE TALK REACT GO]
ART	[A AN THE]
POS	[MY YOUR HIS HER ITS OUR THEIR]
ADJ	[GREEN BIG LUCID INDEFATIGABLE COLORLESS FUNNY]
ADV	[SLOWLY WELL FURIOUSLY STRANGELY QUICKLY]
PREP	[AT ON TO IN AROUND BEHIND TOWARDS BEYOND FOR]
SON	[BOOK BOY SHEEP IDEA WOLF APPLE ROBOT COMPUTER]
NAME	[CHARLEY VICTOR CHRIS JACK ELIZABETH AMERICA]
PRON	[I YOU HE SHE IT WE THEY]

Sample Sentences:

Indefatigable boy react a idea.   I sleep at the computer.
You live quickly in apple.   Elizabeth go in the lucid sheeps.
I talk beyond a wolf around big Charley behind their funny idea in America.

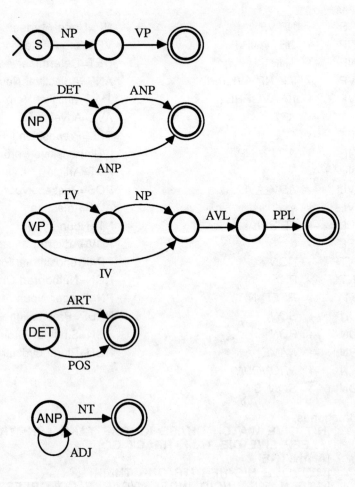

Figure 4–10. **A Recursive Transition Network for the Grammar in Figure 4–9**

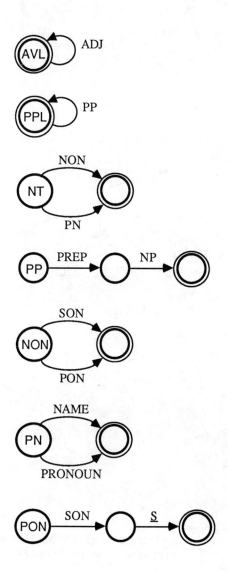

Figure 4–10 (continued).

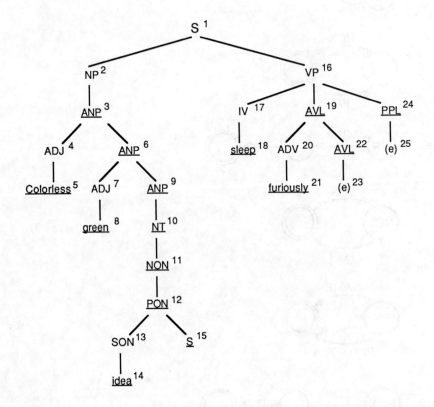

Numbers indicate order in which
a top-down parser generates the nodes

Figure 4–11. **Parse Tree Constructed Using Grammar in Figure 4–10
for the Sentence "Colorless green ideas sleep furiously"**

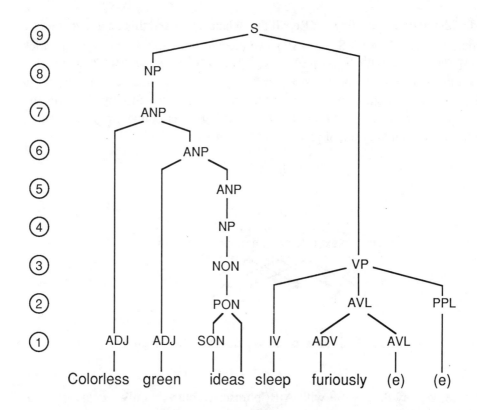

Figure 4–12. **Stages in Bottom-up Parsing of a Sentence**

Weak and Strong Context-free Languages

Thus far our definition of a formal language has been a weak one, namely any finite or infinite set of sentences. However, many have argued that this conception is inadequate for the study of natural languages, in which the structure of a sentence is at least as important as whether we can tell it is in the language. The notion of a strong language is that of a set of *phrase structure trees*, parse trees that specify not just acceptable sentences but the acceptable groupings of each sentence's constituent parts. You can think of such a language as a classical language in which each sentence comes with a defined list of ways in which it may be parsed.

Returning to our $A^n B^n$ language, suppose we also specify the following phrase structure for its sentences: each A_i (the ith occurrence of the letter A) must be paired with the corresponding B_j. Recall that when we parsed this language with the grammar $\{S \to e, S \to S', S' \to ASB\}$, we created trees like Figure 4-6 in which each A_i was paired with B_{n-i+1}. Although the proof is beyond the scope of this discussion, it turns out that there is no context-free grammar that captures the required phrase structure of the new pairing. (We can see this by drawing that pairing, as shown in Figure 4-13; the overlapping lines connecting the terminal symbols seem intuitively out of place in a parse *tree*.)

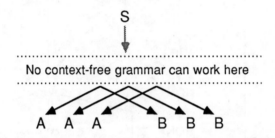

Figure 4–13. **Phrase Structure of a Weakly Context-free Language**

Therefore, we say that A^nB^n with A_iB_i phrase structure is only *weakly context-free*, whereas the same set of strings with A_iB_{n-i+1} phrase structure is *strongly context-free*. At present, there is strong suspicion that English and other natural languages may be only weakly context-free, and consequently require a more complex formalism to represent their syntactic structure.

General Grammars and Augmented Transition Networks

Such a formalism is provided by the general grammar, a logical extension of the context-free grammar. Recall that in a CFG rule, the right hand side can include both terminal and non-terminal symbols, but the left hand side is always a single non-terminal. Allowing unrestricted combinations of all types of symbols on both sides of rules turns the context-free into the *context-sensitive* grammar framework (in Chomsky's original specification, a CSG rule was also required to have no more symbols on the left hand than on the right hand side, but the distinction is minor). CSGs are sufficiently powerful to describe any language for which there exists a computable decision procedure; although there are classes of formalisms intermediate in power between CFGs and CSGs, such as the *indexed grammars*, there is little practical experience with them.

We saw that although the language A^nB^n was too complex for finite automata, there was a simple CFG to describe it. However, the language $A^nB^nC^n$ (*n* As followed by *n* Bs followed by *n* Cs) has been proven impossible to represent with a CFG, and therefore not a context-free language. The following CSG, however will generate $A^nB^nC^n$:

(1)	S	$\to$	e	[A sentence is either the empty string]
(2)	S	$\to$	ASB´C´	[Or an A followed by an S, a B´, and a C´]
(3)	C´B´	$\to$	B´C´	[C´B´ can be rewritten as B´C´]
(4)	AB´	$\to$	AB	[If B´ follows an A it can be rewritten as a B]
(5)	BB´	$\to$	BB	[If B´ follows a B it can also be rewritten as a B]
(6)	BC´	$\to$	BC	[If C´ follows a B it can be rewritten as a C]
(7)	CC´	$\to$	CC	[If C´ follows a C it can also be rewritten as a C]

It is not immediately apparent that this grammar will work. To convince yourself, try a few derivations like the one for "AABBCC" in Figure 4-14 below. Remember that the parse-tree model of grammars that was convenient for CFGs does not apply as well here, since we can replace large patterns of terminal and nonterminal symbols in a single step.

FIGURE 4-14. A DERIVATION WITH A CONTEXT-SENSITIVE GRAMMAR

At each step, the rewritten portion of the string is underlined

S $\to$ ASB´C´	Rule 2: S $\to$ ASB´C´
S $\to$ AASB´C´B´C´	Rule 2: S $\to$ ASB´C´
S $\to$ AAB´C´B´C´	Rule 1: S $\to$ e
S $\to$ AAB´B´C´C´	Rule 3: C´B´ $\to$ B´C´
S $\to$ AABB´C´C´	Rule 4: AB´ $\to$ AB
S $\to$ AABBC´C´	Rule 5: BB´ $\to$ BB
S $\to$ AABBCC´	Rule 6: BC´ $\to$ BC
S $\to$ AABBCC	Rule 7: CC´ $\to$ CC

We can extend our grammar in various ways to handle languages like:

$$A^nB^nC^nD^n, A^{2^n}, \text{ and so on.}$$

We could not do this with CFGs because they could only "remember" essentially one quantity at a time, by replacing one symbol in the input. With CSGs, though, the complex rewrite rules allow the size of the input to actually *increase* during processing, enabling the grammar to use the string being parsed to store all manner of nonterminal symbols. Therefore, CSGs have all the power needed to represent natural languages; unfortunately, their complex structure suggests no obvious parsing algorithms like the top-down and bottom-up methods which mapped so cleanly onto the parse tree formalism of the CFG.

To cope with context-sensitive features of natural languages, Woods developed the *augmented transition network* (ATN), an elaboration of the recursive transition network. Recall that an RTN can change state upon either encountering a specific string of symbols in the input or successfully calling a subnetwork to parse a substring of the input. Once it changes state, it knows only about where it has been in the input to return there, and nothing more. (A finite automaton cannot even backtrack.) This impairs the network's ability to keep track of syntactic features that may arise early in sentences but not be needed until much later in the parsing process, such as the number of a subject for subsequent comparison with the number of a verb.

ATNs get this extended memory capability from sets of *registers*, which can hold partial parse trees (such as completed noun phrase subtrees), feature values (such as the number of a subject or verb), and words (such as clues early in a sentence to some later syntactic aspect). Before traversing an arc to try to change state, the ATN interpreter can use the arc's *conditions* to test the values of certain registers and "peek" ahead in the input stream. Recursive jumps to subnetworks push the current registers onto a stack, and backtracking restores their contents. After successfully changing state, the ATN can perform certain *actions*, including register manipulation, associated with the arc or subnetwork it just traversed. This bundle of facilities enables ATNs to parse the class of general context-sensitive languages.

Although the full details of ATN construction, interpretation, and even compilation are beyond the scope of this discussion, we can look at a small example to get a feel for the power of the ATN formalism. Figure 4-15 shows a fragment of an RTN and the three context-free rules it represents. Note that although the first two rules are clearly for declarative sentences, or statements, the third is for an interrogative sentence, or question. But the RTN does not distinguish between the cases. One way to fix this deficiency would be to create new rules, such as S → DCL and S → Q, and rewrites for the DCL and Q nonterminals that used the patterns from the original "S → ..." rules. However, since more backtracking would surely occur, this solution would negate the improvement in efficiency we got from combining the rules into the RTN in the first place.

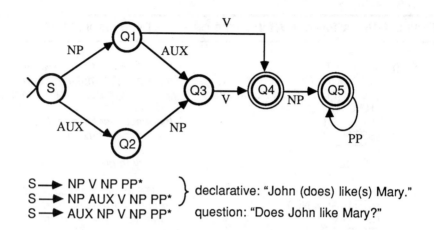

S →→ NP V NP PP*
S →→ NP AUX V NP PP* } declarative: "John (does) like(s) Mary."
S →→ AUX NP V NP PP*   question: "Does John like Mary?"

Figure 4–15. **A Small RTN/ATN**

Figure 4-16 is an annotated listing for an ATN fragment, using the customary Lisp-like parentheses notation, that solves the problem. This example, though it doesn't exercise all the features of ATNs, should demonstrate their power. In particular, the ATN solution provides an elegant computational account of Chomsky's theory of *transformational grammar*, an extension of the context-free grammar that allows various surface-level syntactic transformations to take a single *deep structure*, representing the base propositional content of a sentence, and restate it as, for example, either a question or a declaration. Figure 4-17 compares the parse trees generated for two sentences by the ATN in Figure 4-16; note that the only real difference between the question "Does John like Mary?" and its declarative form "John likes Mary" is in the Q/DCL marker at the surface level of the tree: the deep structure is the same. This profound and useful effect is difficult if not impossible to obtain with pure context-free parsing.

The main drawbacks of the ATN are poor efficiency and readability. Careful design can help to minimize costly backtracking and register shuffling, but as you can see, the sprawling tangles of state diagrams and Lisp code that make an ATN are difficult to understand. However, the great expressive power (though perhaps not strictly required by the problem of parsing natural languages) of the ATN and its related formalisms has given it enduring popularity among AI programmers.

FIGURE 4-16. **A PARTIAL ATN BASED ON THE RTN IN FIGURE 4-15**

```
(S/  (PUSH NP/ T
        (SETR SUBJ *)
          (SETR TYPE (QUOTE DCL))
          (TO Q1))
     (CAT AUX T
        (SETR AUX *)
        (SETR TYPE (QUOTE Q))
        (TO Q2)))

(Q1  (CAT V T
        (SETR AUX NIL)
        (SETR V *)
        (TO Q4))
     (CAT AUX T
        (SETR AUX *)
        (TO Q3)))

(Q2  (PUSH NP/ T
        (SETR SUBJ *)
        (TO Q3)))

(Q3  (CAT V T
        (SETR V *)
        (TO Q4)))

(Q4  (POP (BUILDQ (S+++ (VP+))
            TYPE SUBJ AUX V) T)
     (PUSH NP/ T
        (SETR VP (BUILDQ (VP (V+) *) V))
        (TO Q5)))

(Q5  (POP (BUILDQ (S++++)
            TYPE SUBJ AUX VP) T)
     (PUSH PP/ T
        (SETR VP (APPEND (GETR VP) (LIST *)))
        (TO Q5)))
```

STATE S/: Try to parse an NP
If successful, make the current word
(*) the subject, the sentence type
declarative, and move to state Q1
If not successful, see if the current
word is an auxiliary word; if this
works make AUX the current word,
the type question, and go to Q2

STATE Q1: Is the next word a verb?
Yes, so there is no auxiliary, make V
that verb, and go on to Q4

If the word is instead an auxiliary,
set the correct register and go to Q3

STATE Q2: If we can we parse a NP
here, make the current word the
sentence subject and move on to Q3

STATE Q3: If the current word is a
verb, save it in V and go to Q4

STATE Q4: Try to return a parse tree
built from the current registers; if
that fails, try to parse a NP and
then try to build a VP parse tree in
register VP and go on to Q5

STATE Q5: Try to return a similar tree;
if this doesn't work, try parsing a PP,
appending it to the list in the VP
register, and recursing back to Q5

Does John like Mary?

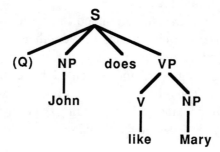

As dictated by transformational grammar, this sentence has the same deep structure as the declarative form *John likes Mary.:*

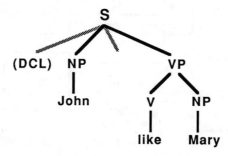

Figure 4–17. **Parse Trees Generated with the ATN in Figure 4–16**

Natural Language Interfaces to Software Systems

The most common application of natural language processing techniques is to user interface design. We will see in Chapter 5 that a good expert system offers some sort of English communication with its users. A database management system (DBMS) is equally well-suited to a *natural language interface* (NLI), and making queries to retrieve information from a database is the application most often associated with applied natural language processing. The technology of NLIs is progressing rapidly, and has reached the point where sophisticated systems are widely available for microcomputers. (Another popular AI DBMS application is the optimization of database queries by using information about the structure of the database to minimize retrieval times.)

In the usual scenario, which is diagrammed in Figure 4-18, several levels of processing separate the user from his database. Were there no NLI present, queries would be entered as programs in a special *query language* (QL), which is just like any other programming language, and executed by either an interpreter or compiler for that language. The NLI just translates queries expressed by the user in English sentences into QL programs, thus shielding the user from the complexities of the QL and simplifying his access to the database.

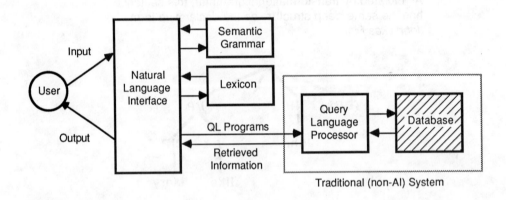

Figure 4–18. **Architecture of a DBMS with a NLI**

Conveniently, when we restrict our language understanding efforts to NLIs in the microworlds of DBMSs, many of the difficulties we have encountered so far vanish. For example, we can fudge the distinction between syntax and semantics by using a so-called *semantic grammar*, a context-free grammar whose rules represent information specific to the problem it addresses. This collapses elements from several levels of linguistic analysis into the syntactic phase, which is conveniently the best understood at this point in the evolution of NLP technology.

Figure 4-19 shows a simple semantic grammar that can handle interaction with our frame database from Chapter 3. Note how its syntactic categories and terminal symbols directly represent concepts in the domain it is to understand and interpret—this is in sharp contrast to the English grammar in Figure 4-9, whose constituents were not slots and fillers but the more abstract nouns, verbs, and prepositional phrases.

FIGURE 4-19.   **SEMANTIC GRAMMAR FOR FRAME DATABASE QUERIES**

Rewrite Rules:

1.1	S	→	ST.
1.2	S	→	QU**?**
1.3	S	→	**QUIT.**
2.1	ST	→	IND **IS** CL
2.2	ST	→	CL **IS** CL
2.3	ST	→	IND**'S** SL **IS** FI
2.4	ST	→	CL**'S** SL **IS** FI
2.5	QU	→	**IS** IND CL
2.6	QU	→	**IS** CL CL
2.7	QU	→	**IS** IND'S SL FI
2.8	QU	→	**IS** CL**'S** SL FI
2.9	QU	→	**WHAT IS** IND'S SL
2.10	QU	→	**WHAT IS** CL**'S** SL
3.1	IND	→	*OBJ*
3.1	CL	→	**A** *OBJ*
3.2	CL	→	**AN** *OBJ*
3.1	SL	→	*OBJ*
3.1	FI	→	*OBJ*

ST=Statement
QU=Query (question)
IND=Individual
CL=Class
SL=Slot
FI=Filler
OBJ=Object

Syntactic Categories:

OBJ → [Any string compatible with the **ObjectName** type in the frame database specification]

A practical system would augment this grammar with routines to handle singular-plural distinctions, quantification (for relative clauses like "how many ..." and "who ..."), and ellipticals. Often, the user will want to ask the same question about several different objects, as in "What are the sales figures for the New England region. For New York?" The latter sentence is barely grammatical, but we know immediately that it is a request for the sales figures for the New York region. One way to get around this problem of taking each sentence as an individual unit, without relation to previous events in the dialogue, is with a *history list*, a simple stack that shows the most recent referents of various pronouns and abbreviated phrases known to the system. We can also add grammar rules like S → NP or S → PP, being sure to have special procedures that access the history list to determine the pragmatics of sentences parsed with them.

A Natural Language Interface in Pascal

A recursive-descent parser in implemented in Pascal can form a front end interface to the frame system database developed in Chapter 3. The file NETNLP is such a program. When you run it, you are repeatedly prompted to type in a sentence, press [Return], and see the program's response. Try entering a few statements, to add information to the database, and some questions, to retrieve it. To exit, type *QUIT*, followed by a period, and press [Return].

   The parser's top-down approach is based very loosely on the RTN in Figure 4-20, which is derived from the semantic grammar in Figure 4-19. Some modifications have been made for the sake of efficiency, such as checking before processing the entire sentence to see whether it ends in a period (signalling a statement), or a question mark (signalling a query). Without this, the parser could get "What is Charley's color?" as input and try all the "ST → ..." rules before getting to the relevant "QU → ..." ones.

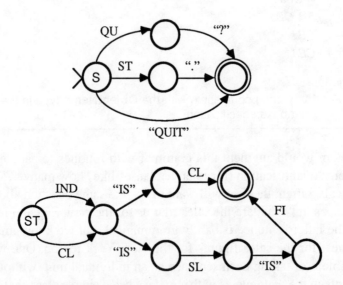

Figure 4–20. **A Recursive Transition Network for the Grammar in Figure 4–19**

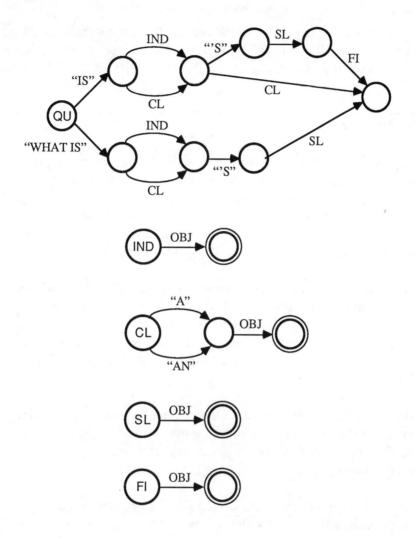

Figure 4–20 (continued).

The most significant departure from the standard NLI structure of Figure 4-18 is the complete omission of the query language. Instead, rather than construct either an explicit parse tree or a QL program, the parser stops as soon as it has success-fully parsed a statement or query and immediately calls the appropriate database access procedure (as defined in SEMANTIC.PAS and in Chapter 3) with the argu-ments it has extracted from the input sentence. Note that these kludges are possible only because neither the frames in the database nor the allowed queries are complex enough to demand an entire language to express them. As designed now, the system can answer questions like "What is California's capital?" but not "Show me all the states whose governors are Republican?" which requires logical deductions in the retrieval process as well as a more sophisticated grammar structure.

Programming Exercises

1. Currently, NETNLP prints out several lines of debugging information when it processes each sentence. Clean up its user interface and improve its robustness with string, input/output, and error handling. Add a display that shows each procedure of the parser as it is called, as well as the strings passed to and from each module. (Graphics enthusiasts might also try displaying and animating a parse tree or RTN as the parsing proceeds.)

2. (After completing exercise 3 in Chapter 3.) Rules 2.5 and 2.6 of the semantic grammar in Figure 4-19 allow queries to the frame system's INST and SUBC links in addition to its slot/filler pairs, but they are not currently implemented in NETNLP. With the unified frame representation and value inheritance procedure in hand, modify NETNLP's parser to handle these queries properly.

3. NETNLP has the same problem any top-down parsing strategy has with left-recursive rules. How can grammars be transformed to eliminate left recursion? Is there any way for the parser to detect runaway left recursion before it happens, without modifying the grammar?

4. Since it calls the appropriate frame database procedures as soon as it has successfully analyzed its input sentence, the parser in NETNLP produces no output. Add the necessary data structures and procedures to create full parse trees. You may have to untangle some of the unwieldy modules in the current version to make sense of the parser's flow of control.

5. (For those interested in databases.) Design a small query language for the frame database, based on the procedures in SEMANTIC.PAS; in particular, allow for calls to the value inheritance procedure, looping, and conditionals. What is involved in planning for disjunctive and conjunctive queries, negation in queries, and other complications? Try to create an interpreter for the query language; remember that you don't need to develop a whole new programming language!

6. (After completing exercises 4 and 5.) Reorganize NETNLP according to the standard NLI architecture from Figure 4-18 by modularizing the program's functions, writing a procedure to convert parse trees from the modified parser into programs in the query language, and piping the program into the QL interpreter. Hints: it may be helpful to develop the modules separately rather than all together in a single large file; also, careful error checking will pay off.

7. A recursive descent parser can be confusing because its grammatical knowledge is distributed throughout the procedures that parse the individual constituents of the language. Design a data structure to represent a recursive transition network for an arbitrary context-free grammar, and implement a general algorithm whose arguments are an RTN structure and a string that "runs" the RTN with the string as input. The program should be able not only to decide whether the string is in the language but also to construct an appropriate parse tree if it is a sentence.

8. (After completing exercise 7.) After further study of parsing with ATNs, augment the general RTN parser and data structures to handle the major extensions of ATNs. Design a textual storage format for ATN specifications, and write a procedure to input them to the program.

9. (After completing exercise 5 in Chapter 3.) We have not extensively discussed natural language *generation*, concentrating mostly on understanding sentences rather than producing them. Extend the program to do intersection search in a lexicon network to return its output in a quasi-natural language format similar to that generated by Quillian's systems.

Summary

Natural language processing is second only to expert reasoning as a commercial application of artificial intelligence, and the role of linguistic communication is one of the most important theoretical issues involved in intelligent behavior itself. The simplest definition of a formal language is a usually infinite set of sentences. Processing a language means understanding a language, or extracting the meaning of its sentences and larger structures at several levels of analysis. Syntax describes the structure of a language and its sentences, semantics assigns a literal interpretation to each sentence, pragmatics attempts to determine the intended meaning of an utterance, and discourse analysis relates a sentence to its local and global contexts.

Parsing is the analysis of strings to determine whether they are sentences in a given language and if so, how they are structured to match the patterns of the language. Classes of languages can be parsed with varying difficulty; regular languages represent only simple repeating patterns, context-free languages have grammars of rewrite rules that impose hierarchical structure on their sentences, and general languages have context-sensitive transformations. It is currently unclear whether natural languages are strongly enough context-free or require more sophisticated formalisms like augmented transition networks to handle problems like subject-verb agreement.

Applying semantic, pragmatic, and discourse analysis are tremendous problems for general natural language comprehension systems. However, natural language interfaces to software systems like database managers need only understand the microworld of the file format and query processor of the programs they serve. By restricting the format of its input, an NLI can utilize a relatively small context-free semantic grammar to collapse the levels of analysis into a simpler process that still provides great functionality from the user's point of view. Clever techniques like history lists can be used to improve the interaction in interfaces and other natural language processing systems.

References

Harris's *Introduction to Natural Language Processing* is a good textbook that covers the major issues and problems of NLP from a classical perspective, with additional material on knowledge representation for NLP and text processing in general. Several Pascal examples developed throughout the text may help you with the programming exercises. Winograd's first volume on *Language as a Cognitive Process* devotes several hundred pages exclusively to syntax. *Elements of the Theory of Computation* by Lewis and Papdimitriou, though mathematically rigorous, gives an excellent introduction to formal languages. Of the general AI textbooks, Charniak and McDermott give two detailed chapters to NLP, covering both ATN parsers and discourse analysis in considerable depth; Winston seems stronger on general issues, semantic grammars, and story comprehension.

The best account of augmented transition networks is still Woods's original "Transition Network Grammars for Natural Language Analysis," which also discusses recursive transition networks and presents an extended example of an ATN and its use in parsing a sentence (Figures 4-15 through 4-17 are based on this paper). Wood's work is reprinted with 37 other landmark articles on NLP in *Readings in Natural Language Processing*, edited by Grosz, Sparck Jones, and Webber. Also in that volume is Early's efficient CFG parser, an outline of Marcus's work on deterministic wait-and-see parsers (WASP) parsers, and "Definite Clause Grammars for Natural Language Analysis," which describes the Prolog language's built-in facility for NLP applications.

"On the Mathematical Properties of Linguistic Theories" by Perrault (also in Grosz, Sparck Jones, and Webber) and "Natural Language Interfaces" by Perrault and Grosz in *Annual Review of Computer Science 1* provide surveys of the theoretical and applied sides of NLP, concentrating on approaches to the parsing problem. While translation was somewhat of a laughing stock of AI for many years, the progress now being made, as well as the history of the field, are reported in Hutchins's *Machine Translation: Past, Present, and Future.* Although neither topic was discussed in Chapter 4, I recommend Berwick's books on linguistic learning, *The Acquisition of Syntactic Knowledge*, and theoretical NLP issues, *Computational Complexity and Natural Language.* Finally, no study of language is complete without a reading of at least one of Chomsky's books; transformational grammar is explained in *Aspects of the Theory of Syntax.*

5. Expert Systems and Knowledge Engineering

Expert Systems are being touted by the popular press as fantastic human-like computer systems that will soon replace experts in all fields from medicine to geology. Many large corporations have formed internal research groups to investigate their potential industrial applications. Is it possible that such programs will revolutionize computer use and industrial practices like their supporters predict?

Although it has by no means yet lived up to the media hype showered on it, expert systems technology is by far the most practical, refined, and commercial result of artificial intelligence research to date. But whereas the prospect of replacing most high-priced expertise with inexpensive, reliable software is not as near as some would have us believe, it is undeniable that expert systems are having a widening impact on business practices.

The goals of this chapter are to:

- Understand what an expert system is, what it is not, and where and when it should be used to solve a problem.

- Review some existing examples of expert systems, discussing how the fruits of university research are being applied to real-world problems.

- Examine what functions and components a program should have to be considered a "true" expert system.

- Look in depth at two different research projects, in medicine and electronics, that have led to such systems.

- Investigate knowledge engineering and the construction of knowledge bases for our own program.

- Consider the limits and faults of expert systems technology.

- Design and implement in Turbo Pascal a generic production system interpreter that can become the core of a complete expert system.

What is an Expert System?

In order to design our own expert system, we first need to decide exactly what constitutes an "expert system" for our purposes. We could adopt a purely functional definition, that an expert system is any computer system that exhibits expert performance in some field (known as the *problem domain*). By such an ad-hoc definition, we could consider the BASIC programming language an expert system in the domain of integer arithmetic, for example; after all, do you know any one who can calculate faster than your computer?

Where, then, does our this definition fall down? I think it fails because it is not mindful of the essential characteristic of expert systems: that they are intended to solve problems in difficult, *unstructured* domains where *knowledge rather than procedure* guides the expert's reasoning. As we would expect, this fits nicely into our discussion in Chapter 2 of what makes programs intelligent. All AI systems get their power from the knowledge they embody rather than the particular algorithm they execute; an expert system goes one step further by concentrating highly specialized knowledge on a single problem to the exclusion of all others.

This key insight, which boils down to "knowledge is power," did not come early to AI researchers. As we have seen, it is at odds fundamentally with the theme of the first fifteen or so years of work in the field, which concentrated on so-called weak methods. By relying on large bodies of specialized knowledge and procedures to achieve good performance, it challenges the idea that some unified theory of intelligence, representable in a relatively simple algorithm, can account for human behavior. But whatever its inelegance, it seems to be working.

So we will adopt the following definition: expert systems are computing systems, or programs, that offer advice or solve problems by reasoning with bodies of knowledge highly specific to a particular domain. The activity of designing and implementing expert systems, especially that of transferring knowledge from experts to programs, is known as *knowledge engineering*. Good knowledge engineers are in great demand today.

Applications of Expert Systems

Almost all of the expert systems in use today tend to solve problems in scientific or engineering domains, although more and more research is underway on professional applications such as law and finance. Let's look briefly at some of the real-world problem domains for which expert systems have been developed.

- **Chemistry** was the very first application area targeted for expert systems development. *Heuristic DENDRAL*, developed starting in 1965 in Stanford University's Heuristic Programming Project, was also the first program to actually be described as an expert system *per se*. It assists chemists in determining the exact or likely structures of molecules based on their chemical formulae and mass spectrograms. Since its completion, DENDRAL has been in daily international use by hundreds of chemists. Subsequent chemical applications include *Meta-DENDRAL* (also for structure elucidation); *CRYSALIS* (x-ray crystallography); and *LHASA*, *SECS*, and *SYNCHEM* (all in synthetic chemistry).

- **Mathematics** was also being explored in the 1960s in Project MAC at MIT. Early programs like *SAINT*, *SIN*, and *MATHLAB*, demonstrated reasonable competence in symbolic integration, the solution of indefinite integrals. Essentially, they were able to solve certain non-numerical problems, operating on expressions with variables regardless of their value. *MACSYMA*, a gigantic and comprehensive symbolic mathematics system, is the product of over 50 man-years of such research. It is expert not only in integration but also in differentiation (see Chapter 4), vector analysis, differential equations, limits, series, linear algebra, and more. The field of symbolic mathematics has become so popular that five technical conferences are held annually to study it, MACSYMA has attracted competition from programs like *Maple*, *REDUCE*, and *SMP*, and microcomputer systems, such as Microsoft Corporation's *muMATH*, are increasingly abundant.

- **Computer Configuration** is the domain of *R1*, developed by John McDermott and his associates at CMU beginning in 1980. Now known as *XCON*, it configures Digital Equipment Corporation VAX minicomputer systems for customer orders, and it is used for virtually every such order received despite the experts' original protestations that it could not possibly work. It checks an order for omissions and errors, lays out the various components in the required cabinetry, and creates floor and cable layouts for the equipment. *XCON* and its growing family of companion programs, such as *XSEL*, is written in *OPS5*, a language designed by Charles L. Forgy especially for expert systems programming.

- **Exploration** is a fertile problem domain. *PROSPECTOR*, created at SRI International in the late 1970s, is designed to assist geologists with a variety of mineral exploration problems. It has knowledge of a dozen models of ore deposit patterns and characteristics. By accepting volunteered information from a user exploring a prospective site and then questioning him on his observations and opinions, it determines the most probable deposits at the site. PROSPECTOR is said to have discovered a molybdenum ore deposit whose lifetime value may approach $100 million. Another expert system in use for exploration is the *DIPMETER ADVISOR*, which analyzes subsurface tilt in oil wells.

- **Electronics** is one application of a new branch of AI research into *qualitative reasoning;* or reasoning about complex physical systems with respect to their salient features rather than numerical parameters. Randall Davis of MIT has developed a program, which we will examine more closely later, that is able to diagnose failures in digital electronic circuits, including not only single part malfunctions but also bridge faults and the like. *DART* is a recent Stanford program for automated diagnosis of physical systems; and while its main application thus far has been electronic circuits, it has also been used in connection with nuclear reactors. *VERIFY* verifies digital designs. This type of program will soon find everyday application in industry.

- **Medicine** has up to now been the most thoroughly explored application of expert systems. Tens of programs have been and continue to be developed. The first of these was Stanford's *MYCIN* system for blood disease diagnosis, begun in the early 1970s, which we will examine in greater depth shortly. Other notable efforts in the field include:

  The *Digitalis Therapy Advisor* (MIT) prescribes a regimen of treatment for patients using the heart medicine digitalis. It is interesting in that an interaction between doctor and program is not a one-time event; the program recommends a dosage schedule and tells the physician when to return for the next consultation so that the prescription can be adjusted as necessary.

  Caduceus (formerly *Internist-I* and *II*, from the University of Pittsburgh) specializes in internal medicine. Using statistical knowledge of 100,000 symptom-disease associations, it displays expert performance on over 500 diseases, or about 85% of internal diseases. It is able to diagnose the presence of multiple diseases, but it does not prescribe treatments based on its findings.

PUFF (Stanford), a consultation program for pulmonary disease, was in 1982 the only medical expert system in regular clinical use for real cases. Surprisingly, it employs only about 55 rules to make its decisions. It is written with *EMYCIN* (Empty MYCIN), a *shell* for expert systems development created by abstracting all the domain-specific knowledge out of the original MYCIN program.

Capabilities and Components of an Expert System

In reviewing these relatively successful expert systems, we have glossed over their structure and behavior to concentrate on their performance, seeing that all have attained at least respectable levels of expertise in their problem domains. While this portends well for the economic future of the expert systems business, we will concern ourselves more with the actual design of the programs.

The first thing to determine when attempting to implement an expert system, or indeed any piece of software, is what capabilities it should have. It used to be enough for an AI program such as an expert system to exhibit "innovative" or "interesting" behavior that had not been seen previously in computers. But by now the field has matured considerably, and users are coming to demand more features from expert systems than a simple question-and-answer session followed by a recommendation or diagnosis.

Today, it is generally agreed that a true expert system must be capable of performing three basic services: not only problem solving but also interactive explanation and knowledge acquisition (learning). Like all software, it should be fast, easy to maintain, and user-friendly. Most systems interact with the operator through either an English language dialog or a Macintosh-style window and mouse environment. At the very least, the user's inputs should be prompted with a list of the applicable possibilities.

In order to deliver this performance, expert systems are normally organized into four modules: the *knowledge base*, the *working memory*, the *inference engine*, and some user interface and support software, for other miscellaneous functions. We can describe the functions and organization of the typical expert system with the schematic diagram in Figure 5-1.

The inference engine is the heart of the expert system, embodying the main control structures and algorithms. Normally, the inference engine operates in a continuous two-step cycle that first settles upon an inference to draw and then executes it. The knowledge base stores the system's total, permanent knowledge of its application domain, while the working memory serves as a temporary cache for information specific to the problem currently being solved.

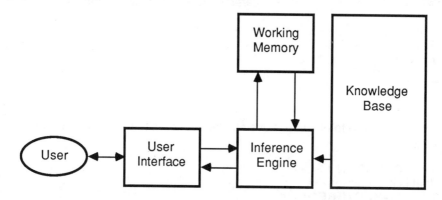

Figure 5–1.   **Architecture of a Typical Expert System**

Case Study 1: Medical Diagnosis

To better understand how an expert system is used, how it works internally, and how the four basic parts facilitate the three basic capabilities, we will look at two quite different expert systems that have been successfully implemented: MYCIN, with its add-on program *TEIRESIAS*, and Davis's electronic circuit diagnostician. We got a glimpse of each earlier, but now we will examine them in greater depth.

We will begin with MYCIN because it is older and illustrative of the more traditional expert system design methods that are most common in today's commercial systems. Having worked on DENDRAL for several years, Stanford's Heuristic Programming Project turned to medical diagnosis for their next effort and produced a series of important experimental programs, including the original MYCIN, the "father of modern expert systems," TEIRESIAS, an addition to the MYCIN environment that facilitated explanation and maintenance, EMYCIN, *NEOMYCIN*, a psychologically motivated reworking of MYCIN, and *GUIDON*, a project that attempted to use expert systems like MYCIN in medical education.

As we know, MYCIN was designed for doctors who need help in diagnosing blood diseases in their patients. To use it, the physician would log on to his computer terminal and run the program, beginning an interactive dialog like the one transcribed in Figure 5-2.

FIGURE 5-2. A CONSULTATION WITH **MYCIN**

---

*The user begins a consultation with MYCIN regarding the case of a patient named
Fred Smith. All relevant information is entered by answering the program's questions:*

- - - - - - - - PATIENT-1 - - - - - - - -
(1) Patient's name (first–last):
** **FRED SMITH**
(2) Sex:
** **MALE**
(3) Age:
** **55**
(4) Have you been able to obtain positive cultures from a site at which Fred Smith
      has an infection?
** **YES**
    - - - - - - - - INFECTION-1 - - - - - - - -
    (5) What is the infection?
** **PRIMARY-BACTEREMIA**
    (6) Please give the date and approximate time when signs or symptoms of the
        primary-bacteremia (INFECTION-1) first appeared. (mo/da/yr)
** **MAY 5, 1975**
The most recent positive culture associated with the primary-bacteremia
(INFECTION-1) will be referred-to as:
    - - - - - - - - CULTURE-1 - - - - - - - -
    (7) From what site was the specimen for CULTURE-1 taken?
** **BLOOD**
    (8) Please give the date and time when this blood culture (CULTURE-1)
        was obtained (mo/da/yr):
** **MAY 9, 1975**
The first significant organism from this blood culture (CULTURE-1)
will be referred to as:
    - - - - - - - - ORGANISM-1 - - - - - - - -
    (9) Enter the identity of ORGANISM-1:
** **UNKNOWN**
    (10) Is ORGANISM-1 a rod or a coccus (etc.):
** **ROD**
    (11) The gram stain of ORGANISM-1:
** **GRAMNEG**
    (12) Have there been POSITIVE cultures from sites which are NOT
        associated with infections about which you are seeking advice?
** **NO**
    (13) Did ORGANISM-1 grow aerobically?
** **YES (0.8)**
    (14) Did ORGANISM-1 grow anaerobically?
** **YES**
    (15) What is the suspected portal of entry of ORGANISM-1
        into this sterile site?
** **GI (0.6)**

Questioning continues in a similar fashion; eventually MYCIN arrives at a conclusion:

My therapy recommendation will be based on the following probable infection(s) and potential causative organism(s):

INFECTION-1 is PRIMARY-BACTEREMIA
<Item 1>   The identity of ORGANISM-1 may be PSEUDOMONAS-AERUGINOSA
<Item 2>   The identity of ORGANISM-1 may be KLEBSIELLA-PNEUMONIAE
<Item 3>   The identity of ORGANISM-1 may be E.COLI
<Item 4>   The identity of ORGANISM-1 may be BACTEROIDES-FRAGILIS
<Item 5>   The identity of ORGANISM-1 may be ENTEROBACTER
<Item 6>   The identity of ORGANISM-1 may be PROTEUS-NON-MIRABILIS

(46) On a scale of 0 to 4, where higher numbers indicate increasing severity how would you rate Fred Smith's degree of sickness?
** 3
(47) Does Fred Smith have a clinically significant allergic reaction to any antimicrobial agent?
** NO
(48) Fred Smith's weight in kilograms (or <number> POUNDS):
** 70

[Rec 1] My preferred therapy recommendation is as follows:
    In order to cover for Items <1 2 3 5 6>:
        Give: GENTAMICIN
        Dose: 119 mg (1.7 mg/kg) q8h IV [or IM] for 10 days
        Comments: Modify dose in renal failure
    In order to cover for Item <4>:
        Give: CLINDAMYCIN
        Dose: 595 mg (8.5 mg/kg) q6h IV [or IM] for 14 days
        Comments: If diarrhea or other GI symptoms develop, patient should be
                        evaluated for possible pseudomembranous colitis.

Do you wish to see the next choice therapy?
** YES
Which, if any, of the above drugs do you wish eliminated from consideration?
** CLINDAMYCIN

[Rec 2] Next best therapy recommendation:
    In order to cover for Items <2 3 4 5 6>:
        Give: CHLORAMPHENICOL
        Dose: 1 gm (15 mg/kg) q6h IV for 14 days
        Comments: Monitor patient's white count
    In order to cover for Item <1>:
        Give: GENTAMICIN
        Dose: 119 mg (1.7 mg/kg) q8h IV [or IM] for 10 days
        Comments: Modify dose in renal failure

At this point the consultation is over.

This transcript reveals several interesting aspects of MYCIN's reasoning. We can see that it collects in working memory a series of statistics about the patient, his symptoms, the infection, the organism, the culture, etc. Note also that the user is prompted clearly for all information, and he only enters information that the program will need to make its decisions. But it sheds no light on either the internal mechanisms of MYCIN's inference engine or the structure of its knowledge base. We still do not know how MYCIN arrives at its conclusions.

Production Rules

MYCIN is often described as a *rule-based* expert system, since its expertise, as embodied in the knowledge base component, consists primarily of a set of *production rules*. (Actually, MYCIN's knowledge base contains a few other data structures, including lists of known organisms and sterile sites, as well as tables of clinical parameters and the like.) Before essaying a formal definition of the term, let's look at a typical production rule, taken straight from MYCIN's knowledge base, shown in Figure 5-3. Below the sample rule is an English rendition of the knowledge it represents. When the program displays its rules to the user, it uses a crudely derived form similar to the rather loose translation shown here. Currently, MYCIN uses about 400 such rules, each of which is assigned a unique number for reference purposes.

FIGURE 5-3. **A TYPICAL MYCIN PRODUCTION RULE (LISP AND ENGLISH)**

```
PREMISE: ($AND  (SAME CNTXT GRAM GRAMNEG)
                (SAME CNTXT MORPH ROD)
                (SAME CNTXT AIR AEROBIC))
ACTION:   (CONCLUDE CNTXT CLASS ENTEROBACTERIACEAE TALLY 0.8)

IF        1)  the stain of the organism is gram negative, and
          2)  the morphology of the organism is rod, and
          3)  the aerobicity of the organism is aerobic,
THEN      there is strongly suggestive evidence (0.8) that the class of the
          organism is enterobacteriaceae.
```

MYCIN's rules are called production rules because they "produce" actions when the conditions of their premises are satisfied. Production rules are a form of declarative knowledge, because a single rule "declares" some quantum of universally applicable knowledge without specifying how it is to be used. In a rule-based system, the inference engine has the primary responsibility for determining when and how the rules will be used. A rule is said to *trigger* when the contents of working memory is such that the rule's premise becomes true. A rule "fires" when its action is performed. In the case of MYCIN, each premise is basically a logical formula that can be described as a conjunction of conditions:

<condition-1> AND <condition-2> AND ... AND <condition-N>

Individual conditions are either boolean functions (similar to Pascal functions that return a boolean value), or simple disjunctions of such functions:

<function-1> OR <function-2> OR ... OR <function-N>

For an example of a rule with a disjunctive condition, see Figure 5-4. (Although only the English version is given, you should be able to reconstruct the internal representation if you want, using Figure 5-3 as a guide.)

FIGURE 5-4. **A MYCIN RULE WITH A DISJUNCTIVE CONDITION**

IF   1) the site of the culture is blood, and
          2) the gram stain is positive, and
          3) the portal of entry is the gastrointestinal tract, and
          4) [A — the abdomen is the locus of infection, or
             B — the pelvis is the locus of infection]
THEN   there is strongly suggestive evidence that enterobacteriaceae is the
         class of organisms for which therapy should cover.

As we also know from Pascal programming, an OR condition will become true when any one of its elements becomes true, whereas an entire AND premise will become true just in case all of its elements become true. The truth value of a boolean function depends on the contents of working memory. MYCIN's working memory is organized into a "context tree," which can be thought of as a set of facts and variable values that apply to the consultation in progress; normally this information is either entered by the user or inferred when a rule fires. Working memory would contain such data as the patient's age and the suspected identities of organisms.

     For an example, consider the sample rule in Figure 5-3. If the three facts given in the list of conditions can all be found in working memory, then MYCIN will perform the action of "concluding," that is, adding a new fact to working memory. The new fact has associated with it a *certainty factor*.

Certainty Factors

MYCIN is designed to cope easily with uncertain evidence (this capability is called *fuzzy reasoning*, or *reasoning under uncertainty*). For example, if it cannot determine exactly which bacteria have caused an infection, it prescribes therapies to cover all of the reasonable possibilities. It does this by associating a certainty factor (CF) with each piece of data in the working memory and with each conclusion it draws in its reasoning process. In Figure 5-2, when the user entered YES in response to Question 13 ("Did the organism grow anaerobically?"), he appended the value 0.8 in parentheses to indicate that he was not completely confident of this information. The value of a CF ranges from -1.0, representing absolute falsehood of a proposition, to 1.0, representing absolute truth or confidence.

Presumably, a fact whose CF were 0.0 would be indeterminate, with no evidence existing to either support or contradict its truth. For a fact to be considered true in the boolean sense, when testing to see whether a rule will trigger, its CF must be greater than some threshold value of perhaps 0.1 or 0.2.

It is important to note that CFs are *not* probabilities. Although intuitive notions of probability can help us think about reasoning under uncertainty, we must keep in mind that associating a CF of 0.6 with a proposition does not imply that it is 60% likely to be true. In reality, it is either true or false, only we do not yet know which one. Indeed, we may never know with absolute certainty (1.0) whether the proposition is true.

How does MYCIN's inference engine use the certainty factors when making decisions? Actually, just a few simple rules are used:

- The CF of an ordinary condition is the CF of the information in working memory that matches it.

- The CF of a disjunctive condition is calculated by taking the *maximum* of the CFs of its elements. This fits our intuition: since just one of the elements need be true, or have a CF greater than the threshold, we should find the highest one possible.

- As you may have guessed, the CF of a premise is calculated by taking the *minimum* of the CFs of its component conditions. Analogously to the above, we reason that a conjunction can only be as true as its "least true" element.

- When a rule fires and draws a conclusion, the data added to working memory by the action are assigned a CF equal to the product of the calculated CF of the premise and the CF associated with the action itself. Also intuitive: if we're only 50% certain of our evidence and 50% certain that a rule applies, we're probably about 25% certain of the inference we can use them to draw.

By adhering to these principles consistently throughout its reasoning, MYCIN will know the relative certainties of the diagnoses it finally makes. Using them, it can adjust the therapies it recommends appropriately. For example, if after a number of rules have been applied, the certainty of a particular organism's presence wound up at 0.01, MYCIN could probably safely ignore it.

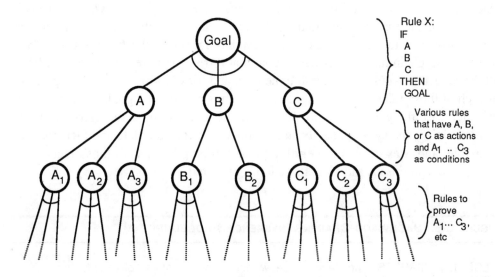

Figure 5–5. **A Tree-structured Model of MYCIN's Reasoning**

Goal-Oriented Reasoning

MYCIN's reasoning seems very orderly: first determine the identity of the infecting organisms, then turn to prescribing a therapy. It follows a *goal-oriented* strategy of choosing a goal and attempting to achieve it. It does this in a top-down way by beginning with the top level goal of treating a patient. To satisfy this objective, it must determine the infecting organism(s) and then prescribe one or more therapies. In turn, to identify the organisms, it must perform certain other tasks, and so on down to the bottom level of asking the user for various data. We can model this reasoning process with a tree-structured diagram, as in Figure 5-5.

This algorithm is known as *backward chaining*, because the system seeks to reason backwards from a conclusion it wants to make towards just those facts it will need to make it. Used in both MYCIN and the programming language Prolog, it is one of the two main control strategies used in rule-based expert systems.

The other, unsurprisingly called *forward chaining*, reasons forwards from whatever facts it may have towards any conclusions it can draw from them. It is used by the OPS5 production rule language. With this strategy, the inference engine collects all the rules that have not yet fired whose premises are satisfied, chooses one, and performs its associated action. It continues this until there are no rules left. Figures 5-6 and 5-7 provide more organized specifications of these two algorithms. One helpful way you can think about these inference procedures is with what I call the proof metaphor. Imagine that, with each conclusion it draws, the inference engine is seeking to *prove* some new fact that has not yet been established to be true. In backward chaining, it starts with a goal that it tries to prove. To prove it, it finds all the rules that would conclude it to be true, and tries in turn to prove the premise of each of those rules until it either succeeds, thus proving the goal, or running out, in which case the goal was unprovable. The process continues recursively. In forward chaining, the system usually starts with all the relevant data and facts that are available, and tries to prove everything that can be proved with those facts. Any time a rule's premise is satisfied, its action is executed.

FIGURE 5-6. BACKWARD-CHAINING INFERENCE PROCEDURE

GLOBAL VARIABLES: Knowledge base, working memory of established facts.
INPUT: The rule from which to begin chaining backwards.
TO COMPUTE: Is it possible to prove the consequent of the rule given the facts?
OUTPUT: The rule's action if it could be proven, NIL otherwise.

1. For each condition in the rule's premise, do the following:
   a. If the condition's CF according to working memory is greater than the threshold given in the condition, then go on to the next condition.
   b. Otherwise, if there are rules in the knowledge base that mention the condition as a conclusion in their action parts, recursively backward-chain on them one by one until the condition is satisfied or there are no more such rules.
2. If all of the rule's conditions were satisfied in step 1, return the rule's action.
3. If any one of the rule's conditions could not be satisfied in step 1, return NIL.

FIGURE 5-7. **FORWARD-CHAINING INFERENCE PROCEDURE**

GLOBAL VARIABLES: Knowledge base, working memory of established facts.
INPUT: None.
TO COMPUTE: Given the known facts, what can be proven with this knowledge base?
OUTPUT: All provable consequent parts of rules in the knowledge base, if any.

1. Create a conflict set consisting of all rules in the knowledge base whose conditions are immediately satisfied by the contents of working memory.
2. If this set is empty, no more inferences can be made, so halt execution.
3. Otherwise, use a conflict-resolution strategy to choose one of the rules in the conflict set (although several rules may trigger, only one is allowed to fire per cycle).
4. Execute that rule's action (this may modify working memory) and go back to step 1.

By now the differences between the two algorithms should be clear, as should be the tradeoff involved in choosing one over the other for a particular implementation or problem. Here's a short guide:

- Backward chaining — use when you have one or more hypotheses about your problem's solution, and you want the expert system to test them. You chain backwards from a hypothesis and the program prompts you for whatever data it needs.

- Forward chaining — use when you have collected all the available data about the problem, but you don't really have any good ideas about its solution. The expert system will draw all possible inferences and eventually find all the existing solutions.

Remember that we noted earlier that MYCIN uses a backward chaining inference engine. However, in the transcript shown in Figure 5-2, we don't see the doctor entering any hypotheses about the patient's illness; rather, the system runs the consultation from the start and makes its own final decisions. MYCIN's behavior resembles "hybrid chaining" algorithm of some sort. How is this accomplished?

In fact, MYCIN does backward chain, but it always starts from the same rule. An English version is shown in Figure 5-8. Basically, this rule supplies the hypothesis that a therapy be administered, causing the system to attempt to "prove" this by looking for an infection and considering the possibility that more than one infection need be treated. It provides a focus for the reasoning without restricting it to one particular goal.

FIGURE 5-8. **MYCIN'S TOP-LEVEL RULE**

IF   1) there is an infection which requires therapy, and
         2) attention has been given to the possibility of additional infections
            requiring therapy,
THEN   compile a list of possible therapies and determine the best therapy
         in this list.

This rule is an excellent example of what can be accomplished in a production system with careful programming. It cleverly integrates declarative knowledge about what constitutes a consultation with a procedural description of how to execute it. In fact, we cannot and should not escape procedural interpretations of production rules, because their declarative content does not tell the whole story of how they will be used.

When MYCIN attempts to prove an action part of a rule, it must prove each of the conjoined conditions (step 1a in Figure 5-6). Declaratively, it makes no difference how those conditions are ordered in the text of the rule, since they all must be proved in any case. But procedurally, we will go about proving them in the order in which they are listed, so the ordering can make a large difference. The same is true of the ordering of rules in the knowledge base, which determines how they will be tried when an action part common to several must be proved (step 1b in Figure 5-6). But even with clever ordering, sometimes ordinary production rules cannot supply enough procedural knowledge to adequately direct the inference engine's reasoning process.

Metalevel Knowledge

Consider again our algorithm for backward chaining from Figure 5-6. Suppose that at step 1b, there are fifty rules that we could conceivably try to use to prove the condition. Which one should we try to prove first? The inference engine has no knowledge itself, so it will probably go through the rules in numerical order. This can result in enormous inefficiencies in large knowledge bases, since significant amounts of time can be spent pursuing lines of reasoning foreseen to be unprofitable by the knowledge engineers who designed the system.

MYCIN's solution to the problem is to order the set of rules that can trigger at any point through the application of one or more *metarules*. Metarules are, by definition, "rules about rules." While ordinary production rules operate on the contents of working memory alone, the metarules also operate on the contents of the knowledge base itself. Figure 5-9 has two examples. Since they have their own CFs, MCYIN's metarules can rank rules according to the certainty that they are applicable in the same way its ordinary rules can rank organisms according to the certainty that they are present.

FIGURE 5-9. **SOME OF MYCIN'S METARULES**

IF   1) the culture was not obtained from a sterile source, and
           2) there are rules which mention in their premises a previous
              organism, which may be the same as the current organism,
THEN it is definite (1.0) that none of them will be useful.

IF   1) the infection is a pelvic abscess, and
           2) there are rules that mention in their premises enterobacteriaceae, and
           3) there are rules that mention in their premises gram-positive rods,
THEN there is suggestive evidence (0.4) that the former should be used before the latter.

Since rules are supposed to represent knowledge, metarules are said to represent *metalevel knowledge*, or knowledge about knowledge; in this case, knowledge about how to apply rules. In the same vein, we could have meta-metarules and so on, but this would probably be overkill. Metarules are effective tools for directing the inference engine but should not be overused, especially in small knowledge bases where the overhead of calling them may negate the savings they are there to produce.

Introspection and Learning

We have seen how MYCIN's knowledge base and inference engine enable it to make rather complex diagnoses, and then to recommend and modify therapies based on those conclusions. These capabilities fulfill the first of the three performance requirements we established for expert systems, that they be able to solve problems. Now we will consider the second and third requirements, namely the abilities to explain its reasoning and to acquire new knowledge.

The "original" version of MYCIN, completed in 1976, contained facilities for explanation, or introspection, and knowledge acquisition, or learning. However, they were primitive compared to those that Davis's TEIRESIAS program brought to the system.

TEIRESIAS is an "add-on module" for rule-based expert systems that was developed in the context of MYCIN. The idea was to make it as domain-independent as possible, so none of its essential knowledge has anything to do with medical diagnosis. Figure 5-10, a transcript of a MYCIN session with TEIRESIAS, should give you a good idea of its capabilities.

FIGURE 5-10. **EXPLANATION AND LEARNING IN MYCIN WITH TEIRESIAS**

In the middle of a session, the user requests explanations from MYCIN:

What is the suspected portal of entry of ORGANISM-1 into this sterile site?
** WHY
[Why is it important to determine the suspected portal of entry of ORGANISM-1 into this sterile site?]

[3.0] ... in order to find out about an organism or class of organisms for which
       therapy should cover.
It has been already established that
       [3.1]   The site of the culture is blood
       [3.2]   The stain of the organism is gram positive
Therefore if:
       [3.3]   The portal of entry of the organism is GI
       [3.4]   [Abdomen is the locus of infection, or
               Pelvis is the locus of infection]
Then
       There is strongly suggestive evidence (0.9) that enterobacteriaceae is the
       class of organisms for which therapy should cover.
[Rule 095]
** HOW [3.4]
[How were you determining that the Abdomen is the locus of infection,
or that the Pelvis is the locus of infection?]

[4.0] At that point Rule 021 was being used.

** HOW [4.0]
[How was rule 021 used?]

       [5.0] It has already been established that
       [5.1] the culture is recent.
Therefore if:
       [5.2] There is therapeutically significant disease associated with the
              occurrence of this organism
Then
       It is definite (1.0) that the site of the culture is the locus of infection in the patient.

As in the first consultation, MYCIN eventually makes its conclusions. Here TEIRESIAS is active, and asks the user whether those decisions are correct:

My therapy recommendations will be based on the following probable infection(s) and potential causative organism(s):

INFECTION-1 is PRIMARY BACTEREMIA
<Item 1>   The identity of ORGANISM-1 may be E. COLI
<Item 2>   The identity of ORGANISM-1 may be PSEUDOMONAS-AERUGINOSA

Are all these identities correct?
** NO
Are there any identities missing?
** YES
Which ones?
** KLEBSIELLA-PNEUMONIAE, PROTEUS NON-MIRABILIS
Are there any identities which shouldn't have appeared?
** YES
Which one(s)?
** PSEUDOMONAS-AERUGINOSA
Do you want to
    1] track down the problem yourself, or
    2] allow me to guide the debugging, or
    3] ignore it for now and fix it another time.
Type 1, 2, or 3.
** 2
We'll start with PSEUDOMONAS-AERUGINOSA first.
The following rules were used in deducing that the identity of ORGANISM-1
is PSEUDOMONAS-AERUGINOSA:

RULE 184
    Since
        [1.1] The category of ORGANISM-1 is not known
        [1.2] The gram stain of ORGANISM-1 is gram negative
        [1.3] The morphology of ORGANISM-1 is rod
        [1.4] The aerobicity of ORGANISM-1 is facultative
    Then there is weakly suggestive evidence (0.3) that the identity of ORGANISM-1
    is PSEUDOMONAS-AERUGINOSA.

Is this rule correct?
** YES
Should its premise have failed for this case?
** YES
Which clause of the premise should have failed?
** CLAUSE 1
Should it have been possible to conclude a category?
** YES
Which one?
** ENTEROBACTERIACEAE
There were no rules successfully invoked in the attempt to deduce that the
category of ORGANISM-1 is ENTEROBACTERIACEAE.
The following (potentially applicable) rules were not executed because the
marked [++] clause failed:

RULE 116
   If   1) The identity of ORGANISM-1 is not known
   ++   2) The gram stain of ORGANISM-1 is not known
        3) The morphology of ORGANISM-1 is not known
        4) The site of CULTURE-1 is CSF
        5) The infection is meningitis
        6) The age of Albert Hall is less than or equal to 2 months
   Then there is weakly suggestive evidence (0.33) that the category of
   ORGANISM-1 is ENTEROBACTERIACEAE.

RULE 050
   If   1) The morphology of ORGANISM-1 is rod
        2) The gram stain of ORGANISM-1 is gram negative
        3) The aerobicity of ORGANISM-1 is facultative
   ++   4) The infection with ORGANISM-1 was acquired while the patient
            was hospitalized
   Then there is suggestive evidence (0.7) that the category of ORGANISM-1
   is ENTEROBACTERIACEAE.

Are all these rules correct?
** YES
Should any of them have been successfully invoked?
** NO
Is there a rule missing?
** YES
Would you like to give me such a rule now?
** YES
Good ...

If:
**   1 THE PATIENT'S INFECTION IS PRIMARY-BACTEREMIA
**   2 THE SITE IS ONE OF THE STERILE SITES
Then:
**   THERE IS EVIDENCE (0.8) THAT THE CATEGORY IS
**   ENTEROBACTERIACEAE

I hate to criticize, Dr. Davis, but did you know that most rules about what the
category of an organism might be, that mention
   the site of a culture; the infection
Also mention —
   [A] The portal of entry of the organism
Shall I try to write a clause to account for [A]?
** YES
How about —
   [A] The portal of entry is gastrointestinal. OK?
** YES

*TEIRESIAS processes the new rule and reruns the consultation non-interactively, try-
ing to determine if the addition of the one rule resulted in a satisfactory diagnosis. In
this case, it did, and receives the expert's approval.*

TEIRESIAS can be invoked in several ways, but the usual procedure is for the user to type either WHY or HOW in response to some question from the system. Recall that whenever MYCIN asks the user something, it is firing a production rule somewhere that directs it to gather a particular piece of data. Therefore, during a typical session, the user will have several chances to interact with the explanation and acquisition facilities.

While the details of the acquisition process are beyond the scope of this overview, we can get a clear picture of the explanation process by recalling our tree-structured model of backward chaining inference. Figure 5-11 shows a fragment of a tree which represents a simple *truth-maintenance system* for MYCIN's reasoning process. If it constructs such a tree over the course of a consultation, indicating which rules were used to prove which actions based on which conditions, the inference engine will always have the information it needs to explain itself.

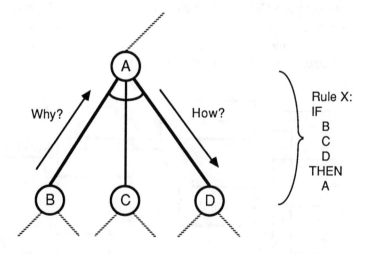

Figure 5–11. **Explanation with the Tree-Model Truth Maintenance System**

Consider node B, which represents one of the conditions in Rule X. Suppose the text of B is "patient's temperature is normal," and that the system accordingly asks for the patient's temperature. In response, the user asks WHY? All the program has to do is look up the tree from B to B's parent, A, to provide the answer "I tried to establish B because I am trying to establish A using Rule X." Similarly, the user could respond HOW? The program need only look at A's children to conclude "I am trying to prove A with Rule X by proving B, C, and D." So the essential trick of explanation requires simply keeping track of inferences with a tree structure and finding a node's parent to answer WHY and its children to answer HOW.

Case Study 2: Digital Electronics Troubleshooting

MYCIN, with its add-ons, derivatives, and imitators, firmly established the production-rule paradigm at the forefront of expert systems development, providing the basic model for most of the subsequent work in knowledge engineering. A characteristic common to the problems to which production systems are being applied is their lack of a unified theoretical framework. One often hears that a domain like physics is unsuitable for expert systems because it is too structured by rigid laws to admit such inexact, unscientific, and shallow reasoning techniques. However, recent work on *qualitative reasoning* is challenging this viewpoint.

As a contrast to MYCIN, we will examine a system developed by Davis that is able to find bugs in digital electronic circuits like the one in Figure 5-12. Here, the problem is to determine which of the five main components in the circuit are malfunctioning, causing the miscomputation of the value output at F.

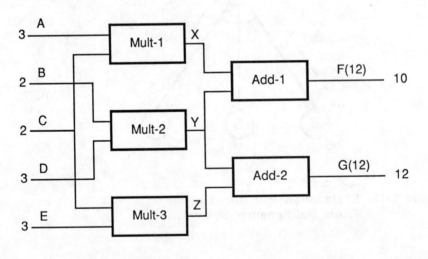

F=AC+BD; G=EC+BD   (expected values in parentheses)

Figure 5-12. **A Problem Solved by Davis's Diagnostic Reasoning System**

The system has built-in knowledge of the *structure* and expected *behavior* of the individual components of the circuit, as well as representations of the device itself. Using *simulation rules*, which are not production rules, the program can predict the outputs of a circuit based on its inputs. A typical rule for an adder is shown in Figure 5-13; note that the rule describes how to infer both inputs and outputs of the device, allowing a reverse simulation. With such a reverse simulation, the program can construct a *dependency record* for each circuit output, showing which subcircuits contributed to its value.

FIGURE 5-13. ONE OF DAVIS'S SIMULATION RULES

ADDER:
    to get sum from (input-1 input-2) do (+ input-1 input-2)
    to get input-1 from (sum input-2) do (- sum input-2)
    to get input-2 from (sum input-1) do (- sum input-1)

With the dependency records constructed and a discrepancy detected between the value of F expected by the simulation and the value actually obtained, the system can begin the diagnostic process. Davis uses a new algorithm called *candidate generation by constraint suspension*, as summarized in Figure 5-14, to accomplish the identification of suspected malfunctioning devices. Central to this procedure is the notion of a *constraint network*, an interpretation of the data structure that describes the circuit as a combination of restrictions on the inputs and outputs of each device in the circuit. The simulation rule in Figure 5-13 constrains the inputs and outputs of the adder with certain mathematical relations between their values.

To illustrate the algorithm, we sketch its operation on the problem shown in Figure 5-12. In steps 1-2, we isolate the discrepancy at F, where the output is 10 rather than the 12 predicted by the simulation. In steps 3-4, we notice that the value at F depends only on the components Add-1, Mult-1, and Mult-2 (the outputs of Add-2 and Mult-3 clearly never influence the inputs of Add-1, whose output is F itself). But why should step 5 work?

Let's first suspend the constraints on Add-1. This means, essentially, that Add-1 is no longer required to act like an adder, in the sense that any combination of its inputs and outputs are acceptable to the simulation process. Now wires X and Y will still both have the value 6 (2 multiplied by 3), and F will still be 10, so we find the combination 6, 6, 10 that accounts for Add-1's faulty behavior as well as the discrepancy detected in the entire circuit. Add-1 is a consistent candidate.

What about Mult-1? If we suspend its constraints, we see by simulating Add-1 backward that X must be 4 (10 - 6). Going backwards through Add-2 from G, we see that Y and Z must both be 6. This means that, since E is 3, C must be 2. However, if C is 2 and A is 3, there is no combination of inputs and outputs for Mult-1 that will put the network in a globally consistent state—either F could not be 10 or G could not be 12, but we have observed both of those values. Therefore, Mult-1 is not a consistent candidate (the same turns out to be true of Mult-2 as well), so Add-1 is likely to be broken.

FIGURE 5-14. CANDIDATE GENERATION BY CONSTRAINT SUSPENSION

GLOBAL VARIABLE: Knowledge base of electronic components and simulation rules.
INPUT: A description of an electronic circuit.
TO COMPUTE: Is the circuit working correctly?
OUTPUT: A set of components that are plausible candidates for malfunction.

1. Insert device inputs into constraint network inputs.
2. Compare predicted with observed outputs and form a set of output discrepancies.
3. For each discrepancy found in step 2, use the dependency record for that output to form a set of components that contributed to its value.
4. Take the intersection of the sets computed in step 3.
5. For each component in the set computed in step 4, do the following:
   a. Turn off (suspend) the constraint modeling its behavior.
   b. Insert values from steps 1-2 at constraint network inputs and outputs.
   c. Re-run the simulation, using both forward and backward rules, trying to find any combination of inputs and outputs for the chosen component that accounts for the observed outputs of the circuit.
   d. If a combination is found, the component is a consistent candidate and should be added to the candidate set.
   e. If no combination can be found, the component is inconsistent and can be ignored.

Davis's program clearly demonstrates expert performance in diagnostic reasoning, but is it a "true" expert system? Although it seems much more algorithmic than and quite different from a rule-based system like MYCIN, closer examination reveals that Davis's system includes an inference engine (primarily the candidate generation algorithm), a working memory (including the constraint network describing the circuit being diagnosed), a knowledge base (for example, simulation rules for various electronic devices), and a user interface (that allows input of a circuit design, test inputs, and observed outputs).

Traditional expert systems are "shallow" in that their knowledge of a problem domain is superficial and requires little understanding of its underlying mechanisms. MYCIN knows nothing about the functioning of the gastro-intestinal tract. By contrast, Davis's system is "deep" because it reasons from first principles about the structure and behavior of electronic components, using that basic knowledge to work with a full model of the problem. It knows that an adder sums its inputs, and that on a lower level it uses two half-adders, which in turn use certain TTL gates, and so on.

Knowledge Engineering

The superiority of reasoning from first principles over shallow production rules is apparent, but the former approach only works well in domains (like electronics) in which the "first principles" are defined at a level of abstraction reasonably close to that of the problems we would like to solve. Knowing the principles that govern the function of an adder helps to debug a circuit that has a faulty adder, but would knowing the principles of cell biology help in diagnosing blood diseases? Medical diagnosis uses shallow knowledge because the deep knowledge involved is hidden too many layers down to be of real use.

In knowledge engineering, we are concerned with discovering and organizing whatever information is relevant to solving the problem at hand. The most basic choice we must make is between the shallow and deep approaches to expertise, keeping in mind that with depth comes increased difficulty of development. While there are many existing shell programs for production-rule expert systems, there are none for deep systems.

Choosing between shallow and deep is just one step in creating a new expert system. Figure 5-15 diagrams the entire knowledge engineering process, showing the five major stages of identification, conceptualization, formalization, implementation, and testing. The arrows pointing backwards indicate the actions that should be taken if difficulty is encountered.

Obviously, the central interaction of the entire process is that between knowledge engineer and *domain expert*, who try to render the special knowledge used to solve problems in the domain in terms conducive to automation. While this transfer of expertise is often a long and very difficult process, the following sample dialog should give you the flavor of what has been termed the "knowledge acquisition bottleneck." The application is toxic chemical spill crisis management:

KNOWLEDGE ENGINEER: Suppose you were told that a spill had been detected in White Oak Creek one mile before it enters White Oak Lake. What would you do to contain the spill? [It is a good idea to start with a concrete example in order to observe the expert in simulated action.]

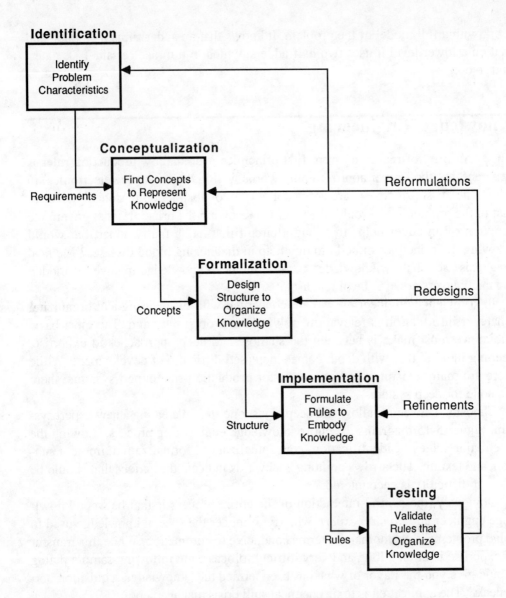

Figure 5–15. **Stages of the Knowledge Engineering Process**

DOMAIN EXPERT: That depends on a number of factors. [A typical response at this point.] I would need to find the source in order to prevent the possibility of further contamination, probably by checking drains and manholes for signs of the spill material. And it helps to know what the spilled material is.

KNOWLEDGE ENGINEER: How can you tell what it is? [The knowledge engineer focuses the interview on the subproblem of identifying the material.]

DOMAIN EXPERT: Sometimes you can tell what the substance is by its smell. Sometimes you can tell by its color, but that's not always reliable since dyes are used a lot nowadays. Oil, however, floats on the surface and forms a silvery film, while acids dissolve completely in the water. [The expert goes on to the next subproblem.] Once you discover the type of material spilled, you can eliminate any buildings that either don't store the material at all or don't store enough of it to account for the spill.

At this point, the knowledge engineer starts using his tools to prototype the expert system. In the case shown above, he chooses the *ROSIE* rule-based language, which has an English-like syntax.

Figure 5-16 shows the rules he writes after completing the above session with the expert. A subsequent session might begin as follows:

KNOWLEDGE ENGINEER: Here are some rules I think capture your explanation about determining the type of material spilled and eliminating possible spill sources. [Shows Figure 5-16.] What do you think?

DOMAIN EXPERT: [After examining the rules.] Yes, that begins to capture it. Of course if the material is silver nitrate it will dissolve only partially in the water.

KNOWLEDGE ENGINEER: I see. Well, let's add that information to the knowledge base and see what it looks like. [Writes a new rule.]

We see here an illustration of the successive-approximation character of knowledge engineering. No successful knowledge base is ever constructed whole out of a single session between knowledge engineer and domain expert. Rather, over the course of many sessions, prototypes are built, refined, and rebuilt until all parties involved are satisfied with the system's performance.

FIGURE 5-16. **ROSIE RULES FOR CHEMICAL-SPILL IDENTIFICATION**

To determine-spill-material:

[1] If the spill does not dissolve in water
     and the spill does not form a silvery film,
   let the spill be oil.
[2] If the spill does dissolve in water
     and the spill does form no film,
   let the spill be acid.
[3] If the spill = oil
     and the odor of the spill is known,
   choose situation:
     if the spill does smell of gasoline,
     let the material of the spill be gasoline
       with certainty 0.9;
     if the spill does smell of diesel oil,
     let the material of the spill be diesel oil
       with certainty 0.8.
[4] If the spill = acid
     and the odor of the spill is known,
   choose situation:
     if the spill does have a pungent/choking odor,
     let the material of the spill be hydrochloric acid
       with certainty 0.7;
     if the spill does smell of vinegar,
     let the material of the spill be acetic acid
       with certainty 0.8.
End.

Performance of Expert Systems

Throughout our discussion of the architecture and engineering of expert systems, we have largely ignored the question of their performance. But unlike many AI programs, expert systems are commercial software products that are expected to deliver on their promises of accuracy and cost-effectiveness in a verifiable way. It is often not enough to just use a system for a while and decide whether its output is of acceptable quality.

One of the first expert systems to undergo performance testing was MYCIN. In 1974, an early version diagnosed 15 real cases of bacteremia, receiving the approval of a panel of experts for 11 of its recommendations. In 1979, a more objective study was conducted on an improved version of the program, yielding the results shown in Figure 5-17. MYCIN's diagnoses on 10 new real cases were anonymously rated acceptable (1 point) or unacceptable (0 points) by 8 experts, so a perfect score would have been 80.

FIGURE 5-17. **MYCIN'S PERFORMANCE BY "HUMAN STANDARDS"**

Ratings by 8 independent experts on 10 cases:

MYCIN	52	Actual therapy administered	46
Faculty member #1	50	Faculty member #4	44
Faculty member #2	48	Resident	36
Infectious disease fellow	48	Faculty member #5	34
Faculty member #3	46	Student	24

Although the differences between MYCIN and the top faculty are statistically insignificant, the program clearly improved upon the actual treatment and the recommendations of a practicing physician. It is not used in hospitals, however, because its domain is quite limited and the computing power required to run a consultation in a reasonable amount of time has only recently become economically feasible.

But even though its therapies are accepted by the medical community, MYCIN has been attacked on more theoretical grounds. J. B. Adams showed that MYCIN's system of certainty factors, however intuitively elegant it may seem, does not correspond to any correct probabilistic model, concluding that its reasoning mechanism is fundamentally flawed (and, by extension, should not be trusted).

The Dreyfus brothers have attacked the rule-based expert system as a practical problem-solving tool on the grounds that a true expert uses nothing like rules. For them, rules (or any paradigm that relies on sequential analysis) are used by beginners and novices, but not experts. Presumably, such experts have "compiled" their early rote learning into sophisticated patterns based on their years of experience—experience which, it is claimed, cannot be assimilated by a computer.

Reasoning with uncertainty, alternative approaches to expertise, and validating the performance of important expert systems are all open problems in artificial intelligence, and will continue to stimulate the applied side of the field for years to come. The early success of expert systems has continued to grow, and it now seems likely that knowledge-based expertise will in one way or another come to be an integral part of computer software for all applications.

A Production System in Pascal

The framework of a rule-based expert system is easily programmed in Pascal. The program *PADVISOR* implements both the backward- and forward-chaining inference procedures with simple propositional production rules. PADVISOR.COM is the executable code, and CHESS.KBS and FACULTY.KBS, which must be put in the same directoryas the PADVISOR executable file, are sample knowledge bases for the program.

To use PADVISOR, simply run the program and answer the first prompt with the name of the knowledge base you wish to consult. You will next be asked for a "context file"; for now just press [Return]. Answer yes for interactive operation, and press [Return] when asked for a goal. The program will now attempt to find the best solution it can, by backward chaining from each top level goal in the knowledge base one-by-one until either one is proved or none remain. You will be prompted with a yes/no question to establish whether any necessary bottom-level facts are true or false.

In PADVISOR, a fact is represented simply as a string, such as "candidate was articulate and knowledgeable during the interview," which can be either true, false, or unknown. There are no variables, and strings must match exactly to be considered equivalent. A *context file* is a series of these strings specifying facts known to be true before the consultation, and a *goal* is a single string specifying a fact the system should try to prove. Forward chaining will take place if you specify a context, backward chaining otherwise. In the latter case, if you specify no goal, the system will try each possible top-level goal in order from the beginning of the knowledge base.

The organization of the knowledge base is key to the operation of PADVISOR. Each rule consists of a series of conjoined condition facts (no disjunctions allowed) and a single action fact, which becomes proven true when the rule fires. Although there are no certainty factors, the production rules are assumed to be listed in *priority order*, such that the most desirable conclusions are listed first. For example, in FACULTY.KBS, the objective is to recommend the best possible faculty position for a candidate; therefore, rules recommending a senior appointment are listed before rules recommending a junior appointment, which are in turn listed ahead of rules concluding facts that are used only as conditions by other rules. In forward chaining, this order is reversed, so that the system will have all possible intermediate facts proven before it reaches the most important goals.

The basic architecture of PADVISOR follows that shown in Figure 5-1, with the exception that there are separate inference engines for backward and forward chaining. The user interface is in ASK_USER, the working memory in PROVEN and DISPROVEN, the knowledge base in RULES (and revRULES, its reverse), and the inference engines in BACKWARDS, FORWARDS, and their associated functions. Knowledge base files are simple text listings of rules, which you should have no trouble deciphering from the examples.

Programming Exercises

1. Enhance PADVISOR's knowledge base structure to number the rules, so that they are prioritized by number instead of just listed in order of priority. Also, allow for multiple actions per rule and disjunctive conditions in rules. What modifications must be made to the inference engines to accommodate these changes, and how do they increase the power of the system? In what other ways can you improve PADVISOR's efficiency, robustness, and friendliness?

2. Add certainty factors to PADVISOR's reasoning process, following either the MYCIN method or a standard probabilistic model such as Bayes's Theorem. Each fact should have an associated CF variable, and each rule should have a CF associated with its conclusion; you will need to modify the data structures for the knowledge base to accommodate them. A global threshold value (as required by the backward chaining algorithm from Figure 5-6), can be used to manipulate the "robustness" of the system's conclusions by mandating that conditions have a certain degree of certainty before they are admitted.

3. Implement an explanation facility similar to MYCIN's, as discussed earlier. If the system is not in interactive mode, explanations will only be available at the top level, after the inference process is complete; otherwise, the user should be able to ask WHY or HOW at any prompt. This will require the construction of a truth-maintenance tree as rules fire, and special care to record only those inferences that were actually made.

4. Create a program to simplify and streamline the maintenance of knowledge bases for PADVISOR, and integrate its functions into PADVISOR. It should be possible to incrementally create, test, and modify (debug) a

knowledge base, completely from within the same program. There need not be a facility for knowledge acquisition, only the ability to easily switch back and forth between the editing and inferencing modules.

5. (After completing #4.) Research the problem of knowledge acquisition to a greater extent than it is covered here. Implement a simple facility in PADVISOR to allow the user to write new rules from within the inference engine itself, preferably using a template-based editor developed above. How far can you go in imitating TEIRESIAS's sophisticated learning capabilities?

6. Modern expert systems can sometimes even learn without user assistance, through an *induction* process that analyzes statistical data about a problem domain in order to form new rules. To what types of problems can such techniques most effectively be applied, and how much must a system know about a domain before it can learn more? Design an implement a simple inductive learning mechanism. (For more information on automatic knowledge acquisition, see Quinlan's "Learning Efficient Classification Procedures and their Application to Chess Endgames.")

7. The main deficiency of PADVISOR is its lack of variables, especially numerical ones. Implement a general variable mechanism for rules, allowing for named variables and arithmetic expressions with comparisons within rules. With your system, it should be possible to write a condition such as "if COST > 30" or "if (ITEMS * COST) > 500," for example. Can you generalize this mechanism to allow for boolean values (true/false), strings, and lists in variables? What are the difficulties of using a language like Pascal for this type of project?

8. (After completing #7.) Having implemented a general variable mechanism, and extended it to cover multiple data types, you can now begin to experiment with metarules by allowing variables to represent individual conditions, actions, or entire rules. Should metarules be segregated from ordinary rules, or can they be combined in the same knowledge base? What new control structures are necessary for metalevel reasoning? At what size threshold does a knowledge base begin to realize benefits from the overhead of metalevel reasoning?

Summary

Expert systems are programs that display expert performance solving problems in domains like medical and electronic diagnosis. One is normally composed of a user-interface, a working memory, an inference engine, and a large database of highly specialized, domain-specific knowledge; it is the prime role of this component that distinguishes an expert system from a more conventional problem-solving system.

The most common method of representing this knowledge is the production system, which encodes expertise in premise-action rules that execute the actions when the conditions in their premises are satisfied. The most common control structures for expert systems are backward chaining, which guides the system from a hypothesized solution through a proof that it is correct, and forward chaining, which goes from a set of observed facts to a solution that is consistent with them. Besides solving problems, expert systems should also be able to provide transparent explanations of their reasoning and to work interactively with experts to enhance their knowledge bases.

Knowledge engineering is the art and process of creating an expert system. It can be divided into five stages of identification, conceptualization, formalization, implementation, and testing, which include the fundamental choice between shallow and deep models of expertise. Expert systems, to gain acceptance among users, must have their performance validated, for which techniques are just beginning to be developed. But although critics of expert systems have accused them of being, among other things, mathematically unsound and fundamentally misguided, their popularity is growing rapidly.

References

Neither Charniak and McDermott's nor Winston's AI textbooks devote much space to knowledge engineering, in fact refusing to use the term "expert system." Instead, they cover basic AI issues like production systems and abductive reasoning that underlie the practice of knowledge engineering. Fortunately, there are several good books on expert systems, including Jackson's *Introduction to Expert Systems*, an excellent overview that discusses the architecture of several example programs in depth, Waterman's *Guide to Expert Systems*, and Hayes-Roth, Waterman, and Lenat's *Building Expert Systems*, which concentrates on knowledge engineering. Waterman and *The Handbook of AI* present the best overviews of existing systems.

MYCIN is the subject of several works, including Shortliffe's *Computer-Based Medical Consultations: MYCIN*, Buchanan and Shortliffe's *Rule-Based Expert Systems: The MYCIN Experiments of the Stanford Heuristic Programming*

Project, and Clancey and Shortliffe's *Readings in Medical Artificial Intelligence: The First Decade*. Davis's contributions to the project, especially TEIRESIAS, are documented in Part I of his and Lenat's *Knowledge Based Systems in Artificial Intelligence*. For an overview of the complete MYCIN project, see "Production Rules as a Representation for a Knowledge-Based Consultation Program" by Davis and Shortliffe.

Davis's later work on electronic diagnosis is covered in "Diagnostic Reasoning from Structure and Behavior," which is reprinted in Bobrow's *Qualitative Reasoning About Physical Systems*. The discussion of knowledge engineering organized around Figures 5-15 and 5-16 is based on material in Chapter 5 of Hayes-Roth, Waterman, and Lenat. For material on the current practice and future of expert systems, see Clancey's "From Guidon to Neomycin and Heracles in Twenty Short Lessons," Davis's essay on "Expert Systems: Where are we and where do we go from here?" and the special issue of the *AI Magazine* (Fall 1986) on knowledge-based systems in manufacturing.

6. HEURISTIC SEARCH

In this chapter we will discuss a paradigm that has been used to solve numerous problems in artificial intelligence and other areas of computer science: *search*. The idea that a problem can be solved by searching for a solution hardly seems exciting or innovative. Isn't that how we always solve problems?

Well, yes and no. Yes in the general sense—we cannot answer a question without finding the answer somewhere first, be it in a book, in our memory, or anywhere else. But no in the sense we introduced in Chapter 2, where we distinguished between problems that have a mechanical, rote method of solution and those that seemed to require some knowledge or creativity to master. As we did in Chapter 5 with expert systems, we can point to a higher class of problems that AI search techniques are used to solve.

The principal goals of this chapter are to:

- Define exactly what is meant by search in AI, and introduce the necessary terminology and basic concepts.

- Look into some practical applications of search in AI programming.

- Present a general search algorithm and investigate various ways to make it more informed and intelligent through heuristic knowledge.

- Analyze the performance of search algorithms, with a view towards understanding how to design heuristics and choose search strategies.

- Program a search algorithm in Turbo Pascal and apply it to the Route-Finding Problem, a variant of the Traveling Salesman Problem.

What Is Search?

The main kind of search we want to discuss is usually called *state space search* because it envisions the attempt to solve a particular problem as an attempt to transform its initial state, or description, into some final goal state, the solution. Sometimes the problem can have one or more intermediate states between the start and goal states. All the possible states of the problem, taken together, are said to form a state space.

For example, suppose we want to search a map to find a route from one city to another. The route will probably take us through other cities. In this case, the state space is the collection of possible locations for our car. The initial state is the city we start in, and the final state is the one we're trying to get to. The other cities on the map represent the intermediate states.

A state space is really just another knowledge-representation formalism, like those discussed in Chapter 3. Each state is a symbolic configuration of some fixed set of elements; how they themselves are represented varies considerably from problem to problem. In our example each state could just be a constant string giving the name of the particular city it represented. The set of states would just be a collection of the cities that the map "knows about."

There is another interpretation of search that we should mention at least briefly: the *problem-reduction* formalism. Here, each state is taken to represent a goal of some sort. An operator decomposes a large goal into a number of smaller subgoals. Typically, there are several ways to satisfy a single goal, so several operators are available at any one time. The tree constructed by applying these operators is also known as an *AND/OR* tree because the operators are applied in logical combination. The most notable application of AND/OR search is in the backward-chaining inference procedure for expert systems, which was discussed in Chapter 5.

We have now learned how we might represent a *problem domain* with a state space formalism, but one more ingredient is needed before we can define a particular problem itself. We know that we are to somehow move from the initial state, referred to as START, to one of the final states, referred to as the GOALS. But how do we get there?

Somewhere it must be specified which *operators* we can apply to transform one state into another. In the route-finding example, the cities are presumably interconnected by a network of roads such that we can drive directly from some cities to some others, but must usually pass through a few on the way. The operators would be the roads connecting the cities. For each state in the space, the operators available would consist of the roads leading out of the city represented by that state. State space search problems are usually depicted with a graph like the one in Figure 6-1, where the vertices, or nodes, represent the states of the problem and each edge represents the application of a particular operator to transform one state into another. This particular graph diagrams an instance of the Route-finding Problem with a very small state space. It now becomes clear that solving this problem involves searching for some sequence of operators which, when applied in order, will transform the START state into the GOAL state. Such a sequence is called a *path* through the state space.

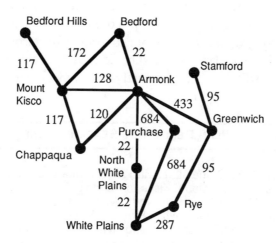

Figure 6–1. **Route Finding Problem State Space**

Note that we have chosen to use a graph rather than a tree to depict a state space because operator cycles are possible. It is easy to see that applying the operator "take Route 128" from Armonk followed by applying it again once at Mount Kisco will return us to a previous state. Our programs must take these problems into account. Some state spaces have only non-invertible operators; that is, operators whose effects cannot be undone by the application of other operators. For such spaces we could use trees.

The illustrative example we have been using so far, the problem of finding routes between cities on a roadmap, corresponds quite obviously to the architecture of a state space. But what about other problems that don't fit so cleanly into the mold? Before you can solve a problem with state space search you must decide what states and operators it contains, but they are often not readily apparent. Some detective work is not infrequently necessary in state space formalization.

Keep in mind throughout the discussion of search that a search graph (or tree) is not necessarily a structure built up as an algorithm executes. It is a way of representing knowledge about a problem domain. We might implicitly construct a tree while searching a state space, but this is because we applied some operators to a state to find out what other states we could reach, and not because we traversed a data structure to a state and then looked at a list of pointers from it to some other states. The search graph is mostly an aid to thinking about a state space search problem.

In problems where we are searching for a path through the state space to a solution, we are actually doing a primitive form of *planning*. By developing a sequence of operators to apply, we make a plan of actions to take starting from a given situation. Figure 6-2 shows a plan that could be derived by searching the map of Figure 6-1 (remember, we still do not know exactly how we would go about searching it).

FIGURE 6-2.   **A SAMPLE PLAN DERIVED BY SEARCHING THE MAP IN FIGURE 6-1**

To get from MOUNT KISCO (the start state) to RYE (the goal state), execute this plan:
  1. Take Route 128 from Mount Kisco to Armonk.
  2. Take Route 22 from Armonk to North White Plains.
  3. Take Route 22 from North White Plains to White Plains.
  4. Take Route 287 from White Plains to Rye.

It differs from the kind of plan people normally make in that it gives no alternatives to cover contingencies, just a course of action to blindly follow. For example, armed only with a plan like the one in Figure 6-2, a PC trying to drive from Armonk to North White Plains would probably apply the operator "take Route 22" even if the intervening bridge across the Kensico Reservoir happened to be out that day. Upon reaching the bridge, even if its program were intelligent enough to realize that something were amiss, it would consult The Plan, attempt to cross, and promptly plunge into the water. But even this type of planning is better than just continuously reconsulting the map along the journey. With such behavior, what would prevent the program from driving all the way to Mount Kisco before discovering that it was no closer to North White Plains?

Usually in search we are interested in discovering such elementary plans, so we must remember the operator sequences as we search them out. Sometimes though, we just need to know what the solution states will be, as in the famous *Eight Queens Puzzle*. For now, we will stick with the Route-finding Problem because its real-world physical existence meshes so neatly with our state space formalism. We will next consider how to conduct the search.

Search Applications

Search is without doubt the most ubiquitous programming and problem-solving paradigm in artificial intelligence today. You might not realize it at first glance, but virtually every AI algorithm involves search, whether by explicitly constructing and traversing a state space or implicitly organizing its reasoning as a search among alternatives. Let's look at a few examples to see how search creeps into AI programming methods.

In Chapter 3, we discussed semantic networks, which have the same graph structure as state spaces. The Value Inheritance Procedure was really only searching the network for an appropriate slot, generating new states whenever it finds INST or SUBC links. A context-free grammar, when drawn as a tree structure as in Figure 4–4, can be viewed as a state space whose operators are computed by the special procedures of a recursive-descent parser. The backward-chaining algorithm from Chapter 5 searches an implicit state space whose operators are the production rules of an expert system. And in Chapter 7, we explore in depth game playing, possibly the most common search application.

Basic Search Algorithms

We turn now to the problem of developing efficient algorithms to search state spaces for solutions. Several possibilities have been developed over the past thirty years, and active research in this area continues. The study of search for its own sake is actually the field of AI that most resembles traditional computer science, often concerning itself with the theoretical analysis of abstract algorithms independent of any particular application.

So this section will perhaps be a little more turgid than most in the book, but if you can endure it, your newfound knowledge of search techniques will give you greater insight into virtually every other application area in AI, since search plays a universal role.

The "British Museum" Procedure

The so-called British Museum Procedure demonstrates just how inefficient a search algorithm can be. It seems that someone once attempted to calculate how long it would take for a monkey, pressing random keys on a typewriter, to generate all the works in the Royal Shakespeare Museum in England (hence the name). In other words, the poor animal is trying to find a sequence of operators—typed characters—that will transform a blank page into a Shakespearean sonnet. It has no knowledge whatsoever to guide its choice of operators.

As you might expect, the calculation resulted in astronomically large numbers that rendered the whole project impractical (as though a scientist would actually place monkeys in front of keyboards to try it!). Just to hit upon "to be or not to be," an 18-character phrase, would have a 1-in-27^{18} probability, or approximately $4.643185 \times 10^{-25}\%$. So the term "British Museum Procedure" has become a derisive moniker for any search procedure that works by generating all the possible solutions and testing to see which one(s) are correct. It is obviously exponential in the number of operators, rendering it intractable for all but the simplest problems, usually those that could be solved easily by inspection. However, it does have a perverse advantage of sorts: given enough time to run, the British Museum Procedure *will* find an optimal solution!

A General Search Strategy

We need to develop a more efficient strategy that focuses the search and conquers such problems as cyclic state spaces. Naturally, we'll begin our search at the root of our tree, the START state.

Suppose, by some stroke of luck, that the START state is also a GOAL state. We can terminate the search successfully without doing anything! If however, as usual, we are not so fortunate, we should generate all the states that can be reached from the START state by applying any single operator. This process is called *expanding* a node in the search tree. It takes any state and returns what are called its *successor* states; for example, a chess program would expand a state by simulating all the legal moves in that board position.

Now, we can apply the two-step method we used on the START state to the members of the list of successors. We choose one of those states and see if it is a goal state. If so, we are finished; if not, we expand that state and merge its successor list with the rest of the states we have discovered but not yet explored. After all, since we have no knowledge of which states are closest to goal states, we can just merge the lists somehow and repeat the process. Figure 6-3 shows how the search tree is gradually formed by the expand operations.

Eventually, we will find a solution if one exists. Figure 6-4 summarizes our generalized search procedure more precisely, with some details filled in. For now we will just use the CLOSED list to keep track of states we have already expanded. If the state space is cyclic, there is nothing to prevent us from reexpanding previously CLOSEd nodes. Nor are any criteria offered for deciding which node to expand. We could expand nodes at random, growing the search tree in all directions, degenerating into a British Museum variant.

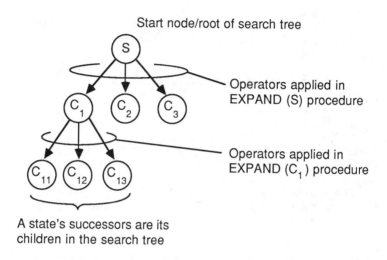

Figure 6–3. **The EXPAND Operation in the Search Tree**

There are two basic approaches to creating the search tree and determining how it will take shape: *depth-first* and *breadth-first*.

Depth-First Search

In depth-first search we go as far *down* into the search tree as possible before backing up and trying alternatives. We can implement it as shown in Figure 6-5 by making just a few small modifications to the general algorithm given previously. By placing the children (successors) of a node at the *front* of the OPEN list in step 3.b.ii, we ensure that when its first node is removed in step 3, it will be a successor of the most recently expanded state. This ensures that search progresses down the tree before across it. And by cleaning out the OPEN list in step 3.b.i, removing states that have already been expanded, we guard against redundant search effort on cyclic state spaces.

To get a better idea of how depth-first search works, let's apply it to a problem in the route-finding domain introduced earlier. Suppose we want to travel by car from Mount Kisco to Rye. We formalize the task as a state space search problem with Mount Kisco as the START node and Rye as the GOAL node.

FIGURE 6-4. SIMPLIFIED GENERAL SEARCH PROCEDURE

INPUT: Two states in the state space, **Start** and **Goal**.
TO COMPUTE: Is there an operator sequence that transforms **Start** into **Goal**?
LOCAL VARIABLES: **Open**, **Closed**, **State-X**, **Successors**.
OUTPUT: YES or NO answer.

1. a. Form a queue consisting of **Start**, call it the **Open** list.
   b. Form an empty queue, call it the **Closed** list.
2. If **Open** is empty (no more states), terminate and return NO.
3. Otherwise, remove a state from the **Open** list and call it **State-X**;
   put **State-X** at the front of the **Closed** list.
   a. If **State-X** is equal to **Goal**, terminate and return YES.
   b. Otherwise, perform the EXPAND operation on **State-X**,
      producing a list of **Successors**.
      i. Merge **Successors** into the **Open** list.
      ii. Go back to step 2.

FIGURE 6-5. DEPTH-FIRST SEARCH PROCEDURE

INPUT: Two states in the state space, **Start** and **Goal**.
TO COMPUTE: Is there an operator sequence that transforms **Start** into **Goal**?
LOCAL VARIABLES: **Open**, **Closed**, **State-X**, **Successors**.
OUTPUT: YES or NO answer.

1. a. Form a queue consisting of **Start**, call it the **Open** list.
   b. Form an empty queue, call it the **Closed** list.
2. If **Open** is empty (no more states), terminate and return NO.
3. Otherwise, remove the first state from the **Open** list and call it **State-X**;
   put **State-X** at the front of the **Closed** list.
   a. If **State-X** is equal to **Goal**, terminate and return YES.
   b. Otherwise, perform the EXPAND operation on **State-X**,
      producing a list of **Successors**.
      i.   Remove from **Successors** any states that are in the **Closed** list.
      ii. Insert **Successors** at the front of the **Open** list.
      iii. Go back to step 2.

Following steps 1 and 2 of our algorithm, we initialize the OPEN and CLOSED lists as follows:

OPEN: (Mount Kisco)
CLOSED: empty

Next we select Mount Kisco and check to see if it's a goal node. Of course it is not, so we place it in CLOSED, expand it, and append its successors to the front of OPEN. We'll put them in alphabetical order to be consistent. We now have:

OPEN: (Armonk, Bedford, Bedford Hills, Chappaqua)
CLOSED: (Mount Kisco)

There aren't any members of CLOSED in OPEN, so we return to step 3. We next see that Armonk is not the goal state, so we put it on CLOSED and add its successors to OPEN:

OPEN: (Bedford, Chappaqua, Greenwich, Mount Kisco,
            North White Plains, Bedford, Bedford Hills, Chappaqua)
CLOSED: (Mount Kisco, Armonk)

Now we must prune down the OPEN list. We remove Mount Kisco, as it is already on CLOSED, and OPEN becomes:

(Bedford, Chappaqua, Greenwich, North White Plains, Bedford,
 Bedford Hills, Chappaqua)

Again, we remove the first element on OPEN and put it on CLOSED. It's still not a goal state, so we have:

OPEN: (Armonk, Mount Kisco, Chappaqua, Greenwich,
            North White Plains, Bedford, Bedford Hills, Chappaqua)
CLOSED: (Mount Kisco, Armonk, Bedford)

After pruning, OPEN becomes:

(Chappaqua, Greenwich, North White Plains, Bedford Hills, Chappaqua)

Now operating on Chappaqua, we get:

OPEN: (Armonk, Mount Kisco, Greenwich, North White Plains,
            Bedford Hills, Chappaqua)
CLOSED: (Mount Kisco, Armonk, Bedford, Chappaqua)

Pruning changes OPEN to:

(Greenwich, North White Plains, Bedford Hills)

Expanding Greenwich gives:

> OPEN: (Armonk, Rye, Stamford, North White Plains, Bedford Hills)
> CLOSED: (Mount Kisco, Armonk, Bedford, Chappaqua, Greenwich)

Pruning reveals OPEN to be:

> (Rye, Stamford, North White Plains, Bedford Hills)

And finally, at long last, we can remove the first element of OPEN and discover Rye, a goal node. The search terminates successfully.

What has our search discovered for us? We know that it is *possible* to transform the state described as "being in Mount Kisco" into the state "being in Rye" by applying some sequence of operators of the form "take <ROUTE> in <DIRECTION>," where <ROUTE> and <DIRECTION> are variables. Unfortunately, we failed to keep track of our path through the state space as we traversed it.

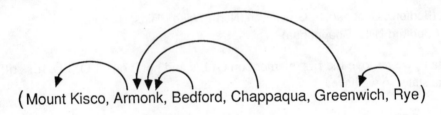

(Mount Kisco, Armonk, Bedford, Chappaqua, Greenwich, Rye)

Figure 6–6. **The Closed List After a Successful Search**

Actually, this fault in our algorithm can easily be overcome if we just associate with each node on the CLOSED list a pointer back to its parent in the search tree, the state of which it was first generated as a successor. (This works because each node in a tree has a unique parent.) With this modification, the CLOSED list at the end of the search would be as shown in Figure 6-6. Had we been doing this all along, it would now be a simple matter to trace the links back from the goal node and find the route. You may also notice that, by rearranging this diagram, as shown in Figure 6–7, we can get a picture of the portion of the search tree that was actually explored during the algorithm's execution.

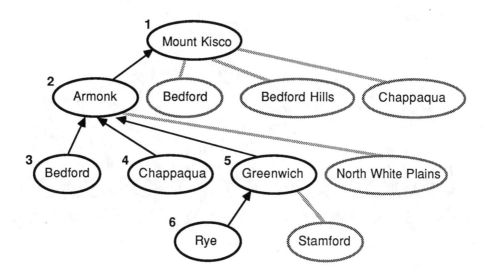

Figure 6–7. **The Search Tree After a Successful Search**

Breadth-First Search

In breadth-first search, we want to expand all the nodes on a given level of the search tree before going on to the next level down. (The *level* of a node is equivalent to the number of direct ancestors it has, so the START state is a level zero node.) Figure 6-8 illustrates the difference: depth-first search descends as far as possible before backtracking and considering alternatives at levels it has already visited, whereas breadth-first search progresses slowly down the tree, one level at a time. Indeed, one could even attach personalities to the algorithms: depth-first represents the risk-taking explorer, breadth-first the conservative incrementalist.

So how do we implement the breadth-first idea? It requires the simplest possible change to the depth-first search algorithm. Instead of inserting the successors of an expanded node at the *front* of the OPEN list, we append them onto the *back*. OPEN now acts like a queue, while before it was more like a stack.

(a) Depth-first Search

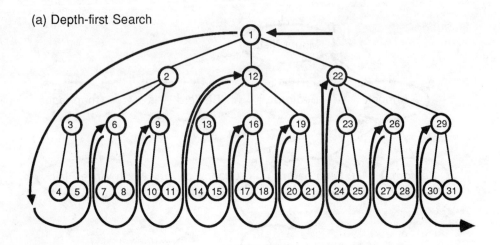

(b) Breadth-first Search

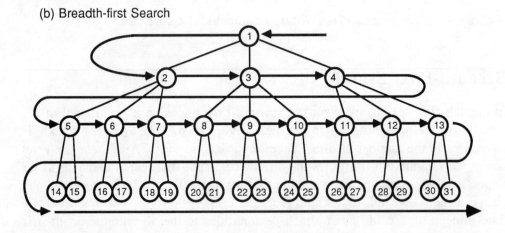

Figure 6–8.   **Breadth-first Versus Depth-first Search:
Order of Expansion**

FIGURE 6-9. BREADTH-FIRST SEARCH PROCEDURE (WITH PLAN OUTPUT)

INPUT: Two states in the state space, **Start** and **Goal**.
TO COMPUTE: Any operator sequence that transforms **Start** into **Goal**.
LOCAL VARIABLES: **Open, Closed, Record-X, Successors**.
OUTPUT: A sequence if one exists, otherwise a NO answer.

1. a. Form a queue of action records consisting of (**Start**-NIL-NIL),
      call it the **Open** list.
   b. Form an empty queue of action records, call it the **Closed** list.
2. If **Open** is empty (no more states), terminate and return NO.
3. Otherwise, remove the first action record from the **Open** list and call it **Record-X**;
   put **Record-X** at the front of the **Closed** list.
   a. If the State variable of **Record-X** is equal to **Goal**, terminate and return the
      plan used, find it by tracing through the pointers on the **Closed** list.
   b. Otherwise, perform the EXPAND operation on **State-X**, producing a list of
      action records called **Successors**; create each action record by associating
      with each state generated its parent (**State-X**) and the operator that was
      applied in the EXPAND operation.
      i.   Remove from **Successors** any records whose State variables are in
           records already in the **Closed** list.
      ii. Append **Successors** to the end of the **Open** list.
      iii. Go back to step 2.

The complete algorithm for breadth-first search is given in Figure 6-9. This time
we have added the messy steps necessary to return a full "plan" rather than just a
true or false answer to whether there is a solution. It is easy to see that the algorithm
produces the correct behavior: since whenever we expand a node we put its successors at the end of the queue, we will always expand them only *after* the siblings
(if any remain) of the expanded node. By applying this rule to each expanded node,
you can visualize the progress of the search and verify the algorithm for yourself.

Let's go through the same example we used for depth-first search with our
breadth-first algorithm. We'll just show the contents of OPEN and CLOSED each
time we reach step 3 (the top of the main loop), omitting the other steps.

1.   OPEN: ([Mount Kisco, •, •])
     CLOSED: empty
2.   OPEN: ([Armonk, 128, Mount Kisco], [Bedford, 172, Mount Kisco],
              [Bedford Hills, 117, Mount Kisco], [Chappaqua, 117, Mount Kisco])
     CLOSED: ([Mount Kisco, •, •])
3.   OPEN: ([Bedford, 172, Mount Kisco], [Bedford Hills, 117, Mount Kisco],
              [Chappaqua, 117, Mount Kisco], [Bedford, 22, Armonk],
              [Chappaqua, 120, Armonk], [Greenwich, 433, Armonk],
              [North White Plains, 22, Armonk], [Purchase, 684, Armonk])
     CLOSED: ([Armonk, 128, Mount Kisco], [Mount Kisco, •, •])

4. OPEN: ([Bedford Hills, 117, Mount Kisco], [Chappaqua, 117, Mount Kisco],
              [Bedford, 22, Armonk], [Chappaqua, 120, Armonk],
              [Greenwich, 433, Armonk], [North White Plains, 22, Armonk],
              [Purchase, 684, Armonk])
    CLOSED: ([Bedford, 172, Mount Kisco], [Armonk, 128, Mount Kisco],
              [Mount Kisco, •, •])

5. OPEN: ([Chappaqua, 117, Mount Kisco], [Bedford, 22, Armonk],
              [Chappaqua, 120, Armonk], [Greenwich, 433, Armonk],
              [North White Plains, 22, Armonk], [Purchase, 684, Armonk])
    CLOSED: ([Bedford Hills, 117, Mount Kisco], [Bedford, 172, Mount Kisco],
              [Armonk, 128, Mount Kisco], [Mount Kisco, •, •])

6. OPEN: ([Bedford, 22, Armonk], [Chappaqua, 120, Armonk],
              [Greenwich, 433, Armonk], [North White Plains, 22, Armonk],
              [Purchase, 684, Armonk])
    CLOSED: ([Chappaqua, 117, Mount Kisco], [Bedford Hills, 117, Mount Kisco],
              [Bedford, 172, Mount Kisco], [Armonk, 128, Mount Kisco],
              [Mount Kisco, •, •])

7. OPEN: ([North White Plains, 22, Armonk], [Purchase, 684, Armonk],
              [Rye, 95, Greenwich], [Stamford, 95, Greenwich])
    CLOSED: ([Greenwich, 433, Armonk], [Chappaqua, 117, Mount Kisco], [Bedford
              Hills, 117, Mount Kisco], [Bedford, 172, Mount Kisco], [Armonk, 128,
              Mount Kisco], [Mount Kisco, •, •])

8. OPEN: ([Purchase, 684, Armonk], [Rye, 95, Greenwich],
              [Stamford, 95, Greenwich], [White Plains, 22, North White Plains])
    CLOSED: ([North White Plains, 22, Armonk], [Greenwich, 433, Armonk],
              [Chappaqua, 117, Mount Kisco], [Bedford Hills, 117, Mount Kisco],
              [Bedford, 172, Mount Kisco], [Armonk, 128, Mount Kisco],
              [Mount Kisco, •, •])

9. OPEN: ([Rye, 95, Greenwich], [Stamford, 95, Greenwich],
              [White Plains, 22, North White Plains],
              [White Plains, 684, Purchase])
    CLOSED: ([Purchase, 684, Armonk], [North White Plains, 22, Armonk],
              [Greenwich, 433, Armonk], [Chappaqua, 117, Mount Kisco],
              Bedford Hills, 117, Mount Kisco], [Bedford, 172, Mount Kisco],
              [Armonk, 128, Mount Kisco], [Mount Kisco, •, •])

10. OPEN: ([Stamford, 95, Greenwich], [White Plains, 22, North White Plains],
              [White Plains, 684, Purchase])
    CLOSED: ([Rye, 95, Greenwich], [Purchase, 684, Armonk],
              [North White Plains, 22, Armonk], [Greenwich, 433, Armonk],
              [Chappaqua, 117, Mount Kisco], [Bedford Hills, 117, Mount Kisco],
              [Bedford, 172, Mount Kisco], [Armonk, 128, Mount Kisco],
              [Mount Kisco, •, •])

At this point, it is a simple matter to refer to the CLOSED list and unwind the correct path by starting with the first action record and tracing through to the last one. If our program had some sort of natural-language generation facility attached, it might produce the following text as output: "Take Route 128 from Mount Kisco to Armonk, then take Route 433 from Armonk to Greenwich, then take Route 95 from Greenwich to Rye."

Note that if we adhere strictly to our algorithm as described in Figure 6-9, step 10 is never actually executed, for as soon as Rye was discovered the loop ended without doing any expanding, pruning, or anything else. We include it so you can see the CLOSED list at the end of the search. Keep in mind also that even though the depth-first and breadth-first algorithms produced the same solution on this particular problem, they don't necessarily have to, nor should they necessarily do so.

Comparing Depth-First and Breadth-First Search

We now have two basic search procedures. Why do we need two? As it turns out, each approach has its own strengths and weaknesses. Consider the question of efficiency. One good way to measure efficiency is the number of states *expanded* during the course of a successful search. (Of course, in an unsuccessful search every node must be visited so we can make sure that none is the goal.) This number is equivalent to the number of interations of the main loop in the algorithms, or the length in records of the CLOSED list at the end of the search process.

To solve our sample problem, the depth-first search expanded 6 states out of 11 in the state space, or 56%, generating 15 successors out of 28 in the state space, or 54% of the total. The breadth-first search expanded 9 states, or 82%, for a total of 24 successors generated, or 86% of the maximum.

Breadth-first search doesn't come out very well in this comparison, does it? Having to expand 50% more states than depth-first, it looks superficially like the less efficient algorithm. But in fact, these results depend entirely on the characteristics of the state space and problem and have nothing to do with the algorithms themselves. Not convinced? Let's consider a couple of modifications.

What if North White Plains were instead named East White Plains? This would change the alphabetical ordering of the states, thereby changing the order in which they were added onto the OPEN list, and hence the order in which they were expanded. With the new state space resulting from this change, depth-first search expands 8 states and breadth-first expands 10, only 25% more.

Now suppose we change the problem specification. We want to go not from Mount Kisco to Rye, but from Mount Kisco to Bedford Hills. Primarily because depth-first search will explore the large part of the search tree rooted at Armonk first, it must expand all 11 states to solve this problem, which breadth-first finishes after only 4!

So now you're wondering what the difference is between the two approaches. The obvious methodological difference is difficult to quantify, but we can make the following observations about the applicability of the two algorithms:

- Depth-first search is *effective* when there are few subtrees in the search tree that have only one connection point to the rest of the states.

- Depth-first search is *dangerous* when such "blind alleys," as Winston termed them, exist, for then the search can pursue many useless paths because of one operator unfortunately chosen early in the process. The closer to the START and farther from the GOAL that choice is made, the more effort wasted. Graph theorists will observe that state spaces with high connectivity are suited to the depth-first approach.

- Breadth-first search is *effective* when the search tree has a low *branching factor*, the average number of successors per state. In this case the tree's levels grow in size relatively slowly, so it pays to take the time to explore each level completely before descending further.

- From a pictorial point of view, depth-first search is best when the GOAL exists in the lower left portion of the search tree; conversely, breadth-first is superior when the GOAL exists in the upper right portion of the search tree. If it is in the upper left, both algorithms will find it easily, and if it is in the lower right, both algorithms will have to explore most of the search tree before finding it. Figure 6-10 illustrates this.

Unfortunately, this is about all we can say. If you have a type of problem that will need frequent searching, consider the state space characteristics mentioned above—branching factor, connectivity, depth of blind alleys, suspected location of the solution—carefully before you begin.

Operators May Not Have Equal Cost

You've probably observed by now that breadth-first search seems to find the shortest sequence of operators that will solve a particular problem (when multiple solutions exist, as in the Route-finding Problem). This property follows from the fact that breadth-first search progresses uniformly down the tree: if there are any GOAL states on level N, resulting from length N operator sequences, they will surely be found before any on level N+1 or below because each level is explored completely before the next deeper one.

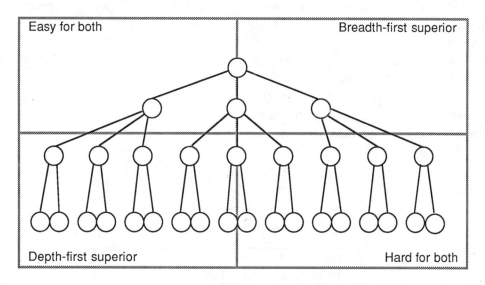

Figure 6–10. **Breadth-first Versus Depth-first Search: Relative Effectiveness**

By contrast, depth-first search can find a solution anywhere. In state spaces with high connectivity (a high ratio of the number of operators applicable per state to the number of states), somewhat of a tradeoff is evident between the speed of arriving at the solution and the size of that solution. Depth-first search will excel (normally, but not always) at the former, and breadth-first search at the latter.

But how much does the size of the solution in *number of operators applied* really matter? In our Route-finding Problem, it is virtually irrelevant because the operators have *different real costs*. Remember, we are trying to solve a real-world problem, and in the real world few people trying to get from one city to another would choose one route over another just because it passed through fewer cities. Rather, they would probably choose the route that required them to travel the shortest total distance or for the least time.

To be as general as possible, we will define a *cost function*, $g(x)$, that assigns to any path x some uniform measure of its cost, or the cumulative expense of applying the sequence of operators that composes it. Such functions are usually defined in terms of abstract units that have no independent significance other than as costs of paths in a particular problem domain. There can be a rough correspondence between the g(x) values and a real-world quantity for the sake of easier comprehension, but the function often combines several disparate factors into one single cost measure. Additionally, it is normal to assign a cost to each possible operator in the state space, and compute g(x) simply by summing the costs of the operators in the path x.

As an example, let's put a new dimension into our Route-finding Problem domain by adding a cartesian coordinate system, as shown in Figure 6–11. Assuming that each city is located at an (h,v) position, and that each route is a straight line between two cities, we can use the familiar *distance* formula to associate with each operator the approximate travelling distance it represents:

$$d^2 = (h_1 - h_2)^2 + (v_1 - v_2)^2$$

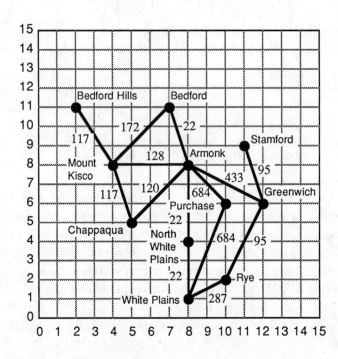

Figure 6–11. **Route Finding Problem State Space with Costs**

Uniform-Cost Search

Now let's see how we can augment the basic search strategies to take variable operator costs into account. We'll look first at the *uniform-cost* search algorithm, also known as *branch-and-bound* search. We will adopt the phrase "extending a partial path" to mean "expanding the state at the end of a path" because we are really just computing all the new paths that can result from the one followed so far. The general idea of uniform-cost search is to always extend the partial path with the least cost. For now, we will rely on our intuitive acceptance of this as a good idea.

To accomplish it efficiently, we must add to each action record [<FROM>, <OPERATOR>, <TO>] a value representing the total cost to reach the <TO> state from the START. This is easily done during the EXPAND operation by just adding the cost of the <OPERATOR> to the total cost of getting to the <FROM> state.

Figure 6-12 gives a precise specification of the uniform-cost search algorithm we will use. It should be obvious that it will always terminate when the *optimal* solution is found, that is, the path of lowest real cost from the START state to a GOAL state. In other words, it finds the goal that is closest to the START. Note that it degenerates to a straight breadth-first search if we simply set $g(x)=1$ for all operators x.

FIGURE 6-12. UNIFORM-COST (BRANCH-AND-BOUND) SEARCH PROCEDURE

INPUT: Two states in the state space, **Start** and **Goal**.
TO COMPUTE: The minimum-cost operator sequence that transforms **Start** into **Goal**.
LOCAL VARIABLES: **Open, Closed, Record-X, Successors**.
OUTPUT: The minimum-cost sequence if one exists, otherwise a NO answer.

1. a. Form a queue of action records consisting of (**Start**-NIL-NIL-0), call it the **Open** list.
   b. Form an empty queue of action records, call it the **Closed** list.
2. If **Open** is empty (no more states), terminate and return NO.
3. Otherwise, remove the first action record from the **Open** list and call it **Record-X**; put **Record-X** at the front of the **Closed** list.
   a. If the State variable of **Record-X** is equal to **Goal**, terminate and return the plan used; find it by tracing through the pointers on the **Closed** list.
   b. Otherwise, perform the EXPAND operation on **State-X**, producing a list of action records called **Successors**; create each action record by associating with each state generated the operator that was used to produce it, its parent (**State-X**), and the sum of the cost of applying that operator and **State-X**'s Cost variable.
      i. For each record in **Successors**, insert it into the **Open** list *in cost order*, so that the records with the lower Cost variables are at the front.
      ii. Go back to step 2 .

Just for practice, let's quickly run through a uniform-cost search solution to the same old Route-finding Problem, with the distance costs we added in earlier in Figure 6-11. Again, we will omit the discussion and just present the contents of OPEN and CLOSED at each iteration; we also include the superfluous last step to see the eventual value of CLOSED.

1.   OPEN: ([Mount Kisco, •, •, 0.0])
       CLOSED: empty
2.   OPEN: ([Chappaqua, 117, Mount Kisco, 3.2],
                [Bedford, 172, Mount Kisco, 3.6], [Armonk, 128, Mount Kisco, 4.0],
                [Bedford Hills, 117, Mount Kisco, 4.2])
       CLOSED: ([Mount Kisco, •, •, 0.0])
3.   OPEN: ([Bedford, 172, Mount Kisco, 3.6], [Armonk, 128, Mount Kisco, 4.0],
                [Bedford Hills, 117, Mount Kisco, 4.2],
                [Armonk, 120,Chappaqua, 7.4])
       CLOSED: ([Chappaqua, 117, Mount Kisco, 3.2], [Mount Kisco, •, •, 0.0])
4.   OPEN: ([Armonk, 128, Mount Kisco, 4.0],
                [Bedford Hills, 117, Mount Kisco, 4.2],
                [Mount Kisco, 117, Chappaqua, 6.4], [Armonk, 22, Bedford, 6.8],
                [Armonk, 120, Chappaqua, 7.4])
       CLOSED: ([Bedford, 172, Mount Kisco, 3.6],
                [Chappaqua, 117, Mount Kisco, 3.2], [Mount Kisco, •, •, 0.0])
5.   OPEN: ([Bedford Hills, 117, Mount Kisco, 4.2],
                [Purchase, 120, Armonk, 6.8], [North White Plans, 22, Armonk, 8.0],
                [Greenwich, 433, Armonk, 8.5])
       CLOSED: ([Armonk, 128, Mount Kisco, 4.0], [Bedford, 172, Mount Kisco, 3.6],
                [Chappaqua, 117, Mount Kisco, 3.2], [Mount Kisco, •, •, 0.0])
6.   OPEN: ([Purchase, 120, Armonk, 6.8], [North White Plans, 22, Armonk, 8.0],
                [Greenwich, 433, Armonk, 8.5])
       CLOSED: ([Bedford Hills, 117, Mount Kisco, 4.2],
                [Armonk, 128, Mount Kisco, 4.0], [Bedford, 172, Mount Kisco, 3.6],
                [Chappaqua, 117, Mount Kisco, 3.2], [Mount Kisco, •, •, 0.0])
7.   OPEN: ([North White Plans, 22, Armonk, 8.0],
                [Greenwich, 433, Armonk, 8.5], [White Plains, 684, Purchase, 12.2])
       CLOSED: ([Purchase, 120, Armonk, 6.8],
                [Bedford Hills, 117, Mount Kisco, 4.2],
                [Armonk, 128, Mount Kisco, 4.0], [Bedford, 172, Mount Kisco, 3.6],
                [Chappaqua, 117, Mount Kisco, 3.2], [Mount Kisco, •, •, 0.0])
8.   OPEN: ([Greenwich, 433, Armonk, 8.5],
                [White Plains, 22, North White Plains, 11.0],
                [White Plains, 684, Purchase, 12.2])
       CLOSED: ([North White Plans, 22, Armonk, 8.0], [Purchase, 120, Armonk, 6.8],
                [Bedford Hills, 117, Mount Kisco, 4.2],
                [Armonk, 128, Mount Kisco, 4.0], [Bedford, 172, Mount Kisco, 3.6],
                [Chappaqua, 117, Mount Kisco, 3.2], [Mount Kisco, •, •, 0.0])
9.   OPEN: ([White Plains, 22, North White Plains, 11.0],
                [Stamford, 95, Greenwich, 11.7],
                [White Plains, 684, Purchase, 12.2], [Rye, 95, Greenwich, 13.0])

```
        CLOSED:   ([Greenwich, 433, Armonk, 8.5],
                   [North White Plans, 22, Armonk, 8.0],[Purchase, 120, Armonk, 6.8],
                   [Bedford Hills, 117, Mount Kisco, 4.2],
                   [Armonk, 128, Mount Kisco, 4.0], [Bedford, 172, Mount Kisco, 3.6],
                   [Chappaqua, 117, Mount Kisco, 3.2], [Mount Kisco, •, •, 0.0])
  10.   OPEN:     ([Stamford, 95, Greenwich, 11.7], [Rye, 95, Greenwich, 13.0],
                   [Rye, 287, White Plains, 13.2])
        CLOSED:   ([White Plains, 22, North White Plains, 11.0],
                   [Greenwich, 433, Armonk, 8.5],
                   [North White Plans, 22, Armonk, 8.0], [Purchase, 120, Armonk, 6.8],
                   [Bedford Hills, 117, Mount Kisco, 4.2],
                   [Armonk, 128, Mount Kisco, 4.0], [Bedford, 172, Mount Kisco, 3.6],
                   [Chappaqua, 117, Mount Kisco, 3.2], [Mount Kisco, •, •, 0.0])
  11.   OPEN:     ([Rye, 95, Greenwich, 13.0], [Rye, 287, White Plains, 13.2])
        CLOSED:   ([Stamford, 95, Greenwich, 11.7],
                   [White Plains, 22, North White Plains, 11.0],
                   [Greenwich, 433, Armonk, 8.5],
                   [North White Plans, 22, Armonk, 8.0], [Purchase, 120, Armonk, 6.8],
                   [Bedford Hills, 117, Mount Kisco, 4.2],
                   [Armonk, 128, Mount Kisco, 4.0], [Bedford, 172, Mount Kisco, 3.6],
                   [Chappaqua, 117, Mount Kisco, 3.2], [Mount Kisco, •, •, 0.0])
  11.   OPEN:     ([Rye, 287, White Plains, 13.2])
        CLOSED:   ([Rye, 95, Greenwich, 13.0], [Stamford, 95, Greenwich, 11.7],
                   [White Plains, 22, North White Plains, 11.0],
                   [Greenwich, 433, Armonk, 8.5],
                   [North White Plans, 22, Armonk, 8.0], [Purchase, 120, Armonk, 6.8],
                   [Bedford Hills, 117, Mount Kisco, 4.2],
                   [Armonk, 128, Mount Kisco, 4.0], [Bedford, 172, Mount Kisco, 3.6],
                   [Chappaqua, 117, Mount Kisco, 3.2], [Mount Kisco, •, •, 0.0])
```

Clearly the main advantage of uniform-cost search is that the first solution it finds is optimal in terms of real cost. One of its disadvantages, as we can see by comparing its trace to the depth-first and breadth-first runs, is that it is not guaranteed to find that solution particularly quickly. With many large problems, the search cost is so high that we would gladly settle for a suboptimal solution if it could be found quickly. An example would be the well-known Travelling Salesman Problem, for which years of research have produced algorithms to find solutions no more than twice as expensive as the optimal solution. But the problem is so intractable that these results are viewed as successes!

However, the biggest flaw in uniform-cost search from an AI point of view is that it is nearly as stupid as depth-first and breadth-first search. It is just intelligent enough to conduct an exhaustive search reasonably well, finding only the optimal solution and no others. Granted, this can greatly reduce the search time when compared with the British Museum Procedure, which finds every solution, but it is still not as efficient as we would like an "intelligent" procedure to be.

We have seen many times throughout our study of artificial intelligence programming that the key to intelligent behavior is focused, domain-specific knowledge. Search is no exception to this rule. The only way to significantly improve our search algorithms is to add such knowledge into the equation, turning our search algorithms into *heuristic search* algorithms.

Intelligent Searching

There are several ways we can do this. We could attach an expert system that would offer advice on which state to expand next, just as metalevel reasoning helps a production-system interpreter decide which rule to apply next. We could try to write programs to streamline the state space itself, removing redundant states and operators to improve overall efficiency. However, we will adopt a "minimalist" approach that tries to offer generality, while remaining within the framework of the search algorithms we have already established.

What is our goal? Ideally, we would like to know, at any given state, which operator would move us closest to a solution. If we knew this magic information throughout the search, for every state in the state space, we would find the optimal path in the optimal way—by expanding just those states that lie on it. This is in sharp contrast with the British Museum Procedure, which in effect expands every state in the entire state space at least once.

Now suppose we knew, for every state in the state space, the minimum cost of getting from it to the goal (the cost of the shortest solution starting from that state). If we would always expand the state that was closest to the goal, we would be making those optimal choices described in the previous paragraph. The good news is that this is possible: we just compute the best state to expand each time by applying the uniform-cost search to each element in OPEN and choose the one with the lowest real cost. The bad news is that this completely self-defeating method is even less efficient than using straight uniform-cost search from the outset. And what happened to the domain-specific knowledge we were talking about?

Best-First Search

Since we obviously can't go back to uniform-cost search, we must find a way to *guess* which path is the most promising to extend another step. We will use the following idea to rank the paths on the OPEN list in order of likelihood to be closest to a goal node: each state at the end of a partial path can be analyzed and assigned a numeric estimate of its distance to the nearest goal node. (As we shall soon see, it is convenient if this estimate is measured on the same abstract scale as the cost function g(x) employed in uniform-cost search).

A *heuristic evaluation function* h(x) accomplishes this by assigning to each state x such an estimate of the minimum cost to reach a goal state. With this function available, all we have to do is sort the OPEN list according to h(x) and the most promising partial path will wind up at the front. Therefore, by always extending the first path in OPEN, at each step we will be pursuing the path estimated to be the closest to a goal. Now that seems like an intelligent thing to do.

Note that the function h(x) is only an *estimator*, and that the only way to make it a perfect predictor is by having it exhaustively search the state space. We must settle for a function that uses heuristic knowledge to judge a state's promise without expanding it. A pretty good heuristic evaluation function for our Route-finding Problem might be the direct "as the crow flies" distance between the cities repre- sented by the current and goal states, without regard to the intervening roads and cities. Presumably, to compute such an evaluation function, the program would have access to a database of longitudes and latitudes, the cartesian coordinate map from Figure 6–11.

Figure 6-13 gives the *best-first* search algorithm outlined above, the classical starting point for heuristically-informed search strategies. The only difference between it and the uniform-cost search is that the OPEN list is not sorted according to accumulated path cost but rather expected remaining path cost, so that the more promising states are always at the front of the list.

Note that, like uniform-cost search, best-first search does not follow a geomet- rically regular route in exploring the search tree. Rather, it jumps back and forth from state to state like an opportunist always looking for something a little bit better, unwilling to stick it out when the going gets tough and the state evaluations look worse). The behavior of these algorithms, while precisely specified, is never- theless unpredictable because they depend on outside knowledge, in the form of cost and heuristic evaluation functions, that is not itself part of the algorithms.

Even so, we can make some observations about best-first search compared to the other methods. First, it is not guaranteed to find an optimal solution, as it goes any- where it thinks a solution might be found, regardless of the real expense. But normally, it finds *some solution* faster than any of the other methods we have seen so far.

However, the most important characteristic of best-first or any other heuristic search method is that *the performance varies directly with the accuracy of the heuristic evaluation function*. If h(x) is equal to the true remaining distance to the nearest goal for all x, then the search is optimal. But if h(x) is inversely related to the real distance for all x—increasing as the real distance decreases and vice-versa—the search will always find the goal node last, after exploring the entire state space. Since many state spaces are infinite, the key is to come up with the best heuristic evaluation possible.

FIGURE 6-13. **BEST-FIRST HEURISTIC SEARCH PROCEDURE**

INPUT: Two states in the state space, **Start** and **Goal**.
TO COMPUTE: Any operator sequence that transforms **Start** into **Goal**.
LOCAL VARIABLES: **Open, Closed, Record-X, Successors**.
OUTPUT: The first sequence found if one exists, otherwise a NO answer.

1. a. Form a queue of action records consisting of (**Start**-NIL-NIL-0),
       call it the **Open** list.
    b. Form an empty queue of action records, call it the **Closed** list.
2. If **Open** is empty (no more states), terminate and return NO.
3. Otherwise, remove the first action record from the **Open** list and call it **Record-X**;
    put **Record-X** at the front of the **Closed** list.
    a. If the State variable of **Record-X** is equal to **Goal**, terminate and return the
       plan used; find it by tracing through the pointers on the **Closed** list.
    b. Otherwise, perform the EXPAND operation on **State-X**, producing a list of
       action records called **Successors**; create each action record by associating
       with each state generated the operator that was used to produce it, its parent
       (**State-X**), and the value returned by the heuristic evaluation function h(x).
       i. For each record in **Successors**, insert it into the **Open** list *in heuristic
           order*, so that the records with the lower estimated distances to **Goal** are at
           the front.
       ii. Go back to step 2.

The A* Algorithm

Let us now turn to the last major search algorithm we will discuss in this chapter: the *A* (pronounced "Ay star") algorithm. A* is a heuristic strategy, like best-first search, that always terminates with the optimal solution. A* is created by making subtle changes to the general search algorithm of Figure 6-3.

First, we introduce a new function called f(x), which is defined to be equivalent to g(x) + h(x), which are defined as for uniform-cost and best-first search. We can think of f(x) as an estimate of the cost of a minimal-cost solution path constrained to go through x. By using this function to order the nodes on the OPEN list, we judge them based on a combination of the work already done to reach them and the expected additional work to reach the goal. Even intuitively, f(x) seems a "fairer" measure of the a desirability of being in state x than either g(x) or h(x) alone.

In fact, we can see that the A* algorithm always terminates with the optimal path just in case h(x) is an *admissible* heuristic evaluation function. Admissible functions have the property that h(x) is less than or equal to the real distance to the nearest goal for all states x. Normally, A* is specified to require admissible heuristics, so the algorithm itself is also said to be admissible. A complete description is given in Figure 6-14.

FIGURE 6-14. **THE A* OPTIMAL HEURISTIC SEARCH PROCEDURE**

INPUT: Two states in the state space, **Start** and **Goal**.
TO COMPUTE: The minimum-cost operator sequence that transforms **Start** into **Goal**.
LOCAL VARIABLES: **Open, Closed, Record-X, Successors**.
OUTPUT: The minimum-cost sequence if one exists, otherwise a NO answer.

1. a. Form a queue of action records consisting of (**Start**-NIL-NIL-0),
       call it the **Open** list.
    b. Form an empty queue of action records, call it the **Closed** list.
2. If **Open** is empty (no more states), terminate and return NO.
3. Otherwise, remove the first action record from the **Open** list and call it **Record-X**;
    put **Record-X** at the front of the **Closed** list.
    a. If the State variable of **Record-X** is equal to **Goal**, terminate and return the
       plan used; find it by tracing through the pointers on the **Closed** list.
    b. Otherwise, perform the EXPAND operation on **State-X**, producing a list of
       action records called **Successors**; create each action record by associating
       with each state generated the operator that was used to produce it, its parent
       (**State-X**), and the sum of the cost of applying that operator, **State-X**'s Cost
       variable, and the value returned by the heuristic evaluation function h(x).
       i. For each record in **Successors**, insert it into the **Open** list *in optimal order*,
           so that the records with the lower Cost+Estimated Remaining Distance are
           at the front.
       ii. Go back to step 2.

The Behavior of A*

Remember, A* is not guaranteed to find the optimal path with the least amount of effort; as we know, only an algorithm with the perfect heuristic function (h(x)=h'(x) for all x) can do that. But it is obvious that A* will find the optimal path—just let h(x)=0 for all x. Certainly this is an underestimate of h'(x), since operators cannot have negative cost. So f(x)=g(x), and the algorithm degenerates into uniform-cost search, which we know to find optimal solutions.

Now suppose h(x) varies with x, but is still always an underestimate. Consider the situation at any step in the search process. The OPEN list is sorted according to f(x), with lower-valued states in front. At this point, suppose we remove the first path and find that it cannot be extended because it ends at a goal state. How do we know for sure that this is the optimal path?

The path, which we will call P, is a complete one, leading all the way to a goal, so h'(P) = 0. By the admissibility constraint, h(x) must be less than or equal to h'(x), so h(x) must equal 0 as well. Therefore, f(P) = g(P) + 0, so f(P) = g(P), and the estimate of P's cost turns out to be perfect—the real cost. Now every partial path x that came after P in the OPEN list has f(x) ≥ f(P), since the list was just sorted in that order. However, again by the admissibility constraint, for all these x, f(x) must always be less than or equal to the actual cost f'(x). Since f(P) is less than all these known *underestimates* f(x), it is bound to also be less than all the real costs. Therefore, P is optimal.

We can also now see the significance of the admissibility constraint, which figured twice in the above proof. Suppose h(x) were not admissible; e.g., it could possibly return estimates higher than the real costs for some states. It is easy to see then that we would have no way of knowing whether the path found by A* were optimal, because another still lurking somewhere in the OPEN list could actually be much closer to a goal than the heuristic evaluation function says it is. Under this uncertainty, we would have no choice but to, having found one solution, continue extending the paths in the OPEN list until either a better solution is found or all the paths grow longer than the solution.

It turns out that A* is the best known general-purpose search algorithm that finds optimal solutions. Like that of best-first search, its performance depends greatly on the quality of h(x), the heuristic evaluation function.

A New Search Example

As a final example in our comparison of searching algorithms, let's examine a problem that is a little more abstract than the Route-finding Problem: the infamous *eight-puzzle*. This puzzle, a classic problem domain for state space search research, is a scaled down version of the 15 squares game. You are required to align 8 numbered, movable squares in order within a 3x3 grid. On each move, one of either 2, 3, or 4 bordering squares is slid into the empty space. The states of the problem are configurations of the puzzle and the operators are moves into the empty space. Figure 6-15 shows a typical start state and the desired goal state, which has the empty square in the center and the numbered tiles arranged sequentially clockwise around it starting from the upper left corner.

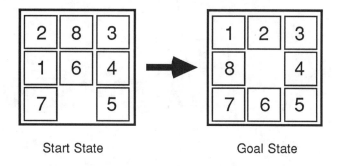

Start State   Goal State

Figure 6–15. **The Eight-puzzle as State-Space Search**

Figures 6-16, 6-17, and 6-18 show the search trees generated by the depth-first, breadth-first, and A* search algorithms. (We omit the uniform-cost search since, as in many abstract problems, all the operators have equal cost.) The depth-first search descends to a fixed depth of six levels before backtracking, and the A* search uses a state-evaluation function $f(x) = g(x) + h(x)$, where $h(x)$ equals the number of tiles not in their final position in a given state x.

Measuring Search

Two popular measurements of search algorithm performance are the *penetrance* and *effective branching factor*. Penetrance is computed simply by dividing the length of the solution path found by the total number of nodes in the search tree ($P = L/N$); naturally, larger penetrances are to be preferred, since they indicate that search concentrated on the nodes on the solution path. Effective branching factor describes, independent of the length of the solution path, the "bushiness" of the search tree—the average number of children explored for each node in the tree, or the extent to which search deviated from the solution path. Since a search using the perfect heuristic $h(x)=h'(x)$ would have a branching factor of 1 (because we would always only explore the child that was on the optimal search path), we want our search tree branching factors to be as close to unity as possible.

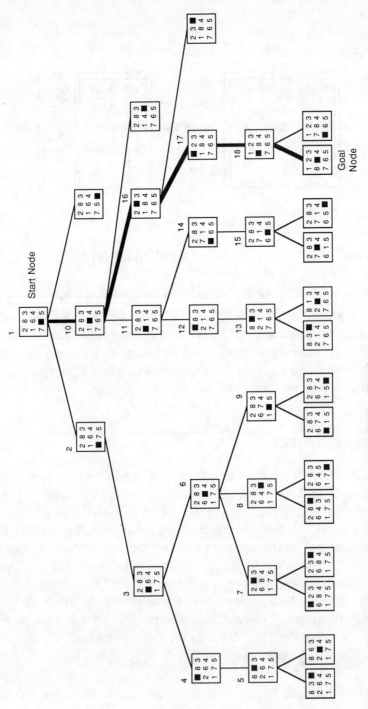

Figure 6-16. Depth-first Search on the Eight-puzzle

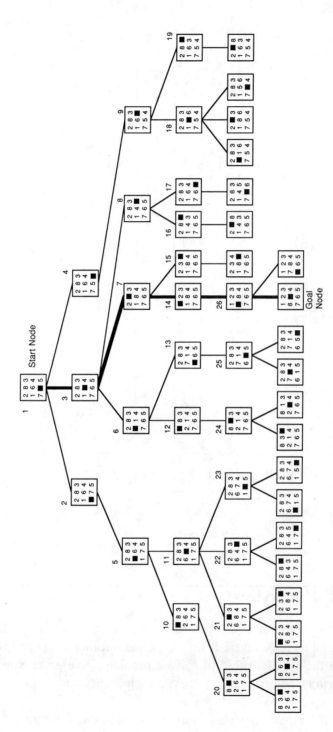

Figure 6-17. Breadth-first Search on the Eight-puzzle

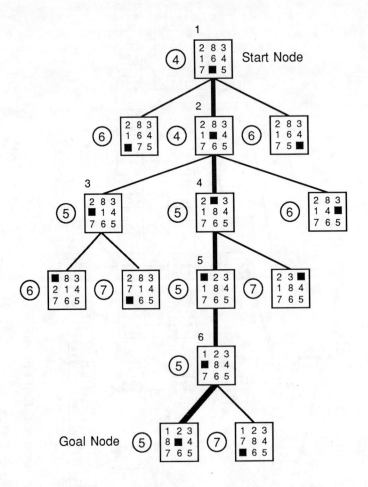

Figure 6–18. **A* on the Eight-Puzzle**

Design of Heuristics

Heuristics, being informal and rather intuitive, are by nature difficult to study and systematize, and therefore there is little concrete information I can give you. If you decide to use the A* algorithm to solve a problem, give great care to the development of accurate heuristics. Keep these principles in mind:

- Prefer the *most informed* heuristic evaluation function. A heuristic evaluation function $h_1(x)$ is considered to be more informed than another function $h_2(x)$ if both are admissible and $h_1(x) > h_2(x)$ for all states x. This is easy to see, since if both functions are underestimates, we would normally prefer the one that comes closest to the actual cost without ever exceeding it. (I say "normally" prefer because the quest for more informed heuristics can often lure us into the trap of wasteful computation.)

- Good heuristic evaluation functions are efficiently computed. If you have to spend as much time evaluating a state as it would take to expand fifty others, consider a weaker heuristic (or even uniform-cost search).

An example of these first principle can be found for the eight-puzzle. Our original heuristic simply counted 1 for each out-of-position tile, a trivially admissible function when we observe that any move in the puzzle can put at most one tile in the right place. Consider the alternative of counting each out-of-position tile's distance in moves to its proper location in the goal state. This heuristic is more informed because the amount contributed to its value by each tile ranges from 1 to 4 instead of being just a constant 1 (you should be able to convince yourself that it is also admissible). However, in comparing this heuristic to the original, we must weigh carefully the advantage of reducing the amount of search with the disadvantage of losing more time in evaluating each state.

Ironically, while it has been shown to be the optimal general-purpose algorithm for finding optimal solutions, A* is rarely the optimal algorithm for finding a quick solution. According to Judea Pearl, "in many problems A* spends a large amount of time discriminating among paths whose [real] costs do not vary significantly from each other ... [in this case,] the admissibility property becomes a curse rather than a virtue."

Choice of Search Algorithm

So just as we are thinking that A* will be the perfect answer to our search needs, this observation raises again the question of which search algorithm to choose for a particular problem. Depth-first and breadth-first search, in their pure forms, are museum pieces of little practical use. Their main application, outside of graph theory and algorithm analysis, is to the analysis of control strategies used in AI programs. For actually solving state space search problems, a heuristic method is essential to keep the size of the search tree as manageable as possible.

So the only real choice is between strict A* and the use of an inadmissible heuristic, resulting in best-first search. For relatively small state spaces, conser-

vative programmers, or problems that demand the optimal solution (many do), A*
is generally preferable. The more complex the problem becomes, the more willing
you will be to settle for a second-best solution if it can be found quickly and
cheaply. In this case, maximize the power of your heuristics even if they sometimes
violate the admissibility constraint and overestimate the true costs.

Let's explore this possibility by going back once more to the eight-puzzle. We
saw that we could improve upon our original heuristic with a more informed one
that was more expensive to compute. However, when we apply either to a more
difficult eight-puzzle than the one in Figure 6-15, which can be solved in five
moves, we immediately see their weakness. In a more difficult position, such as the
one in Figure 6-19, these heuristics will provide too little information to effectively
counter the tendency to exchange two out-of-position tiles that must be later
removed from their proper positions. (An extremely pathological case in this
respect is the *Rubik's Cube*, whose solution can sometimes necessitate temporarily
removing over two thirds of the squares from their proper positions.)

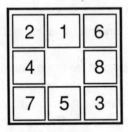

Figure 6–19. **A Difficult Eight-puzzle**

Nils Nilsson introduced an extremely powerful heuristic for the eight-puzzle which
involved "allotting 2 for every tile not followed by its proper successor and 0 for
every other tile, except that a piece in the center scores 1." This "sequence score"
was given 75% weighting in combination with the sum-of-distances measure. Even
though the resulting function was proved inadmissible, a best-first search using it
was able to solve the puzzle in Figure 6-19 in 18 moves (coincidentally the optimal
solution) with a search tree of only 44 nodes. For comparison, Figure 6-20 gives
the penetrance and branching factor statistics for the eight-puzzle searches we have
considered so far, including this last inadmissible one, which on a harder problem
outperformed A* in both measures!

FIGURE 6-20. **SOLVING THE EIGHT-PUZZLE WITH HEURISTIC SEARCH**

	Breadth-first	Depth-first	A*/easy puzzle	Best-first/hard puzzle
Penetrance:	5/46 (0.108)	5/34 (0.147)	5/13 (0.385)	18/43 (0.419)
Branching Factor:	1.86	1.70	1.34	1.08

The A* Algorithm in Pascal

It is fairly easy to use heuristic search to solve problems in Pascal. The *HSEARCH* program implements the full A* algorithm and applies it to the Route-finding Problem. It gets the map data from a file called MAPDATA.TXT, which must be in the same directory. To create this file, rename either of the MAPDATA1.TXT or MAPDATA2.TXT examples.

The format of MAPDATA.TXT is as follows: for each city on the map, a series of lines of text begins with the city's name, followed by its horizontal and vertical coordinates on separate lines, followed by its neighboring cities and the routes to them. Looking at MAPDATA1.TXT, which corresponds to the state space in Figure 6-11, you should be able to create your own map. When run, HSEARCH prompts for the starting and goal cities and goes into the search. As it works, it prints out certain debugging information. After the optimal solution is displayed, you must press [Return] to exit the program.

Internally, HSEARCH conforms to the standard heuristic search architecture shown in Figure 6-21, implementing the A* algorithm with three main procedures: AStar, Expand, and Insert. OPEN and CLOSED are linked lists of [TO, ROUTE, FROM, COST] action records; since these are global variables, the main procedures take no arguments. Their functions closely follow the A* algorithm outlined in Figure 6-14.

Programming Exercises

1. What modifications to HSEARCH would you make to implement different search algorithms, such as best-first or uniform-cost? You should only need to change the procedure that orders the elements in the OPEN list; the code to unwind a plan from the CLOSED list will remain essentially the same. What about depth-first and breadth-first search?

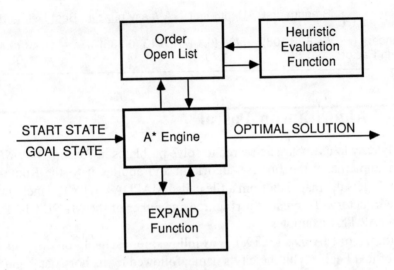

Figure 6–21. **Architecture of HSEARCH Program**

2. Within the A* framework, suppose we desire not just the optimal path, but the *n* best paths (using the same cost metrics)? Is it sufficient to just continue running A* until we accumulate *n* paths, or are additional modifications necessary? Hint: there may be a problem with pruning the OPEN list.

3. The current straight-line distance heuristic seems to work quite well; why is this? Can you improve this estimator to avoid problems such as the pathological case that might arise with the map in Figure 6-22, in which three cities are "closer" to City B than is City A, but all paths to B must run through A?

4. (For graphics enthusiasts.) Add a module to the program to draw out the map, and insert code to display the progress of the search on the map as it takes place; for example, the path currently being expanded could be highlighted on the display, or a separate window could continuously display the OPEN list.

5. Develop a state space representation for a different problem domain from the Route-finding Problem. Good candidates are the Eight Puzzle, the

Towers of Hanoi, the Eight Queens Problem, or a blocks world planning situation. In such abstract domains, the EXPAND operation must do all the work of generating successors, which often cannot be represented as simply as a list of neighbors. What sorts of heuristics can you develop for these problems?

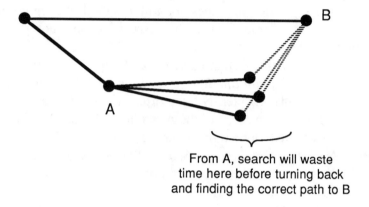

Figure 6–22. **A Pathological Route-Finding Problem**

Summary

Heuristic search is the central problem-solving paradigm in artificial intelligence, occurring in applications ranging from value inheritance to expert systems. Problems are suitable for solution by search when they can be represented within the state space formalism, as can the Route-finding Problem and the eight-puzzle, but are unsuitable otherwise, as in the case of sorting or matrix multiplication. Breadth-first and depth-first are the two basic search algorithms, but they do not discriminate between operators with unequal costs. Uniform-cost search does, and finds optimal solutions, but still incorporates no intelligence, in the form of knowledge about the structure of the problem-space. Best-first search adds that knowledge by ordering states to be explored according to a heuristic evaluation function that estimates the "distance" from a state to the goal state. A* combines uniform-cost and best-first search to find optimal solutions in an informed way, but can get bogged down in difficult problems. Analyses of search algorithms have revealed that A* and best-first are the only practical choices, but that heuristic search by itself is always a relatively weak problem-solving method.

References

Being the primary problem-solving strategy in AI, heuristic search is prominently covered in all AI textbooks. Almost uncharacteristically, Charniak and McDermott give a restrained exposition that does not go through all the algorithms and techniques. Winston is more traditional in this respect, but does not go far beyond the material presented here.

Figures 6-16, 6-17, and 6-18 are taken from Chapter 3 of Nilsson's *Problem-Solving Methods in Artificial Intelligence*, and Figure 6-20 is an expanded version of a similar table in that chapter. Nilsson offers an excellent analytical review of search fundamentals and the state of the AI art in the 1970, when the A* algorithm had just been discovered. For a more complete, rigorous, and up-to-date treatment, see Pearl's *Heuristics: Intelligence Search Strategies for Computer Problem Solving*. Pearl's *Search and Heuristics* reprints several recent papers in the field. *The Handbook of AI* discusses various algorithms and applications.

7. GAME PLAYING

Computer games are common today, from coin-operated units in shopping malls to home video game machines to entertainment software for personal computers. It is no longer remarkable to have a digital opponent ready to play you on a moment's notice. In exploring the application of heuristic search to game playing, our goals in this chapter will be to do the following:

- Investigate a general search-based game playing algorithm and extend it to improve its efficiency and performance.

- Explore some of the many tricks that game programmers use to counter the combinatorial explosion that hinders the effectiveness of heuristic search.

- Examine how search is applied in computer chess, a frontier application of game playing and problem solving research.

- Design and implement a complete game program in Turbo Pascal.

Game playing is the most practical direct application of the heuristic search problem-solving paradigm. We will consider only two-player, *discrete, perfect-information* games in this chapter, as they are both interesting and easily mapped onto the state-space formalism. Examples include chess, checkers, and tic-tac-toe.

We call such games discrete because they contain a finite number of states, or configurations. They have perfect information because both players have access to the same information about the game in progress. For example, all of the elements of a game of chess, the pieces and their positions, are readily apparent to both players. By contrast, most card games like poker are not perfect-information games because the players do not necessarily know who holds which cards, or which have not been dealt. Although we will stick to two-player games because they are easier to think about and more common to play, it has recently been shown that many of the basic concepts of two-player games will generalize to multi-player games.

Typically, the distinguishing characteristic of the games that we will consider is that they demand the skill of "looking ahead" at future positions to succeed, whereas games of chance are just that or little more. In perfect-information games, although you can do worse, you cannot do any better than your opponent allows you to do; in games of chance it is possible to make only objectively correct decisions from the outset and still lose to a lucky opponent.

There is a natural correspondence between such games of skill and state-space problem formalism: states are legal board positions, operators are legal moves in such positions, and the goal states are "winning positions." It seems simple enough, but there are problems. How do we know, when searching a game tree, whether we are finding a winning or losing (winning for the opponent) position? How do we keep track of which moves lead to a win and which to a loss? This all results from the key difference between search in game playing and search in "planning" applications: in the former we must *deal explicitly with an adversary* who has the same goal that we have.

So, as you might expect, standard state-space search algorithms do not translate well into game-playing strategies, although the underlying heuristic search principle does. We will first consider a weak general game-playing algorithm, and then improve its performance with more efficiency and heuristic power.

MINIMAX and Game Trees

The basic game playing strategy is the recursive MINIMAX algorithm, so named because it tries to minimize its opponent's advantage while at the same time maximizing its own. MINIMAX operates on a *game tree*, a structure similar to a search tree, whose paths represent all the possible legal move sequences from the root position, which represents the current board configuration. The root of the tree is the game's starting position.

The leaves represent all the possible final positions of the game. For most games, these can be assigned values of either 1, -1, or 0 depending on whether they are winning, losing, or drawn *with respect to the player whose turn it is to move*. It is important to remember that in MINIMAX notation, everything is expressed relative to the player whose turn it is to move. Each level of the game tree corresponds to a player's turn to move. Level 0, which contains only the root position, has the "first player" on move, Level 1 the second, Level 2 the first again, and so on.

The key idea in MINIMAX search is this: the player whose turn it is wants to *maximize* the position score he can reach against the best possible play by his opponent. Ideally, he would like to find a move, by searching down the game tree, such that he can reach a winning score of 1 no matter what moves his opponent chooses. To do this analysis, he makes the assumption that his opponent is thinking the same way, and will try in turn to *minimize* that same score (ideally, to -1 in all cases). Since the players take turns, each level of the game tree can be thought of as either a maximizing or a minimizing level depending on whose turn it is to move.

Figure 7-1 shows a complete game tree for a very simple game called *Last One Loses*, in which the objective is to force the opponent to remove the last stick from a pile. At each move, a player may draw one, two, or three sticks. Here we start with four sticks. Figure 7-2 shows the MINIMAX procedure itself. It is remarkably simple, especially since in practice we really only need to discover the best move in a given position, rather than the entire line of best play to the end of the game.

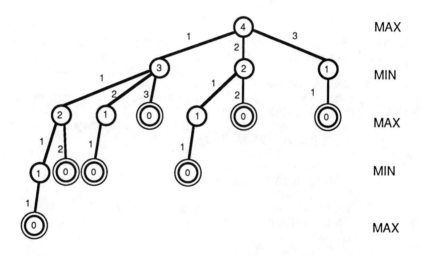

Figure 7–1. **A Game Tree for Last One Loses**

Let's run through the execution of MINIMAX on the four-stick Last One Loses game. Remember that, as in state-space search, rarely do we actually have a built-up game tree data structure in memory to work with; it is constructed implicitly by the pattern of execution of the algorithm.

FIGURE 7-2. **THE MINIMAX ALGORITHM**

INPUT: The current position and the player on move, either MIN or MAX.
TO COMPUTE: The line of best play for both sides from that position.
OUTPUT: The value of the final position of the game given the computed line of play.

1. If the position is a final one for the game (terminal), return the result of the game relative to the player on move.
2. If MIN is on move, then:
    a. Generate the successors of the current position.
    b. Apply MINIMAX to each of those positions with *MAX* to move.
    c. Return the *minimum* of the results.
3. If MAX is on move, then:
    a. Generate the successors of the current position.
    b. Apply MINIMAX to each of those positions with *MIN* to move.
    c. Return the *maximum* of the results.

```
MINIMAX (4,MAX)                     The opening position, with MAX to play
  Successors: 3,2,1                 We can take 1, 2, or 3 sticks here
  1 MINIMAX (3,MIN)                 Applying MINIMAX to the first child
    Successors: 2,1,0               Again we can take up to 3 sticks
    1.1 MINIMAX (2, MAX)
        Successors: 1,0             But here we can take just 1 or 2 sticks
        1.1.1 MINIMAX (1,MIN)
              Successors: 0         And here there is only one legal move
              1.1.1.1 MINIMAX (0,MAX)
                       Return +1
              Return: +1
        1.1.2 MINIMAX (0,MIN)
              Return: -1
        Return: +1                  Maximum of (+1,-1)
    1.2 MINIMAX (1,MAX)
        Successors: 0
        1.2.1 MINIMAX (0,MIN)
              Return: -1
        Return: -1
    1.3 MINIMAX (0,MAX)
        Return: +1
    Return: -1                      Minimum of (+1,-1,+1)
  2 MINIMAX (2,MIN)
    Successors: 1,0
    2.1 MINIMAX (1,MAX)
        Successors: 0
        3.1.1 MINIMAX (0,MIN)
              Return: -1
        Return: -1
```

```
      2.2  MINIMAX (0,MAX)
              Return: +1
         Return: -1                    Minimum of (-1,+1)
    3  MINIMAX (1,MIN)
         Successors: 0
         3.1  MINIMAX (0,MAX)
                Return: +1
           Return: +1
       Return: +1                      Maximum of (-1,-1,+1)
    Output is +1, indicating a forced win for the first player.
```

Refining MINIMAX

We can easily extend the basic MINIMAX algorithm to convert it from a playing mechanism to a planning one—returning its estimate of the complete line of best play for both sides—by having the procedure attach its recommended best move in each position to the value of the position it returns. A list of moves will be constructed by linking these moves together as they are passed up the game tree. In our example, the best line of play would be for the first player to draw 3 sticks, forcing the second to draw the one remaining stick, thereby losing.

It is quite wasteful to reanalyze the entire game tree each move, as the basic MINIMAX algorithm does. Each time we choose a move, we should save the portion of the tree stemming from it, and rooted in the position it brought about, to be reused after the opponent moves.

The main problem with our MINIMAX algorithm as stated is its utter impracticability for all but the most simplistic games, like Last One Loses. By performing an exhaustive lookahead to the end of the game, it generates a game tree that includes every legal position. While this works in our example, chosen purely for its simplicity, it cannot for games like checkers or chess. A few back-of-the-envelope calculations reveal that the number of possible chess games is so astronomically huge—on the order of 10^{120}—that if every atom in the universe had been analyzing positions at picosecond speeds since the Big Bang, the analysis would just be getting started!

Cutting Off Search with Static Evaluations

One way to remedy this situation is to cut off the search at a certain level of depth. Since we have no certain foreknowledge of the game's outcome and so cannot return an absolute won-lost decision, we must instead apply a *static evaluation function* to each leaf position. Such a function assigns to a legal game position a numeric value in the range somewhere between losing for the player on move and winning for the player on move, however those events are measured. The numbers computed by the static evaluation function are normally positive to indicate an advantage for the player on move and negative to indicate an disadvantage, and actual final game positions are evaluated as positive infinity, +∞, and negative infinity, -∞. (Remember, we express everything relative to the player on move.)

Like the analogous heuristic evaluation function in state-space search, the static evaluation function is a rough calculation, using heuristic estimates based on the positional, static characteristics of the board position to judge its worth. Our conclusions about planning heuristics also apply to game-playing heuristics: they should strive for the optimal balance between accuracy and speed of calculation. Note that since we are usually more concerned about victory than optimality in game playing, there is no admissibility issue to worry about. Figure 7-3 shows the positional component (which gets added to the material differential) of a fairly good static evaluation function for chess positions, taken from the successful *Chess 4.7* program developed by David Slate and Larry Atkin at Northwestern University in the 1970s. Even if you are not a chess player, you can appreciate the scope and complexity of the function, which concentrates the total positional knowledge of the system, as well as the work that went into testing and refining it.

FIGURE 7-3. **STATIC EVALUATION FUNCTION FROM *CHESS 4.7***

---

100 points approximate the value of a single pawn. Square brackets around a quantity abbreviate "number of". Add together the following terms:

• For each friendly pawn:
  -8   if the pawn is doubled
  -20 if the pawn is isolated
  -4   if the pawn is backward and the square in front is attacked by one enemy pawn
  -8   if the pawn is backward and the square in front is attacked by two enemy pawns
  If the pawn is passed:
    (pawn's rank) *
      +1.6 if pawn is blocked by an enemy piece, or
      +1.9 if square in front of pawn is attacked by an enemy piece, or
      +2.6 if square in front of pawn is attacked by a friendly piece, or
      +2.3 otherwise
    +1.6 * (pawn's rank - 2) if pawn belongs to a local majority
    +3.9 * (pawn's rank - 2) if pawn is a c-pawn
    +5.4 * (pawn's rank - 2) if pawn is a d-pawn
    +7.0 * (pawn's rank - 2) if pawn is an e-pawn
    +2.3 * (pawn's rank - 2) if pawn is an f-pawn

• For each friendly knight:
    +1.6 * (6 - (2 * ((4.5 - knight's rank) + (4.5 - knight's file))))
    +1.2 * (5 - (sum of the knight's rank and the distance from enemy king)
     -9.4 if the knight is on its first rank

• For each friendly bishop:
    +2.4 * ([squares attacked by bishop and not occupied by friendly pawns] - 7)
    -11 if the bishop is on its first rank

• For each friendly rook:
    +1.6 * [squares attacked by rook]
    -1.6 * (lesser of rook's rank and file distances from enemy king)
    +22 if the rook is on the seventh rank
    +8 if the rook is connected to another rook
    +8 if the rook is on a fully open file
    +3 if the rook is on a half-open file

• For each friendly queen:
    +0.8 * [squares attacked by queen and not attacked by any enemy piece]
    -0.8 * (lesser of queen's rank and file distances from enemy king)

• For the king:
    Importance * Guardedness, where:
      I = [non-pawn enemy pieces] - (2 if an enemy queen is on the board)
      G = (-3.1 if king is more than 1 square from a corner on the friendly side) +
          (-0.8 if king cannot move) +
          (either -3.1 if no friendly pieces are adjacent to the king, or
          -1.6 if just one friendly piece is adjacent to the king) +
          (-4.1 if king's file has no friendly pawn(s)) +
          (-3.6 if files adjacent to kings have no friendly pawns) +
          (for each square adjacent to the king,
          -1.2 * ([enemy attackers of the square] -1))

Cutting off the search at a given depth by using static evaluations enables us to choose between depth of search, which we intuitively take to correspond directly to quality of play, and time spent searching. But even so, looking just a few moves ahead with MINIMAX can be costly. Suppose the branching factor in game trees for chess is about 20; that is, that in the average chess position the player on move has 20 legal move options. Then to look ahead 6 ply (6 half moves, or 3 full moves by each player), we must statically evaluate approximately 3,200,000 positions, the number of leaves in the game tree, and then apply MINIMAX to each of its 168,421 interior nodes!

Even at 160,000 evaluations per second, the speed of today's best chess computers, it would take more than 22 seconds to look just 3 moves ahead. Extending the search to 3 1/2 moves would increase the search time to 422 seconds, or

7 minutes. Since tournament chess is played at about 3 minutes per move, such performance is disappointing.

Alpha-Beta Pruning

Fortunately, there are more ways to improve the algorithm, one of which in particular can achieve dramatic reductions in the number of positions expanded and evaluated. The well-known and widely used *alpha-beta pruning* technique seeks to prune provably unpromising branches of the game tree, by discovering moves that need not be analyzed and ignoring them, thereby saving valuable search time. It has been proven that theoretically, alpha-beta pruning in the MINIMAX strategy can double the search depth while examining the same number of positions. Since in the extreme case it prunes nothing and degenerates to pure MINIMAXing, it can do no worse than improve on that algorithm's performance.

How does α–β pruning achieve any reduction at all, let alone such a miraculous one? The key lies in using the information provided by the static evaluation function to determine that certain moves cannot *possibly* lead to a better result than has already been found in searching the game tree. By making many such local decisions, we can accumulate a substantial global savings.

Let's look at an example of when α–β pruning should take place. Figure 7-4 is a game tree with the path of a 3-ply MINIMAX search drawn in: each downward arrow marks a call to the MINIMAX procedure, and each upward arrow indicates a value being returned by that procedure. The terminal nodes are labelled with their static evaluations, and the interior nodes show the backed-up values returned by the MINIMAX calls.

Figure 7-5 shows the same tree in the middle of the search. At the point labelled A, on the way up from terminal node 1.2.1, the *maximizing* player (MAX) has just examined a move that brings about a position whose static value is +7 (remember, our belief in this analysis is predicated on our faith in the static evaluation function as an accurate measure of the advantage or disadvantage of a position). Therefore, he knows that if the game should reach the position at point A, he can play a move that will give him a +7 advantage.

However, at node 1, the *minimizing* player (MIN) had already discovered a move, leading to node 1.1, that promises a score no greater than +5. Keeping this in mind, think what would happen if we stopped the search at point A without examining any more of node 1.2's successors. The value +7 would be returned, but at node 1, MIN would choose the left successor, with a value of +5. Therefore, MAX should only continue to analyze at point A as long as there is a chance that its value drop below the +5 that MIN already knows he can get from node 1. But since that node is a MAX node, its real value will *never decrease*, so it will never go below +7, much less below the requisite +5.

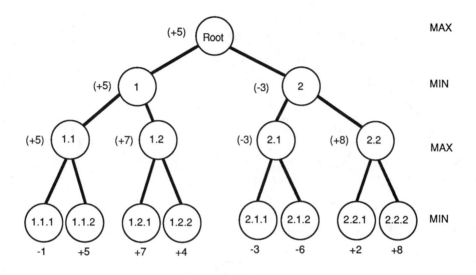

Figure 7–4. **Minimaxing a Game Tree with Static Evaluations**

Given these conclusions, once we ascend to point A, we can safely abandon the search, *cutting off* all the other successors of node 1.2. We never bother to examine node 1.2.2, though we did examine it with straight MINIMAX in Figure 7-4. This is because we are trying to find the best move at node 1, so we are not interested in any nodes that are bound to be worse than the best one we have found so far.

Figure 7-6 shows the situation some time later in the same search. MAX is analyzing the alternative move in the root position, knowing that he has already found a move, represented by the left branch from the root, leading to a score no worse than +5. Furthermore, at the point labelled B, MIN has found a move giving a score of -3. And since node 2 is a MIN node, its value will never increase. So since MAX can already get +5, and node 2's value can never be greater than -3, there is no point continuing the search at point B. We can cut off node 2's remaining successors and return the value -3 to the root, which will return a final value of +5 for the entire search.

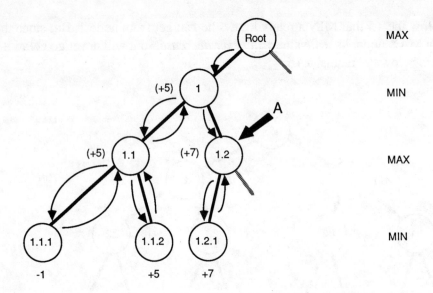

Figure 7–5.   **Making a Beta-Cutoff**

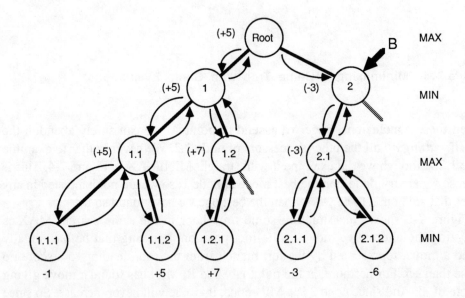

Figure 7–6.   **Making an Alpha-Cutoff**

Figure 7-7 shows the whole game tree with both cutoffs. In this case, out of 8 terminal/leaf positions, we performed a static evaluation (the most costly part of the search process) on only 5, for a 37.5% savings. If the tree were deeper, we would have eliminated the entire subtrees stemming from the right children of nodes 1.2 and 2, and probably realized additional savings from prunings deeper in the other subtrees. Note also that if the tree were broader, with 1.2 and 2 having more children, we could prune all of them. Such cutoffs are the essence of the algorithm, enabling us to completely ignore entire variations with absolutely no decrease in the quality of play.

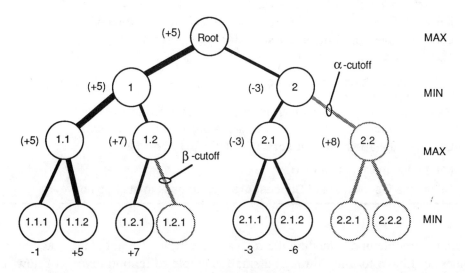

Figure 7–7. **Alpha-Beta Pruning Results**

Figure 7-8 gives a more specific formulation of the general alpha-beta algorithm in the MINIMAX procedure. Alpha-beta pruning is named after the two variables α and β that represent the thresholds beyond which search can stop (cutting off the remaining children), with α being the static evaluation of the best position the MAX player can currently force, and β being, conversely, the best that MIN can get. Accordingly, as shown in Figure 7-7, an *α-cutoff* occurs at a MIN node, and a *β-cutoff* occurs at a MAX node.

FIGURE 7-8. THE ALPHA-BETA PRUNING ALGORITHM

INPUT: The current **Position**, the player on move (either MIN or MAX), α, β, the
          current **Level** of search, and the maximum search depth **MaxSearchDepth**.
TO COMPUTE: The line of best play for both sides from that position.
LOCAL VARIABLES: **Successors**, α_c, β_c.
OUTPUT: The static evaluation of the position after **MaxSearchDepth**-ply given the
          computed line of play.

1. If **Level** equals **MaxSearchDepth**, then compute the static evaluation function
   on **Position** and return the result.
2. If MIN is on move, then:
   a. Generate a list of the **Successors** of the current **Position**.
   b. If $\alpha > \beta$ or **Successors** is empty, terminate and return β (α-cutoff).
   c. Let β_c = AlphaBeta(**Successors**[1], MAX, α, β, **Level**+1).
   d. Let β = the minimum of (β, β_c).
   e. Delete the first element of **Successors** and go back to step 2b above.
3. If MAX is on move, then:
   a. Generate a list of the **Successors** of the current **Position**.
   b. If $\alpha > \beta$ or **Successors** is empty, terminate and return α (β-cutoff).
   c. Let α_c = AlphaBeta(**Successors**[1], MIN, α, β, **Level**+1).
   d. Let α = the maximum of (α, α_c).
   e. Delete the first element of **Successors** and go back to step 3b above.

If you have trouble understanding the α–β algorithm, you're not alone. Each time
it comes up I have to think through a small example to remind myself of how it
works. Winston wrote that "Even seasoned game specialists still feel magic in the
α–β procedure," adding that "each individual conclusion seems right, but somehow
the global result is strange and hard to believe."

Analysis of α–β Pruning

Having been known for some time, the α–β algorithm is well-studied in terms of
performance and efficiency. We will retrace some of that analysis to get a better
feel for its operational characteristics.

   It turns out that α–β pruning works best when the successors of every state are
ordered exactly according to their correctness; that is, when the search will always
examine the absolute best move in any given position first. It has been shown that

under these optimal conditions, the number of leaf positions statically evaluated will be approximately $2b^{d/2}$, where b is the branching factor (as defined in Chapter 6) and d is the depth of the game tree. With normal MINIMAX search, all b^d leaf nodes must be evaluated before a decision can be reached. Therefore, we can search to twice the depth with the same number of evaluations, or to the same depth with the square root of the number of evaluations performed by MINIMAX. For example, searching 3 full moves at a branching factor of 10 evaluates 2000 positions with optimal α–β pruning, or 1000000 with MINIMAX only. Unfortunately, the question is somewhat academic—after all, if the moves are always perfectly ordered, we can just choose the first in the list with full confidence that it is the absolute best move in the position!

So, we now know that the improvement over MINIMAX offered by the addition of α–β pruning depends on how closely the ordering of the legal moves possible in each position corresponds to the correct ordering. If the ordering were exactly the reverse of the correct one, α–β pruning would be of no help at all, for we would always have to MINIMAX every successor of a position before finding the best move. Pearl has shown that even random successor ordering yields a significant improvement, permitting search to go about 33% deeper than would basic MINIMAX with the same number of evaluations. And each small improvement we make over random ordering will increase this percentage, thereby improving a program's performance.

Alternatives to α–β Pruning

It is clear that α–β pruning is a significant improvement to straight MINIMAX searching, but is it the best we can hope for? A theoretical result says that it is asymptotically optimal, meaning that as the total size of the search tree increases, the number of nodes evaluated by α–β increases at as slow a rate as possible. However, there are procedures that will always choose the same moves as α–β but will sometimes not evaluate nodes that α–β would. Chief among these algorithms are *Scout*, *SSS**, and *B**.

The first two are MINIMAX-family algorithms that use different strategies from α–β to prune unnecessary lines of search, but often at significantly higher costs in storage space. B*, the only non-MINIMAX algorithm in practical use for chess, was invented by Berliner and is the basic control mechanism used by his HiTech system. Instead of assigning a single static evaluation to each position in the game tree, it computes both *optimistic* and *pessimistic* estimates. The key invariant is that at any position in the analysis, a move is only selected as best when its pessimistic evaluation exceeds the optimistic evaluation of all the alternatives. Enhancements to B* by Andrew Palay, using probability distributions instead of ranges for the estimates, have been shown comparable or superior to α–β pruning in many practical situations.

Enhancements to the α–β Algorithm

We have a general-purpose game playing algorithm, MINIMAX with α–β pruning, and two ways to add specific knowledge into the system: the static evaluation function and the move-ordering algorithm. In general, the former is suited to the application of knowledge about the static characteristics of positions. In chess, as we saw in Figure 7-3, this would give prime weight to a point count of the material on the board, then add and subtract small amounts based on positional factors such as pawn structure defects, piece mobility, king safety, and other salient features.

Through the move-ordering algorithm, we can endow the system with some basic knowledge about the dynamic aspects of positions: try captures first, piece moves next, and pawn moves last, for example. This can be further modified by sorting the capture moves according to the value of the piece captured, and so on. Note that normally we order the moves based solely on the merits of the move itself without considering the position that will result; evaluating positions is a job of the static evaluation function.

We now have a basic framework for studying game-playing programs. While the discussion has been oriented towards the example of chess, which is the best-studied game to which computers have been applied, it applies to most two-player, discrete, perfect information games. As we delve into deeper game playing concepts, such as quiescence search and iterative deepening, we will continue to use chess for our examples.

Quiescence Search

The tactical skills of a game playing program are embodied in the search algorithm itself, which provides the ability to look ahead at future positions. Strangely enough, this very capability, central to the machine's ability to play, engenders a serious performance problem called the *horizon effect*.

Consider this situation: the computer is on move in a game of chess against a human opponent. In the position on the board, it is clear that the computer must lose some material no matter how it plays. For example (see Figure 7-9), a bishop is pinned and attacked by a knight, and it has no defense. Now suppose the α–β

algorithm is programmed to analyze the game to a depth of 4 ply, or 2 full moves. It sees that it can give up the bishop immediately, and that this will result in at best a score (static evaluation) of about -3.0 pawns. However, it also notices that it can sacrifice two pawns on the other side of the board instead; in this case, it will achieve a score of -2.0 after 3 moves. Of course, the machine chooses the latter course, loses the two pawns, and then discovers that it still must lose the bishop. When the smoke clears, it winds up down a bishop and two pawns. But it could have been down just a bishop if it had had the foresight to give it up immediately when it was irretrievably lost.

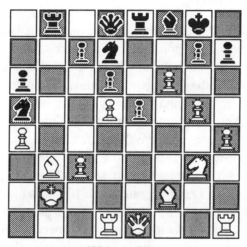

White to Move

Figure 7–9.   **The Horizon Effect**

This phenomenon, which used to occur with alarming frequency in computer chess, is called the horizon effect. The machine "convinces itself" that it is not losing the bishop because the loss is pushed beyond the search depth, or horizon, of the program's lookahead capability. One can easily observe this by watching the computer's play when it is faced with a forced checkmate. It will give up as many of its pieces as possible as long as such moves push the checkmate beyond the horizon. At this point in the game, the horizon effect is harmless, but, as we have seen, in other situations it can severely impair the machine's playing ability.

Fortunately, there is a solution to the problem. The main idea of a *quiescence search* is to extend the search process in volatile positions, continuing to look ahead until a state of quiescence is reached. Normally, the quiescence search begins at the predetermined maximum search depth and continues to examine forcing moves, like captures and checks in chess, until there are no more. In theory, this would avoid the horizon effect in the example we discussed above by enabling the machine to see from the outset that it would really lose more material by sacrificing the pawns than by giving up the bishop immediately. A quiescence search may also help the machine to calculate long, forcing combinations, thereby improving its tactical ability. Indeed, it is in tactical situations where today's chess computers demonstrate their greatest abilities.

Iterative Deepening

Another problem with the algorithms and heuristic enhancements we have seen thus far is that there is no way of predicting, in advance of a search, how many positions will be evaluated. Since the number of static evaluations is roughly proportional to the amount of real time the search will consume, a game program that is to compete under the same rules and time limits as human beings must have a method of managing its search so as never to be caught in a time forfeit.

Most modern programs manage the search explosion with the *iterative deepening* enhancement to the α–β pruning algorithm. As the name suggests, this procedure searches the game tree in a breadth-first fashion (remember that standard MINIMAX and α–β operate depth-first to a predetermined fixed depth). After constructing one level of the search tree, the program can pause to check how much time it has left, then decide whether to proceed with the search. The key to iterative deepening lies in preserving the important α–β information from level to level, and with it the efficiency of the pruning algorithm.

Killer Move Heuristic

Chess programmers, forever seeking new ways to improve the playing strengths of their programs, have devised many small heuristic "tricks" that are used to cut down on the amount of search without modifying the basic α–β algorithm itself. One proven example is the *killer move heuristic* (KMH), which operates in the move-ordering phase of the search. Suppose a chess program must choose its move in a position in which its opponent is threatening checkmate on the move (for example, see Figure 7-10).

Executing the normal α–β algorithm, the program will generate a list of moves it can legally play in the given position. With the KMH implemented, after examining a few moves to a depth of 2 or 3 ply, the program takes note of the fact that in most of those cases, the same move by its opponent causes a radical change in the evaluation of subsequent positions; in the example, a change from an approximately even position to a losing one for the program. Since this move is obviously strong, the KMH instructs the move generator to put it at the front of the legal move list for the opponent for all subsequent positions (in this search) in which that move is legal. Remembering that α–β performs best when the moves are perfectly ordered (best to worst), you can easily imagine how, by searching strong paths first, the KMH can cause more cutoffs to occur down the search tree than would normally be made without it.

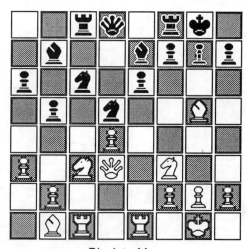

Black to Move

Figure 7–10   **The Killer Move Heuristic**

Game Playing in Pascal

To illustrate α–β pruning and the other basic game playing concepts discussed in this chapter, we have developed a complete *CHECKERS* program in Pascal. When run, the program will introduce itself and then ask for the depth of search. Type the number of ply to which you wish the game tree searched by the computer, and press [Return]. The computer plays Red, and you play Black and move first. Figure 7-11 shows the initial game position and the standard checkers numbering scheme used by the program to input your moves and output its own.

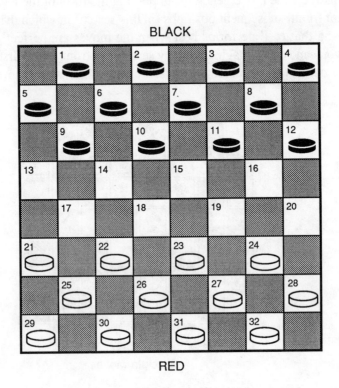

Figure 7–11. **Checkers Program Notation**

The game begins with the computer prompting you for the first move; type the starting square, press [Space], type the ending square, and press [Return]. Jumps are not compulsory, and you can stop in the middle of a jump sequence. When the computer determines its move, it announces it and asks for your response. This continues until the game ends, at which point you must press [Return] to exit. Since the program has neither a visual display nor any of the bells and whistles found in commercial game programs, you should have a checkers set at hand to play a complete game.

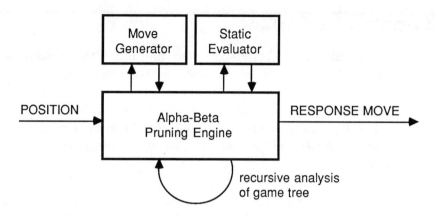

Figure 7–12. **Architecture of CHECKERS program**

CHECKERS is based on the MINIMAX algorithm with standard α–β pruning, searching to a predetermined depth with no iterative deepening or quiescence search. The program's architecture is based on the vanilla model diagrammed in Figure 7-12: an α–β engine takes the current board position as input, recursively explores the game tree stemming from that position, and produces a response move as output. Assisting the main module are a move generator, which takes a position and computes all the possible successor positions, and a static evaluator, which takes a leaf position and computes its static value. The evaluation function built into the program (in function Status) is:

0.7 * (friendly kings - enemy kings) + 0.3 * (friendly pieces - enemy pieces)

While this is clearly a very simplistic measure (especially in comparison with Figure 7-3), it does encourage two key behaviors we would desire in a checkers program: winning enemy checkers and making kings.

The CHECKERS source code is long, but most of it comprises the move generator module (GenBoards and associated procedures). Games, with their convoluted rules and restrictions, require special care in generating legal moves, and it is here that most programs spend the much of their time. CHECKERS uses an array of possible moves for a checker in each square on the board, plus several procedures to handle jumps, make kings, and so on.

Procedure AlphaBeta is the longest in the program, and it should demonstrate the complexity of translating an innocuous algorithm into working code, much of which is devoted to actually determining best moves rather than just α and β values. Since the program always plays Red, the values of the MIN and MAX players have been hard-coded into the algorithm (MAX=Red, MIN=Black).

Programming Exercises

1. CHECKERS could be brought more into line with standard checkers rules. It does generate only legal moves, but it does not recognize stalemate (for example). Rewrite the move generator and evaluation function to make them more efficient and add stalemate and final position recognition. Try adding a compulsory jump requirement and investigate how it decreases the size of the game tree. Allow the user to play either Red or Black.

2. (For graphics enthusiasts.) As we have seen, the user interface is an important part of any AI program. A game playing program must have some way of displaying the current board position. Modify CHECKERS to print out the board after each move and improve its interaction with the human player.

3. The static evaluation module is the main source of knowledge for a game program, but CHECKERS has a particularly weak function. What positional knowledge should the program have? Try to add one or more of the following factors: preferring checkers in corners, on the sides, and on the back rows, immobilizing enemy checkers, and searching for checkers with open paths to the last row.

4. Commercial chess programs are required to play under the strict time limits used in tournaments. Add a time limit to CHECKERS, and use iterative deepening to manage the search. After doing this, you should be able insert some simple code to print out, during the analysis, the current line of best play and the backed-up value of the board position currently being analyzed.

5. CHECKERS is quite susceptible to the horizon effect. Add to the static evaluation function a test for positional quiescence by looking for remaining jumps. What exactly should you do with jumps found at the horizon? Modify the program to analyze those moves further, perhaps using the existing α–β procedure. How will the resulting improvement in playing quality compare with the expense of performing the quiescence search, and would it not be more profitable to just extend the global search depth?

6. The threat of a multiple jump is a killer move. CHECKERS's tactical knowledge, embodied primarily in the move generator, could be augmented with a better ordering of generated moves and the killer move heuristic. Implement both. What are the problems of incorporating these enhancements?

7. Currently, CHECKERS includes some debugging code that prints various messages during execution of the α–β procedure. Clean up this code to gather statistics on the algorithm's performance, including the numbers of cutoffs, and analyze the results to help improve the move generator. How would straight MINIMAX searching compare to the current α–β version of CHECKERS?

8. Replace the α–β procedure with either B*, Scout or SSS* (you will need additional sources on these algorithms). In general, how difficult are these other algorithms to implement? Do they improve the program's performance, or are they only valuable with very large game trees? How deep can CHECKERS search the tree before its time consumption becomes unreasonable?

9. Convert CHECKERS to play a different two-player perfect-information game, such as Chess, Othello, or Go. Does the current approach to move generation work well in more complex situations? How does the profile of time consumption by the various program modules change for different games? Analyze the differences in complexity between the various games considered.

Summary

Game playing is a common but often-overlooked application of heuristic search in artificial intelligence. It differs from simple "planning" search in two main ways: the astronomical size of the typical state-space prevents its complete exploration, and programs must know how to deal with an adversary. The standard game playing algorithm, MINIMAX, exhaustively searches the entire game tree, which is analogous to a search tree.

α–β pruning is the most significant of many extensions to MINIMAX; by discovering nodes whose values can never contribute to its choice of move, it enables large sections of the tree to be cut off and never explored. Within the α–β

framework, performance can be improved further by refining the static evaluation function and the move-ordering function, most notably with iterative deepening, quiescence search, and the killer move heuristic.

References

Charniak and McDermott's coverage of game-playing includes the MINIMAX and SSS* algorithms, whereas Winston presents a detailed example of α–β pruning. Neither text, however, goes into depth on modern algorithms or practical techniques. Nilsson's *Problem-Solving Methods in Artificial Intelligence* looks at game trees as special cases of AND/OR graphs instead of standard state-spaces. Pearl's *Heuristics: Intelligent Search Strategies for Computer Problem Solving* offers detailed mathematical and probabilistic analyses of several algorithms, including α–β pruning, SSS*, and Scout. Recent results are gathered in Bramer's *Computer Game-Playing: Theory and Practice*.

Figures 7-3, 7-4, 7-5, 7-6, and 7-7 are adapted from a basic discussion of search in game playing in Holding's *The Psychology of Chess Skill*, which offers an interesting perspective on chessplaying and problem-solving expertise in general. Ongoing computer chess research is reported in the *Advances in Computer Chess* series, of which four volumes have been published (1-3 edited by Clarke, 4 by Beal). The generalization of MINIMAX to multiplayer games was reported by Luckhart and Irani in "An Algorithmic Solution of N-Person Games."

Frey's *Chess Skill in Man and Machine*, 2nd edition, has been the standard work on computer chess, including papers on the Chess 4.x series, Belle, and Cray Blitz. HiTech is documented in various sources, including Ebeling's 1986 ACM Distinguished Dissertation *All the Right Moves: A VLSI Architecture for Chess*, Palay's *Searching with Probabilities*, and Berliner and Ebeling's "The SUPREM Architecture: A New Intelligent Paradigm," which attempts to generalize HiTech's success to other AI applications. The B* algorithm was introduced by Berliner in "The B* Tree Search Algorithm: A Best-First Proof Procedure."

8. FUTURE DIRECTIONS

In the last six chapters, we have examined some of the fundamental issues and problemsin contemporary knowledge-based AI. The basic ideas of knowledge representation and search were illustrated with applications to natural language processing, expert systems, and game playing. However, this is not a complete picture of current work in artificial intelligence and its related fields, which includes research into computer vision, machine learning, and cognitive modelling techniques such connectionism. These advanced topics, less well-understood than those of "classical" AI, are the subject of this final chapter, a look at future directions in the exploration of intelligence.

Computer Vision

Imagine for a moment that we are interested in creating a robot to simulate a human being. We have some of the basic information we need to endow it with common-sense knowledge, capabilities for natural language communication, expert problem-solving, rudimentary planning, and a little entertainment from game playing. But so far we can only talk to our machine through its keyboard and display screen. The logical next step is *perception*, the ability to receive input from the external world in its own media: sights, sounds, smells, and so on.

While "odor processing" (if it even deserves study) may be beyond today's AI and engineering techniques, both speech and image understanding have been extensively pursued since the late 1960s. Commercial applications that have evolved since then include voice-activated word processors, optical text scanning, and robots that sort containers, for example. But despite the enormous industrial potential of these technologies, perception seems to have an even more "natural," and uniquely human aura than such purely cognitive abilities as planning and problem-solving.

195

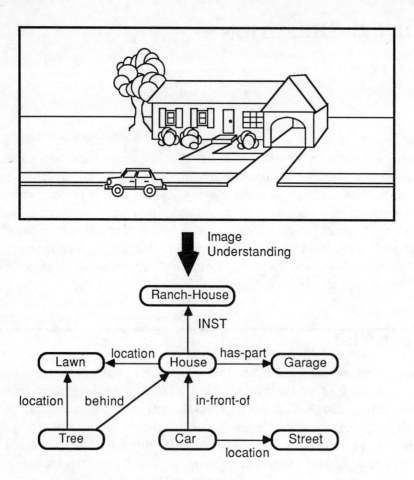

Figure 8–1. **The Visual Process**

The Vision Problem

Although a complete treatment of speech understanding is unfortunately not possible in this book, we can give an overview of the problems in computer vision. The basic objective is this: given a *bitmap*, a two-dimensional image of a scene, construct a description of the scene which specifies the objects that produce the image, including their shapes, sizes, colors, and locations. Figure 8-1 gives an example of the input to and output from a complete vision system.

Essentially, the visual process is one of converting the very low-level information provided as raw input from the "senses" into a very high-level abstraction of the relevant and useful objects encoded in the input. In our specification, exactly what constitutes an "object" has been left rather vague, for we would not want to arbitrarily exclude levels of detail that might be interesting in one situation but irrelevant noise in another. For example, in counting the cars on a road to analyze traffic patterns we do not care about license plates, but in looking for a stolen vehicle they are the most important features.

Representation in Vision

In converting from one level of description (the bitmap) to another (such as a semantic network, as in Figure 8-1), we must employ a structured representational framework such as that invented by David Marr. Basing his conjectures on constraints derived from both computational necessity and biological studies of natural vision systems, he proposed the following four-level model of the representations that should be used in an artificial vision system. Figure 8-2 gives some examples of how various scenes and objects might appear in each of the representations.

Image
- Consists of intensity values in a gray scale (color can be safely ignored) for each point in a bitmap of the scene.
- Represents the observed light intensities.

Primal Sketch
- Consists of zero-crossings, blobs, terminations and discontinuities, edge segments, virtual lines, groups, curvilinear organization, and boundaries.
- Makes explicit important aspects of the two-dimensional image, especially the intensity changes (indicating edges) and their geometrical distribution (potentially composing objects) and organization (defining shapes).

2 1/2 Dimensional Sketch
- Consists of surfaces with local orientations, distances from the viewer, and discontinuities in depth and surface orientation.
- Makes explicit the depth and orientation characteristics of the surfaces in the scene from a viewer-centered frame of reference.

3 Dimensional Model Representation
- Consists of 3-D structural models in a hierarchical organization, with each model based on a configuration of a few main axes.

- Describes the various shapes in the scene in an object-centered perspective using a modular system of primitives that represent volume and surface information.

(Image)

(Primal Sketch)

(2 1/2 Dimensional Sketch)

(Three Dimensional Model)

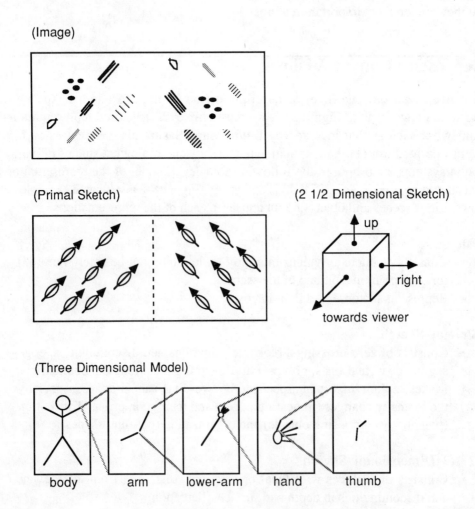

body   arm   lower-arm   hand   thumb

Figure 8–2. **Levels of Representation in Visual Processing**

Marr's separation of visual processing into these levels, as well as several intermediate versions, was motivated by his observations of the constraints physical law places on what surfaces can exist in nature. However, the enormous computations necessary to convert each level into the next are extremely difficult to implement efficiently.

Edge Detection

To make vision problems more tractable for today's computer systems, several simplifications are often made. First, the domain is restricted to the familiar blocks world, resulting in scenes of only straight-edged geometric figures, perhaps with occlusions or shadows to complicate things. Second, we skip several of the intermediate representations, intending to produce a conceptual description more directly from the input. To complete our brief survey of computer vision, we will examine the classical problem of *edge detection*, which aims to eliminate noisy data from the bitmap and transform it into a line drawing.

Given an intensity bitmap, in which each *pixel*, or picture element, in the image is represented by an integer indicating its "grayness," the first step of many vision systems is to determine which parts of the image form edges, indicating potential boundaries between two surfaces. As Figure 8-3 shows, this is not a trivial task. Although you can clearly perceive two leaves, one occluding part of the other, from the original image, this fact is not readily apparent from the intensity array, where there is no obvious change in intensity at the edge between the two surfaces. This would seem to indicate that a purely bottom-up, data-driven process of edge detection is not solely responsible for surface separation. Our high-level knowledge of leaf shape and structure seems to generate an expectation that an edge should exists in the image, so the visual system "fills it in" even though it is not there. However, this automatic interaction of bottom-up and top-down constraints in human vision is difficult to realize in computer models.

Detecting edges is most commonly done by passing the image intensity array through one or more *filters*, functions that are applied to each element in the array, and then scanning through the array for certain readily apparent regularities. As demonstrated in Figure 8-4, the idea is to make the intensity changes at surface borders, which can be difficult to perceive in the original image, explicit. We outline one such method, known as "sombrero filtering" or *Gaussian convolution*, in Figure 8-5 below (although we use a one-dimensional intensity array for simplicity, the technique is trivially extended to normal two-dimensional images).

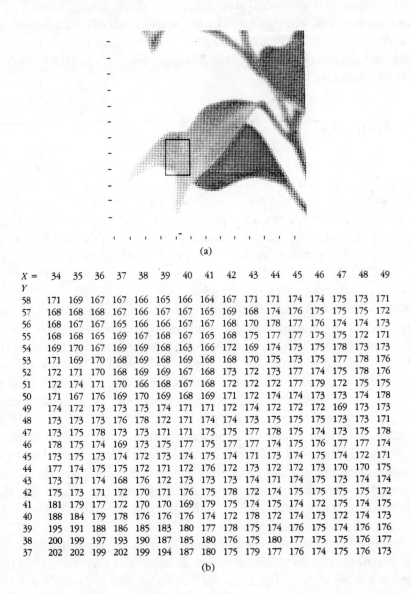

(a)

X =	34	35	36	37	38	39	40	41	42	43	44	45	46	47	48	49
Y																
58	171	169	167	167	166	165	166	164	167	171	171	174	174	175	173	171
57	168	168	168	167	166	167	167	165	169	168	174	176	175	175	175	172
56	168	167	167	165	166	166	167	167	168	170	178	177	176	174	174	173
55	168	168	165	169	167	168	167	165	168	175	177	177	175	175	172	171
54	169	170	167	169	169	168	163	166	172	169	174	173	175	178	173	173
53	171	169	170	168	169	168	169	168	168	170	175	173	175	177	178	176
52	172	171	170	168	169	169	167	168	173	172	173	177	174	175	178	176
51	172	174	171	170	166	168	167	168	172	172	172	177	179	172	175	175
50	171	167	176	169	170	169	168	169	171	172	174	174	173	173	174	178
49	174	172	173	173	173	174	171	171	172	174	172	172	172	169	173	173
48	173	173	173	176	178	172	171	174	174	173	175	175	175	173	173	171
47	173	175	178	173	173	171	171	175	175	177	178	175	174	173	175	178
46	178	175	174	169	173	175	177	175	177	177	174	175	176	177	177	174
45	173	175	173	174	172	173	174	175	174	171	173	174	175	174	172	171
44	177	174	175	175	172	171	172	176	172	173	172	172	173	170	170	175
43	173	171	174	168	176	172	173	173	173	174	171	174	175	173	174	174
42	175	173	171	172	170	171	176	175	178	172	174	175	175	175	175	172
41	181	179	177	172	170	170	169	179	175	174	175	174	172	175	174	175
40	188	184	179	178	176	176	176	174	172	178	172	174	173	172	174	173
39	195	191	188	186	185	183	180	177	178	175	174	176	175	174	176	176
38	200	199	197	193	190	187	185	180	176	175	180	177	175	175	176	177
37	202	202	199	202	199	194	187	180	175	179	177	176	174	175	176	173

(b)

Figure 8-3 **The Difficulty of Detecting Edges**

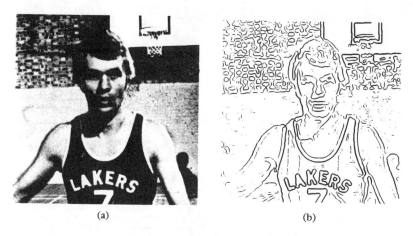

(a)   (b)

Figure 8-4. **Highlighting Edges in a Real-World Image**

FIGURE 8-5. SOMBRERO FILTERING EDGE HIGHLIGHTING ALGORITHM

INPUT: Intensity array I of gray-scale brightnesses.
OUTPUT: List Z of zero-crossings indicating possible edges.

1. Compute A, the average-intensity array, as follows: $A_i = (I_{i-1} + I_i + I_{i+1}) / 3$.
2. Compute F, the average-first-difference array, as follows: $F_i = (A_{i+1} - A_{i-1}) / 2$.
3. Compute S, the average-second-difference array, as follows: $S_i = (F_{i+1} - F_{i-1}) / 2$.
4. For each pair of adjacent elements $[S_i, S_{i+1}]$, if one is positive and the other negative, add the index pair [i, i+1] to the list Z of zero-crossings.

The output of this algorithm happens to be a list of *zero-crossings*, or points at which the values in the S array change sign; however, other phenomena like steep slopes and peaks can be useful in detecting edges. Figure 8-6 illustrates its operation on a simple four-pixel image with two surfaces, denoted by intensities of 1 and 0, and an edge between them. Note that for the purposes of computing the leftmost and rightmost elements, we follow the common practice of creating a dummy border around the image, calculated by simply duplicating the real border values. It turns out that two-dimensional convolution is as simple as running this algorithm once in the x-direction, for each row in the array, then once in the y-direction, for each column, and summing the results.

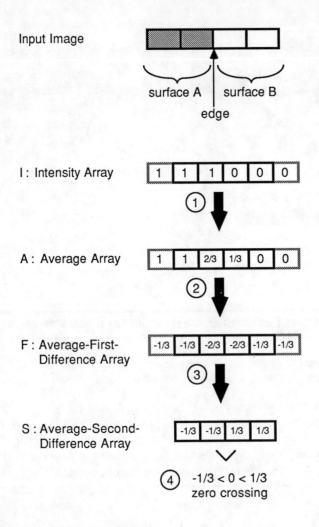

Figure 8–6. **Example of Edge Detection Algorithm**

We should note, before moving on to learning, that computer vision is the area of AI research that has seen the most productive interaction with neurobiology and cognitive psychology. The edge detection technique presented here is motivated by and comparable to that used by primate retinae, in which thousands of cells simultaneously perform the averaging and differencing processes. When we discuss connectionism, we will see an example of how a biologically plausible model of parallel computation can explain some phenomena of higher level vision.

Machine Learning

Throughout our discussion of AI thus far, there may have been a disturbing question lingering in the back of your mind: "what about learning?" Most people would consider learning an essential ingredient in intelligent behavior, if not the deciding factor in distinguishing an intelligent entity from an unintelligent one. And although they did not all put it at the top of the list, most of the definitions of intelligence from Figure 2-1 at least mentioned learning or adaptation. It even seems sometimes that the ability to learn—to improve performance over time—might be the "missing link" in artificial intelligence, a problem which, if solved, would lead to the solution of many other outstanding problems.

Learning takes several forms, of which we will examine a few in detail later on. They include rote learning, being instructed, learning by analogy, learning from examples, learning by observation and discovery, and learning from experience (practicing). That which is learned can include random data items, single facts, structured concepts, grammatical rewrite rules, production rules, static evaluation functions, and entire procedures. In each case, the process of learning tends to increase the system's knowledge, enabling it to perform better in the future.

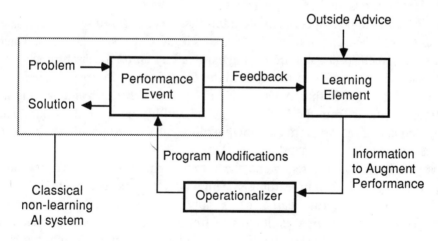

Figure 8–7. **General Learning Paradigm**

In a general learning model, which is diagrammed in Figure 8-7, an AI system is functionally divided into a *performance element* (PE) and a *learning element* (LE), which need not be structurally distinct. The PE performs the normal problem-solving task of the program, and the LE integrates available outside advice and feedback from the PE's actions to formulate possible modifications to the PE that will improve its performance. However, a problem often occurs in *operationalizing* the output of the LE; that is, in converting the representations used in the learning process into ones suitable for the performance process. In simple systems, the operationalization step can be avoided with the *single-representation trick*, which ensures that both the LE and PE always manipulate the same concept representations; however, in complex systems it can be easier to decide what changes should be made than to actually implement them.

Rote Learning

The simplest of all forms of learning is rote learning, which essentially boils down to memorization. Although most commonly used to teach the alphabet and similar things to young children, it can be an effective way of ensuring that a problem-solver will improve at least slightly with experience. We will consider standard search-based applications, such as expert systems and game playing programs. As an exercise, you should try adding the rote learning capabilities described below to the PADVISOR and CHECKERS programs from Chapters 5 and 7.

Game Playing. In heuristic search programs that will be reused several times, an application of rote learning immediately suggests itself. Consider Figure 8-8, which diagrams a fragment of a game tree being explored by an α–β search procedure. When the search descends to node A, from the root of the entire tree, A's value is computed by searching further to the maximum depth of the search and backing-up the static evaluations from the leaf nodes as defined by the α–β algorithm. The learning element of the program can now memorize the board position in node A and its associated value, +12 in this case.

Some time later, in a different game, the search might encounter the exact same position *as a leaf node*. A non-learning system would have to recompute the static evaluation of A, but the rote learner can simply retrieve the +12 value from its memory. This technique, first explored in Arthur Samuel's pioneering checkers program, gives two advantages: first, time is saved by retrieving information from a knowledge base rather than regenerating it over and over again (the prepare/deliberate tradeoff in practice); second, the stored value of +12 is more reliable than a computed static evaluation, since it was originally created by searching an entire subtree rooted at A. Samuel found that continuously running his programs using this simple learning method led to gradual but significant performance improvements over time.

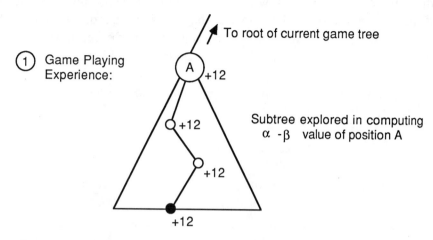

① Game Playing
    Experience:

To root of current game tree

A +12

Subtree explored in computing
α -β   value of position A

+12

+12

+12

② Learning Experience:
    Memorize the associated pair [A, +12]

③ Later Game
    Playing Experience:

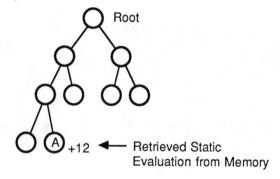

Root

A +12 ← Retrieved Static
          Evaluation from Memory

Figure 8–8. **Rote Learning in Game Tree Search**

Expert Systems. Recall our tree model of expert system reasoning. In a single consultation experience, the inference engine proceeds from a start state, such as a set of symptoms for a patient, to a goal, such as a recommended diagnosis, by executing several rules that lead from the problem to its solution. It is easy to see how such a system could learn by *chunking* the start and goal states together into a new production rule that is added to the system. Repeated execution of this operation, diagrammed in Figure 8-9, will create many rules whose premises are symptoms themselves and whose actions are final diagnoses. In subsequent sessions, these rules can be used to solve problems in one step instead of several. Since it operates in domains in which search cutoffs are unnecessary, chunking improves efficiency but not reliability. Therefore, it can be the basis for a general model of single-task practice, and has been so used by Newell in his *Soar* project.

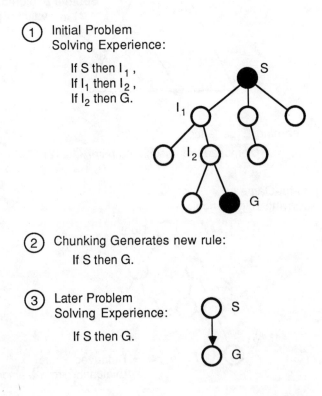

(1) Initial Problem
Solving Experience:

If S then I_1,
If I_1 then I_2,
If I_2 then G.

(2) Chunking Generates new rule:
If S then G.

(3) Later Problem
Solving Experience:

If S then G.

Figure 8–9. **Learning by Chunking in Production Systems**

However, chunking can run into the well-known *credit-assignment problem*, which confronts a learning element which must decide which parts of the performance element contributed to the successful solution, and therefore should be rewarded Suppose a doctor gives MYCIN a set of observed symptoms, MYCIN makes its diagnosis, and the LE prepares to chunk a new production rule. Some of the symptoms may never have been accessed by the rules that fired, but they will be chunked into the new rule nevertheless, unless the LE can properly decide which were useful and filter out the others; one possible solution is to have the inference engine mark each working memory element as it is tested by a triggered rule.

But beyond credit-assignment, which is a problem for all learning systems, these simple learners face a basic problem of inflexibility. Just as the performance elements to which we have seen them applied suffer from a sort of tunnel vision within their own highly specialized problem domains, rote learning elements can only augment performance to a maximum. Once all possible evaluations or all possible chunks are formed, further learning is impossible; furthermore, the continual piling up of knowledge can slow the search process of the PE. For example, the complexity of a game like chess might make it more space- and time-efficient to modify the evaluation function rather than store [position, evaluation] pairs. Rote learning cannot accomplish such conceptual manipulations.

Concept Learning

In *concept learning*, the goal is to induce from a set of examples a classification procedure for the general concept they define. This procedure, like a decision procedure for a language, will decide whether any given test case is an instance of the learned concept. Such concepts are fundamental to activities of classification, decision, and discrimination that characterize many aspects of human behavior, including reading, speaking, and problem solving.

A common representation for concepts is the *feature vector*, which is basically a frame whose name is the name of the concept, whose slots are the attributes that compose the concept, and whose fillers are the particular attribute values unique to the concept. For example, a blocks world concept could have features like shape, color, size, material, texture, and so on: [TETRAHEDRON SMALL BLACK PLASTIC SMOOTH]. Any feature value can be replaced by a more general description, as in [TETRAHEDRON * * * *], with * matching any value, to indicate a tetrahedron with any size, color, material, and texture. Likewise, a smooth plastic object would be [* * * PLASTIC SMOOTH].

EPAM Models

A useful representation for classification procedures is a *discrimination network*, such as the EPAM (Elementary Perceiver And Memorizer) model of Edward Feigenbaum and Herbert Simon. Each step of the decision process is represented by a node in the network, which corresponds to a yes/no comparison between a test feature and a feature of the concept. The search of the network branches either left or right from the node depending on the result of the comparison. Leaf nodes indicate the concept name that has been decided.

Figure 8-10 shows a simple EPAM net that can decide whether an object is in the SMALL-OR-CIRCULAR category. Given the feature vector [LARGE CIRCLE], we would start at the root, see that the SMALL? test fails, go down the left branch, satisfy the CIRCLE? test, go down the right branch, and see that a large circle is indeed small or circular. Given [LARGE SQUARE], after reaching the CIRCLE? test, we would turn left and discover that no, we do not have an instance of the represented concept.

The real fun with EPAM begins when we use it to induce new classifications from scratch. We can present the system with either positive or negative examples of the concept to be learned. It begins with the performance task, running the discrimination net on the training instance, and comparing the result with the intended result for the concept. (The network always starts out as a single NO leaf node, since it has had no examples of any concepts.) If the results are equal, no learning is necessary; if they are different, the network must be modified.

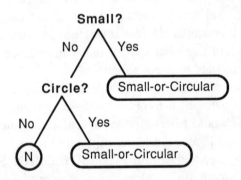

Figure 8–10. **A Simple EPAM Discrimination Network**

The necessary modification consists of removing the leaf node that was reached in the performance task and replacing it with a test for any feature that is present in the example but which was not tested during the classification process. Then, with a positive example, the NO branch from this new test node is made to point to the previously excised leaf, and the YES branch points to a new Y-leaf. In the negative case, the branches are simply reversed. Figure 8-11 shows how an EPAM net learns the concept SMALL-OR-CIRCLE from three examples, two positive and one negative.

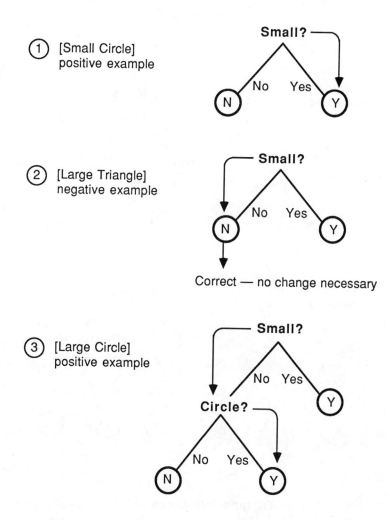

Figure 8–11. **Learning in an EPAM Discrimination Network**

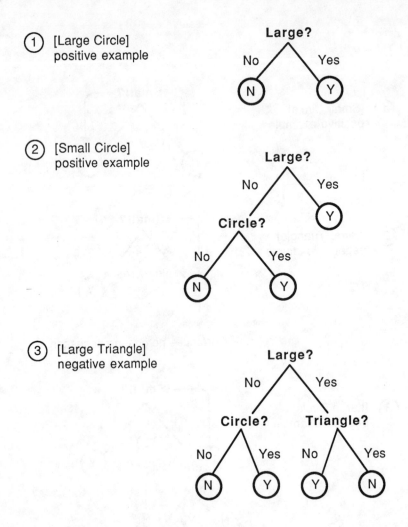

① [Large Circle]
positive example

② [Small Circle]
positive example

③ [Large Triangle]
negative example

Figure 8–12. **The Order of Training Influences the Concept EPAM learns**

Although it did a good job of explaining paired-associate learning and other data on "verbal learning behavior" (its original purpose), EPAM has several weaknesses as a general concept-learning mechanism. First, it literally has no idea what it has learned: try looking at an unfamiliar EPAM net and figuring out what concepts it can classify. It is possible, but the answer is hidden in the structure of the test nodes. Second, the order of the training instances can influence the concept that is learned;

Figure 8-12 shows how rearranging the examples from Figure 8-11 creates a completely different net, representing not SMALL-OR-CIRCULAR but perhaps NON-LARGE-CIRCLES-OR-LARGE-NON-TRIANGLES. EPAM is also open-ended, has no structural knowledge of the concept domains presented to it, and can change performance depending on the order in which it considers the features in the example concepts.

Version Space Models

Tom Mitchell's work on *version space* models answers some of the criticisms of EPAM. He created a procedure, the *candidate-elimination algorithm*, that could learn single concepts (not disjunctions, like CIRCLE-OR-SQUARE) with structured feature spaces from positive and negative training examples. Unlike EPAM, the result of the learning is a simple description of the concept, and does not depend on order of presentation. Each feature is explicitly limited to a predefined set of values, which are organized in individual inheritance networks, one per feature. Figure 8-13 shows a sample shape hierarchy for a three dimensional blocks world domain; moving down the tree specializes a feature value, whereas moving up generalizes it. The most general value, denoted by *, is at the root.

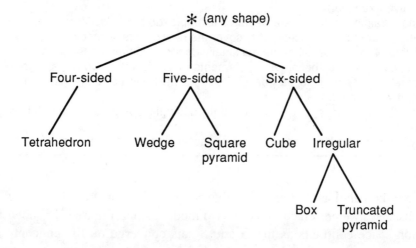

Figure 8-13. **An Inheritance Hierarchy for the Shape Feature**

The version space itself is the set of all possible concepts, or all possible combinations of features. We generalize a whole concept by creating a new concept description, of which one or more feature values is a generalization of the original value. We can specialize concepts in a similar way. A concept is said to *cover* another concept if each of its feature values is identical to or more general than the corresponding values in the covered concept. Candidate-elimination uses this by maintaining two sets, G and S, that represent the necessary and sufficient conditions, respectively, for membership in the category being learned. When these sets converge to become equal, the version space is said to have collapsed, and a single necessary and sufficient condition for the concept has been discovered. Figure 8-14 gives the full candidate-elimination algorithm.

FIGURE 8-14. CANDIDATE-ELIMINATION CONCEPT LEARNING ALGORITHM

---

1. Initialize the G set to contain the maximally general concept description. Initialize the S set to contain all of the most specific concepts in the version space.
2. If the next training instance is a positive example, do the following:
   a. Remove from G all concepts that do not cover the new example.
   b. Update S to contain all of the maximally specific common generalizations of the new instance and the previous elements in S. (In other words, generalize the elements in S as little as possible so that they will no longer cover this new positive example.)
3. If the next training instance is a negative example, do the following:
   a. Remove from S all concepts that cover the new counterexample.
   b. Update G to contain all of the maximally general, common specializations of the new instance and the previous elements in G. (In other words, specialize the elements in G as little as possible so that they will no longer cover this new negative example.)
4. If G=S, the version space includes only a single concept, so the learning is complete.
5. Otherwise, more training instances are necessary, so go back to step 2.

To see how the candidate-elimination algorithm works, consider the same set of training instances we presented to the EPAM model earlier. Figure 8-15 shows how the version space contracts as the G and S sets converge on the concept to be learned. In practice, we can take advantage of the fact that after the first *positive* example, the S set will be specialized to include only that example (work it out to assure yourself that this is true), to initialize S directly to [SMALL CIRCLE]. G remains unchanged, since the maximally general concept [* *] covers all specific concepts.

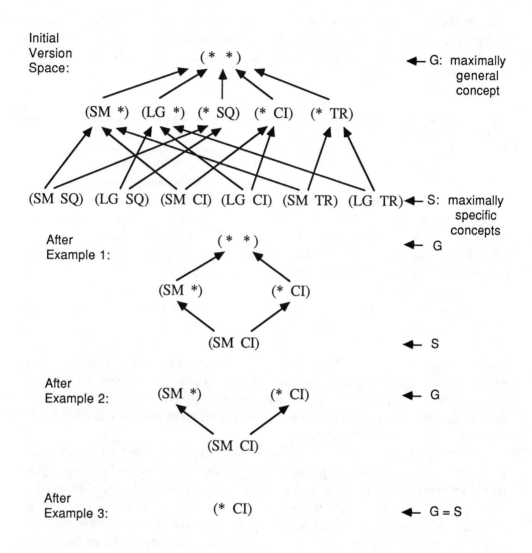

Figure 8–15. **Version-space Learning**

The second example, a negative one, causes G to be updated so that none of its member concepts cover [LARGE TRIANGLE]. This can be done by specializing the first feature, the size, to SMALL, or by specializing the second feature, shape, to either CIRCLE or SQUARE. We therefore update G to be {[SMALL *], [* CIRCLE]}, but we omit [* SQUARE] because it does not cover the elements of the S set (we can think of this concept as having been eliminated from the entire version space by the first example, as shown in the second frame of Figure 8-15). Finally, a positive example of [LARGE CIRCLE] removes the inconsistent [SMALL *] from G and generalizes with the other positive example to make S {[* CIRCLE]}. At this point, both G and S describe the concept "circle," so the learning has ended.

Connectionism

Our glimpses of computer vision and machine learning should have you convinced that integrating the processes of perception and induction with cognition is one of the most difficult facing the designers of intelligent systems. The information-processing paradigm seems almost inherently foreign to the low-level operations necessary to transduce sensory inputs to symbolic descriptions, or the flexibility and repetition characteristic of skill acquisition. The methods of *connectionism*, a sophisticated, biologically-motivated approach to cognitive modeling, are emerging as promising alternatives.

In connectionist models, also known as *parallel distributed processing* (PDP) systems, the fundamental object is not the symbol but the *unit*, a tiny processor whose only ability is to sum several input values and output a function of that sum. Each unit can have an arbitrary number of inputs, all potentially different, and an arbitrary number of outputs, all the same. Units, also known as nodes, are connected to each other via *weighted links*, which send the outputs of nodes to the inputs of other nodes; the weight specifies the relative influence of the value carried by the link on the unit to which it is carried.

To illustrate these basic ideas, we will consider the small connectionist network shown in Figure 8-16, whose job is to compute the exclusive-or function. (XOR takes two one-bit inputs, a datum and a mask, and inverts the datum if the mask is set; its truth table is $\{00 \rightarrow 0, 01 \rightarrow 1, 10 \rightarrow 1, 11 \rightarrow 0\}$, the same as the boolean function $\sim AB + \sim BA$.) XOR is of historical interest to the development of neurally-inspired computational systems, because it was the inability of the early, single-layer *Perceptron* model to learn this simple propositional function that discredited all non-symbolic models in the eyes of many AI workers.

In this network N, each unit computes the straight sum of its input values multiplied by their connection weights. For example, the value of node N_3 is $(1 \times N_1 + -1 \times N_2)$, where N_i is the current value of node i in the network. It then outputs that value only if it is greater than the unit's *threshold*, which in this case has been set globally to 0. Now suppose we initialize N_3 through N_5 to be zero, $N_1 = 0$, and $N_2 = 1$. Running the network one step causes N_3 to compute the value $1 \times 0 + -1 \times 1 = -1$, and N_4 to compute $-1 \times 0 + 1 \times 1 = 1$; note that N_5 would compute a 0 since all its inputs were initialized to 0. The problem is not solved yet, so we go a second step. N_3 and N_4 compute the same values as before, but N_5 now computes $1 \times 0 + 1 \times 1 = 1$, the correct answer for 0 XOR 1. Note that the input from N_3 to N_5 remained at 0, not the -1 actually computed by N_3, because -1 is less than the 0 threshold value established for the units; by convention, no matter what its threshold, a unit outputs 0 if it cannot reach it.

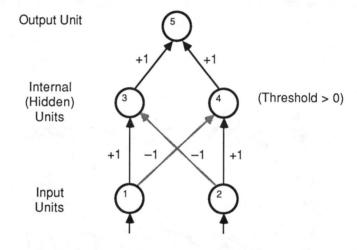

Figure 8–16. **A Connectionist Network to Compute the XOR Function**

Many generalizations have been made to our simple network model; most importantly, the function computed by a unit can be more complex than a simple summation. We will look at some of the issues and refinements in connectionist systems by examining their application to speech production, perception, and the sequential processing of traditional AI.

Applications to Speech Production

Perceiving and producing human-quality speech have been thorny problems for traditional AI research, but connectionist approaches have recently made progress in both areas. Since we shortchanged language generation in Chapter 4, we will consider here the problem of *speech production*, which at a low level requires converting a representation of a word in memory into a set of *phonemes*, or elementary sounds, to be passed on to a sound generation system. The two experiments we will examine also serve to illustrate the uses of *error propagation learning* and *feedback* in PDP systems.

For the XOR function from Figure 8-16, we used a simple three-level layered network in which the input was represented as a pattern of initial activation values placed on the input units, and the output was a similarly encoded pattern arriving on the output unit after a two-step parallel computation. We can generalize this model, known as a *feedforward network*, as shown in Figure 8-17. A theorem (whose proof is beyond the scope of this book) has shown that such a network needs only one level of hidden units between the input and output to have the basic computational power of a Turing Machine, which is equivalent to any serial computer.

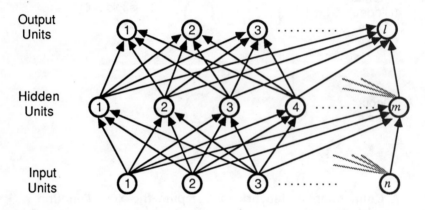

Figure 8–17. **A General Three-level Feedforward Network**

In his *NETalk* program, Terrence Sejnowski connected the output of such a network directly to a speech synthesizer that could translate phonemes into the appropriate waveforms to drive a speaker. The inputs were set to patterns for various words. However, unlike our XOR network, his was completely randomly connected at the start of the experiment: the weights on the links between levels 1 and 2 and 2 and 3 were randomly assigned. Naturally, on the first run, the output was a gibberish completely unrelated to the input string. However, by comparing the incorrect output values to the hand-calculated correct phonemes, an error signal could be computed for each output unit. This signal value measured the absolute degree to which the unit's final value was in error.

Using this measure, a *learning rule* called backward propagation error correction can be used to adjust the weights of the links between the levels by computing the error signals for the hidden and input units as well as the output units. If two connected units each committed relatively little error, their connection strength is increased; pairs in which both had gross discrepancies have their weights weakened. By repeating this procedure with thousands of word trials, the network reached a state of reasonable competence at pronouncing "ordinary" English words, including many that were *not* among its original training set. This happened because the averaging process induced by successive small adjustments in weight tended to fix the links according to the most common pronunciations of each syllable. Therefore, exceptions to general rules, such as foreign words and names, were learned very poorly; nevertheless, the experiment showed that simple multilayer networks could learn significant behavior patterns.

Gary Dell approached the speech production problem from a psychological viewpoint, and designed a network that did not learn but did produce output that contained the same sorts of errors that human speakers often make. These "slips of the tongue" include *lexical bias*, a tendency to make mistakes that result in real words rather than nonsense strings, and *phoneme repetition*, in which a phoneme used in one word may wrongly intrude on a different word spoken later in the sentence. For example, the phrase "deal back" could accidentally be pronounced as "deal *beak*," a nonsense phrase but one that still contains legitimate words (lexical bias) and features the duplication of the *æ* sound (phoneme repetition).

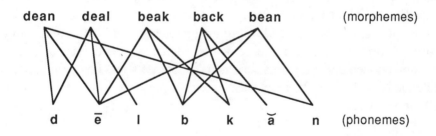

Figure 8–18. **A Speech-production Model**

Figure 8-18 shows a fragment of Dell's network. Its differences from NETalk include the use of two levels instead of three, *feedback* between the levels not present in simple feedforward models, and most importantly, *local representations* rather than the *distributed representations* favored by NETalk. Local nets are similar to semantic networks, where each node represented a distinct concept, whereas distributed nets represent each concept as a pattern of activation values over many units. The latter have the advantage of robustness, since the loss of one unit will not eliminate a crucial concept, but the former are easier to interpret and understand. In our example, a unit stands for either a morpheme (word) or a phoneme.

To utter a word, the corresponding morpheme node is given a standard initial activation. Link weights are all +1, and activation flows bidirectionally through them, the network being prewired so that each morpheme is connected to all the phonemes that compose it. After the network runs for a few cycles, the phoneme nodes with the highest values communicate with the motor system to produce the appropriate sounds. Suppose the network begins at rest, with all unit values equal to 0, and we want to say the word *deal*. We give its node a value of 1, which is propagated to the *d*, *e*, and *l* nodes, which also acquire values of 1. On the next step, all three phonemes feed their values back to *dean*, making it 4, as well as to all the other morphemes containing them. Therefore, *dean* becomes 2 and *beak* and *bean* become 1. As this continues, every morpheme and phoneme will be activated, but since the correct phonemes will gather the majority of the energy, the proper sounds will be produced.

Now suppose we activate *back*. A similar process will occur, but the network will start with residual values from the previous production run for some of the units (a constant decay rate ensures that units will not increase in value forever, and the most recently spoken word and phonemes are completely deactivated to prevent their continual repetition). If these residuals are large enough, they will unintendedly participate in the activation process. Lexical bias derives from the fact that over-activated phoneme nodes can only develop from continual feedback in loops with words at the morpheme level; illegal phoneme combinations cannot be sufficiently reinforced to create nonsense words. Phoneme repetition occurs when a very common phoneme that remains activated overcomes a less common phoneme in the intended word, since the repeated phoneme's presence in more morphemes creates more feedback for it.

Perceiving in Parallel

What would happen if we inverted Dell's speech production network and applied it to the problem of recognizing words in printed text? Instead of words feeding forward to phonemes and phonemes feeding back to words, we would have the situation diagrammed in Figure 8-19, where visual features activate letter nodes, which in turn activate word nodes. This three-level feedforward network, designed by David Rumelhart and James McClelland, is improved by adding representations for *local constraints* using the mechanism of *lateral inhibition*.

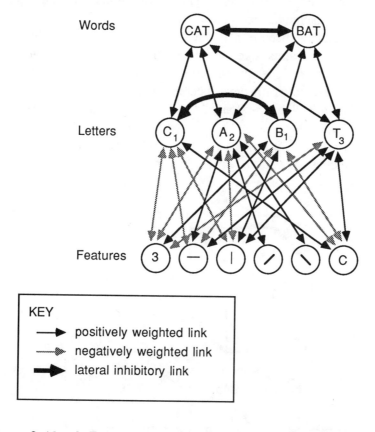

Figure 8–19. **A Fragment of an Interactive Constraint-satisfaction Model of Word Perception**

Suppose we activate the feature for a straight vertical line by placing a letter "T" in the visual input of such a system. Activation will spread forward to the *B* and *T* letter nodes, which will pass energy on to the *CAT* and *BAT* word nodes. Feedback will spread, as in the speech model, to enhance these initial steps and involve other units in the processing. We can think of the units as representing "competing hypotheses" about the nature of the input stimulus, each trying to acquire activation and increase its value so as to win out in the end. But unlike Dell's model, this one will not allow activation to increase unbounded. Some hypotheses are mutually inconsistent, such as those represented by the C_1 and B_1 nodes at the letter level: the perceived letter cannot be *both* an initial C and an initial B (the subscripted "1" refers to the first position in the whole word). This constraint is built into the system by a negatively weighted link between the competing units, analogous to the lateral inhibition found in the human nervous system.

Connectionist systems have been remarkable in illustrating the point that computing with many local constraints, like the lateral inhibition between letters and words in this model, can produce results that are also consistent with the implicit global constraints, such as two words never becoming simultaneously overactive. David Waltz and Jordan Pollack have extended these ideas in a complete system for sentence understanding, in which competing interpretations of ambiguous phrases gradually resolve their differences as the network relaxes into a steady state (with no units changing appreciably in value).

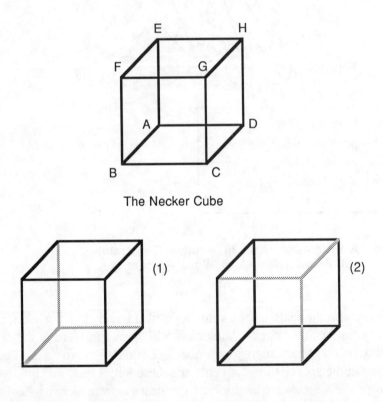

The Necker Cube

Figure 8–20. **Two Mutually Inconsistent Interpretations
of the Necker Cube**

Finally, a rather whimsical example of higher-level phenomena in vision as modelled by a connectionist network. Figure 8-20 should remind you of the famous *Necker Cube* illusion, which if stared at long enough seems to "flip" between the two orientations of corner G being closer to the viewer (1) and corner A being closer (2). Naturally, there are some local constraints between the positions of the corners that must be satisfied in each interpretation of the cube, and they can be modeled by a network using local representations, as shown in Figure 8-21 (due to Jerome Feldman). With a simple activation rule, the network will rapidly settle into the correct state if it starts completely at rest except for a tiny value in a single node on either side; if the two sides start with equal values, an inconsistent state will be reached. With a more complex rule that includes a decay factor, the model can be made to automatically shift interpretations back and forth over time, much as human beings seem to do after staring at the cube for some time.

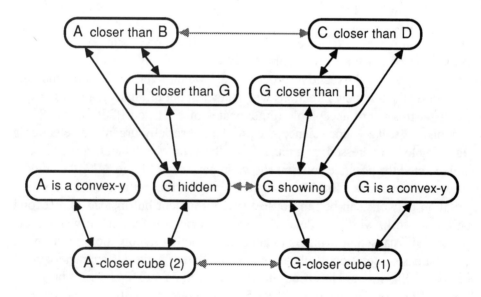

Figure 8–21. **A Simple Network to Model Interpretation of the Necker Cube**

The Problem of Sequential Processes

It is apparent that connectionist models, with their built-in learning methods, are powerful tools for perceptual operations like speech production, visual recognition, and many others not discussed here. It is no accident, then, that these are the tasks we intuitively associate with massively parallel processing and the tasks about which the most neurobiological knowledge has been accumulated. However, proponents of the PDP approach claim more for it than the ability to explain low-level perceptual processing in an elegant way; indeed, they suggest it as a general, natural, and simple model of computation that can be applied as well to cognitive tasks like planning and problem-solving, traditionally thought of as goal-oriented and sequential.

The common picture of a connectionist system is the one we depicted in discussing visual perception: a network of excitation and inhibition settles by relaxation into a stable state that satisfies all the relevant local constraints. Once there, it will not move until its inputs are revised or the normal entropy of the system jars it out of quiescence. As shown in part (a) of Figure 8-22, in which the input comes from and the output goes to an omnipresent "environment," such a system can respond well to stimuli but can not obviously initiate action on its own. It would seem that a higher-level executive process must watch over and control the networks, pointing them in new directions when they run out of inputs to process.

Of course, this is not acceptable to advocates of a unified PDP theory. Since connectionism is still a young science, the problem of serially-organized behavior is just beginning to be addressed, as it must. Rumelhart and McClelland have proposed and implemented the possible solution shown in part (b) of Figure 8-22: the "model of the world" network. In this dual-net system, the output of a standard interpretation network can be fed not to the environment but instead to a second simulation network, which models what *would* happen if the output went to the environment and caused new inputs to appear. Predicting hypothetical reactions in this way is a basic operation of planning and simulation activities characteristic of goal-oriented behavior, and has been shown promising in a PDP checkers program. Work now in progress is extending these ideas to cover many traditional AI concepts like frame-based knowledge representations and production rules.

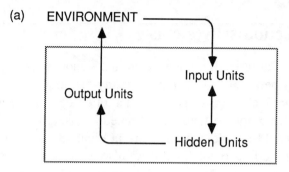

Perceptual Processing

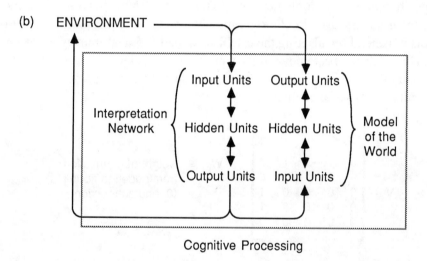

Cognitive Processing

Figure 8–22.   **Interpretation and Simulation with the "Model of the World" in a Connectionist System**

Programming Connectionist Systems

Looking at the models we have examined, it might seem like a chore to set up the data structures and programs necessary to simulate a many-processor network. However, the wonder of linear algebra lets us get around a lot of algorithm design if we represent the network as a square matrix of connection weights, as diagrammed in Figure 8-23 (derived from the XOR network in Figure 8-16). The link from N_i to N_j has weight $W_{i,j}$. So far, so good, but if we also represent the pattern current values of each unit in a vector V whose size is the number of nodes, we can calculate the total input to each unit by simply multiplying W by V, giving a new vector I. From I we can compute the output value of each node by simply applying the output function to each element of I. This WV=I simplification can remove much of the drudgery from PDP programming and aid our analysis of connectionist models in general by adapting the established mathematical framework of linear algebra. However, the best known matrix multiplication algorithms are not terribly efficient, and we still must compute each input to each unit separately—a fundamental limitation of serial computers.

$$W = \begin{bmatrix} 0 & 0 & -1 & -1 & 0 \\ 0 & 0 & 1 & 1 & 0 \\ 0 & 0 & 0 & 0 & 1 \\ 0 & 0 & 0 & 0 & 1 \\ 0 & 0 & 0 & 0 & 0 \end{bmatrix}$$

$W_{i,j}$ = weight of connection from node i to node j (0 if no connection)

Figure 8–23.   **A Matrix Representation of the XOR Network**

To get around this "von Neumann bottleneck" of serial processing and achieve the speeds necessary for intelligent computers, W. Daniel Hillis of Thinking Machines Corp. has designed the massively parallel *Connection Machine*, a computer with up to hundreds of thousands of tiny processors not unlike those found in PDP networks. Using a hypercube architecture in which each processor is connected to 16 neighbors, any unit in a 64K processor machine can send a message, such as an output value, to any other unit in at most 16 steps. With each processor having its own memory and computing in parallel with the others, the Connection Machine can perform tasks like NETalk many times faster than a DEC Vax minicomputer can simulate them. What is really exciting, however, is that comparisons with the human brain indicate that a Connection Machine of comparable power will be available well within our lifetimes.

To conclude this discussion of connectionism, let us keep in mind that PDP networks have many appealing similarities to the networks of neurons that compose the human and other brains. Positively-weighted links remind us of excitatory synaptic junctions, negative ones of inhibitory synapses, inputs of dendrites, outputs of axons, and threshold values of the axon hillock. However, there is more to the brain than ion channels and neurotransmitters. It is probably not a "hormone of intentionality" or some other exotic agent, but rather a large body of detail that is just not yet understood. Philosophically, connectionist models lie at the junction of artificial intelligence, cognitive psychology, and neurobiology; scientifically, they have some distance to go before they become accepted as the key to understanding intelligent behavior.

References

Firschein and Fischler's *Readings in Computer Vision: Issues, Problems, Principles, and Paradigms* gathers over 50 recent papers in vision, but the only real textbook in vision is Ballard and Brown's *Computer Vision*. The field's classic, Marr's posthumous *Vision* (the source for Figures 8-3 and 8-4) outlines not only an influential theory of early vision but also a metatheory of how all AI research should be done. Winston's AI text offers the clearest explanation of edge-detection and many aspects of higher-level visual processing; Tanimoto's *The Elements of Artificial Intelligence* is also strong on vision. Pinker's *Visual Cognition* presents a representative sample of psychological vision research.

The field of learning has been defined by two outstanding volumes by Michalski, Carbonell, and Mitchell, *Machine Learning* and *Machine Learning Volume II* The 38 detailed papers presented in these volumes are supplemented by the 77 short contributions to *Machine Learning: A Guide to Current Research*. Samuel's checkers program, EPAM, and version space are all well-documented by the *Handbook of AI*. For a detailed discussion of an attempt to go beyond the taxonomizing and special mechanisms common in learning research, see "Chunking in SOAR: The Anatomy of a General Learning Mechanism," and *Universal Subgoaling and Chunking*, both by Laird, Rosenbloom, and Newell. Frontier research in abstracting concepts and laws from data is discussed in *Scientific Discovery: Computational Explorations of the Creative Process* by Langley, Simon, Bradshaw, and Zytkow.

The new "bible" of connectionism and neural network models is the two-volume *Parallel Distributed Processing: Explorations in the Microstructure of Cognition* by Rumelhart and McClelland. Earlier but still very relevant work is covered in Hinton and Anderson's *Parallel Models of Associative Memory*. NETalk is covered in "Toward Memory-Based Reasoning" by Stanfill and Waltz, and Dell's speech-production model is discussed in his paper "Positive Feedback in Hierarchical Connectionist Models: Applications to Language Production." Hillis describes the Connection Machine and its uses in his 1985 ACM Doctoral Dissertation Award winning *The Connection Machine*.

APPENDIX 1:   BIBLIOGRAPHY

This bibliography is divided into six sections for convenience of reference: *AI Textbooks*, which includes books giving an academically-oriented overview of AI in general or of one particular aspect, such as expert systems or natural language processing; *Monographs*, which are non-textbooks on any AI-related topic, many of which present research results in highly specific areas; *Articles, Papers, and Technical Reports*, mostly proceedings papers and journal articles by AI researchers or other short pieces of interest; *Anthologies*, simply collections of articles, papers, and technical reports; *AI Languages*, books on Lisp, Prolog, OPS5, and other programming languages commonly used for AI work; and *Pascal and Programming*, which lists a few sources relevant to this book but not specifically to AI or its related fields.

Note that the sources listed here are a superset of those consulted in the preparation of this book, and that I have only read a small fraction of them myself. They are organized here to provide you with a representative listing of current research and practice in AI. After studying this book, you should be able to understand and benefit from the majority of the references cited here.

Finally, although I have tried to create a mix of publications on all fields of AI, the list is slanted towards knowledge representation, natural language processing, expert systems, heuristic search, and game playing. Vision, learning, and connectism are covered to a lesser extent, followed by areas like automatic programming, cognitive science, education, logic, planning, and robotics. Other criteria for my choices, though they certainly do not all describe each selection were accessibility, currency, and respect within the field.

AI Textbooks

Ballard, D. H. & C. Brown. *Computer Vision*. Englewood Cliffs, NJ: Prentice-Hall, 1982.

Banerji, R. B. *Artificial Intelligence: A Theoretical Approach*. Amsterdam: North Holland, 1980.

Barr, A., E. A. Feigenbaum, & P. R. Cohen. *The Handbook of Artificial Intelligence*, in 3 volumes. Los Altos, CA: William Kaufmann, 1981.

Bundy, A. *Artificial Inteligence: An Introductory Course*. Amsterdam: North Holland, 1978.

Chang, C-L. *Introduction to Artificial Intelligence Techniques*. New York: JMA, 1985.

Charniak, E. & D. McDermott. *Introduction to Artificial Intelligence*. Reading, MA: Addison-Wesley, 1985.

Charniak, E., C. K. Riesbeck, & D. V. McDermott. *Artificial Intelligence Programming*, 2nd edition. Hillsdale, NJ: Lawrence Erlbaum Associates, 1987.

Frenzel Jr., L. E. *Crash Course in Artificial Intelligence and Expert Systems*. Indianapolis, IN: Howard W. Sams, 1987.

Harris, M. D. *Introduction to Natural Language Processing*. Reston, VA: Reston, 1985.

Jackson Jr., P. C. *Introduction to Artificial Intelligence*, 2nd enlarged edition. New York: Dover, 1985.

Jackson, P. *Introduction to Expert Systems*. Wokingham, UK: Addison-Wesley, 1986.

Nilsson, N. J. *Principles of Artificial Intelligence*. Palo Alto, CA: Tioga, 1980.

Raphael, B. *The Thinking Computer*. San Francisco: W. H. Freeman, 1976.

Rich, E. *Artificial Intelligence*. New York: McGraw-Hill, 1983.

Schank, R. C. & C. K. Riesbeck. *Inside Computer Understanding: Five Programs Plus Miniatures*. Hillsdale, NJ: Lawrence Erlbaum Associates, 1981.

Shapiro, S. C. *Encyclopedia of Artificial Intelligence*. New York: Wiley, 1987.

Simons, G. L. *Introducing Artificial Intelligence*. New York: Wiley, 1985.

Stillings, N. A., M. H. Feinstein, J. L. Garfield, E. L. Rissland, D. A. Rosenbaum, S. E. Weisler, & L. Baker-Ward. *Cognitive Science: An Introduction*. Cambridge, MA: MIT Press, 1987.

Tanimoto, S. L. *The Elements of Artificial Intelligence: An Introduction Using LISP*. Rockville, MD: Computer Science Press, 1987.

Waterman, D. A. *A Guide to Expert Systems*. Reading, MA: Addison-Wesley, 1986.

Winograd, T. *Language as a Cognitive Process, Volume I: Syntax*. Reading, MA: Addison-Wesley, 1983.

Winston, P. H. *Artificial Intelligence*, 2nd edition. Reading, MA: Addison-Wesley, 1984.

Monographs

Alty, J. & M. Coombs. *Expert Systems: Concepts and Examples*. Manchester, UK: NCC Publications, 1984.

Anderson, J. R. *The Architecture of Cognition*. Cambridge, MA: Harvard University Press, 1983.

Baron, R. J. *The Cerebral Computer: An Introduction to the Computational Structure of the Human Brain*. Hillsdale, NJ: Lawrence Erlbaum Associates, 1987.

Barton, G. E., R. C. Berwick, & E. S. Ristad. *Computational Complexity and Natural Language*. Cambridge, MA: MIT Press, 1987.

Berwick, R. C. & A. S. Weinberg. *The Grammatical Basis of Linguistic Performance: Language Use and Acquisition*. Cambridge, MA: MIT Press, 1984.

Berwick, R. C. *The Acquisition of Syntactic Knowledge*. Cambridge, MA: MIT Press, 1985.

Bishop, P. *Fifth Generation Computers*. New York: Wiley, 1986.

Boden, M. A. *Artificial Intelligence and Natural Man*. New York: Basic Books, 1977.

Brown, D. & B. Chandrasekaran. *Design Problem Solving: Knowledge Structures and Control Strategies*. Los Altos, CA: Morgan Kaufmann (Pitman), 1986.

Buchanan, B. G. & E. H. Shortliffe. *Rule-Based Expert Systems: The MYCIN Experiments of the Stanford Heuristic Programming Project*. Reading, MA: Addison-Wesley, 1984.

Budd, T. *Little Smalltalk*. Reading, MA: Addison-Wesley, 1987.

Chomsky, N. *Aspects of the Theory of Syntax*. Cambridge, MA: MIT Press, 1965.

Chomsky, N. *Lectures on Government and Binding*. Dordrecht, Holland: Floris Publications, 1981.

Chomsky, N. *Rules and Representations*. New York: Columbia University Press, 1980.

Chomsky, N. *Syntactic Structures*. The Hague: Mouton, 1957.

Chorfas, D. N. *Applying Expert Systems in Business*. New York: McGraw-Hill, 1987.

Clancey, W. *Knowledge-Based Tutoring: The GUIDON Program*. Cambridge, MA: MIT Press, 1986.

Cohen, P. R. *Heuristic Reasoning About Uncertainty: An Artificial Intelligence Approach*. Los Altos, CA: Morgan Kaufmann (Pitman), 1985.

Davis, E. *Representing and Acquiring Geographic Knowledge*. Los Altos, CA: Morgan Kaufmann (Pitman), 1986.

De Groot, A. D. *Thought and Choice in Chess*. The Hague: Mouton, 1965.

Dreyfus, H. L. *What Computers Can't Do*, 2nd edition. New York: Harper and Row, 1979.

Ebeling, C. *All the Right Moves: A VLSI Architecture for Chess*. Cambridge, MA: MIT Press, 1986.

Ennals, R. *Artificial Intelligence: Applications to Logical Reasoning and Historical Research*. New York: Wiley, 1985.

Ernst, G. & A. Newell. *GPS: A Case Study in Generality and Problem Solving*, ACM Monograph Series. New York: Academic Press, 1969.

Fahlman, S. E. *NETL: A System for Representing and Using Real-World Knowledge*. Cambridge, MA: MIT Press, 1979.

Feigenbaum, E. A. & McCorduck, P. *The Fifth Generation*. Reading, MA: Addison-Wesley, 1983.

Fischler, M. A. & O. Firschein. *Intelligence: The Eye, the Brain, and the Computer*. Reading, MA: Addison-Wesley, 1987.

Fogel, L., A. Owens, & M. Walsh. *Artificial Intelligence Through Simulated Evolution*. New York: John Wiley & Sons, 1966.

Forsyth, R. & C. Naylor. *The Hitch-Hiker's Guide to Artificial Intelligence*. London: Chapman and Hall/Methuen, 1985.

Forsyth, R. & R. Rada. *Machine Learning: Applications in Expert Systems and Information Retrieval*. New York: Wiley, 1986.

Gardner, H. *The Mind's New Science: A History of the Cognitive Revolution*. New York: Basic Books, 1985.

Gazdar, G., E. Klein, G. K. Pullum, & I. Sag. *Generalized Phrase Structure Grammar*. New York: Blackwell, 1985.

Genesereth, M. R. & N. J. Nilsson. *The Logical Foundations of Artificial Intelligence*. Los Altos, CA: Morgan Kaufmann, 1987.

Gevarter, W. *Artificial Intelligence, Expert Systems, Computer Vision, and Natural Language Processing*. Park Ridge, NJ: Noyes Publications, 1984.

Gloess, P. Y. *Understanding Artificial Intelligence*. New York: Alfred, 1981.

Graham, N. *Artificial Intelligence, Making Machines "Think"*. New York: Tab, 1979.

Harmon, P. & D. King. *Expert Systems: Artificial Intelligence in Business*. New York: Wiley, 1985.

Harris, L. R. & D. B. Davis. *Artificial Intelligence Enters the Marketplace*. New York: Bantam, 1986.

Hart, A. *Knowledge Acquisition for Expert Systems*. New York: McGraw-Hill, 1986.

Hartnell, T. *Exploring Artificial Intelligence on Your Personal Computer*. New York: Bantam, 1985.

Haugeland, J. *Artificial Intelligence: The Very Idea*. Cambridge, MA: MIT Press, 1985.

Hillis, W. D. *The Connection Machine*. Cambridge, MA: MIT Press, 1985.

Hofstadter, D. R. *Gödel, Escher, Bach: An Eternal Golden Braid*. New York: Vintage, 1980.

Holding, D. H. *The Psychology of Chess Skill*. Hillsdale, NJ: Lawrence Erlbaum Associates, 1985.

Horn, B. K. P. *Robot Vision*. New York: McGraw-Hill, 1984.

Hunt, V. D. *Artificial Intelligence and Expert Systems Sourcebook*. London: Chapman and Hall, 1986.

Hutchins, W. J. *Machine Tranlsation: Past, Present, Future*. New York: Wiley, 1986.

Jenkins, R. A. *Supercomputers of Today and Tomorrow: The Parallel Processing Revolution*. New York: Tab, 1986.

Johnson, W. L. *Intention-Based Diagnosis of Errors in Novice Programs*. Los Altos, CA: Mogan Kaufmann (Pitman), 1986.

Kearsley, G. *AI and Instruction*. Reading, MA: Addison-Wesley, 1987.

Keravnou, E. T. & L. Johnson. *Expert Systems: A Case Study in Fault Diagnosis*. New York: McGraw-Hill, 1986.

Konolige, K. *A Deduction Model of Belief*. Los Altos, CA: Morgan Kaufmann (Pitman), 1987.

Korf, R. *Learning to Solve Problems by Searching for Macro-Operators.* Los Altos, CA: Morgan Kaufmann (Pitman), 1985.

Kosslyn, S. M. *Image and Mind.* Cambridge, MA: Harvard University Press, 1980.

Krutch, J. *Experiments in Artificial Intelligence.* Indianapolis, IN: Howard W. Sams, 1981.

Kuhn, T. S. *The Structure of Scientific Revolutions.* Chicago: University of Chicago Press, 1962.

Ladd, S. *The Computer and the Brain: Beyond the Fifth Generation.* Toronto: Bantam/The Red Feather Press, 1986.

Laird, J., P. Rosenbloom, & A. Newell. *Universal Subgoaling and Chunking: The Automatic Generation and Learning of Goal Hierarchies.* Boston: Kluwer, 1986.

Langley, P., H. A. Simon, G. L. Bradshaw, & J. M Zytkow. *Scientific Discovery: Computational Explorations of the Creative Process.* Cambridge, MA: MIT Press, 1987.

Levine, R., D. E. Drang, & B. Edelson. *A Comprehensive Guide to AI and Expert Systems.* New York: McGraw-Hill, 1986.

Levy, D. *The Joy of Computer Chess.* Englewood Cliffs, NJ: Prentice-Hall, 1984.

Marcus, M. *A Theory of Syntactic Recognition for Natural Language.* Cambridge, MA: MIT Press, 1980.

Marr, D. *Vision.* New York: W. H. Freeman, 1982.

McCorduck, P. *Machines Who Think.* San Francisco: W. H. Freeman, 1979.

Mellish, C. S. *Computer Interpretation of Natural Language Descriptions.* New York: Wiley, 1984.

Michie, D. *On Machine Intelligence,* 2nd edition. New York: Wiley, 1986.

Miller, P. L. *A Critiquing Approach to Expert Computer Advice: ATTENDING.* Los Altos, CA: Morgan Kaufmann (Pitman), 1984.

Minsky, M. & S. Papert. *Perceptrons: An Introduction to Computational Geometry.* Cambridge, MA: MIT Press, 1969.

Minsky, M. *The Society of Mind.* New York: Simon & Schuster, 1986.

Mischkoff, H. C. *Understanding Artificial Intelligence.* Indianapolis, IN: Sams, 1985.

Moto-Oka, T. & M. Kitsuregawa. *The Fifth Generation Computer*. New York: Wiley, 1985.

Naylor, C. *Build Your Own Expert System*. New York: Wiley, 1985.

Negoita, C. *Expert Systems and Fuzzy Systems*. Menlo Park, CA: Benjamin/Cummings, 1985.

Newborn, M. *Computer Chess*. New York: Academic Press, 1975.

Newell, A. & H. A. Simon. *Human Problem Solving*. Englewood Cliffs, NJ: Prentice-Hall, 1972.

Palay, A. J. *Searching with Probabilities*. Los Altos, CA: Morgan Kaufmann (Pitman), 1985.

Papert, S. *Mindstorms*. New York: Basic Books, 1981.

Partridge, D. *Artificial Intelligence: Applications in the Future of Software Engineering*. New York: Wiley, 1986.

Pearl, J. *Heuristics: Intelligent Search Strategies for Computer Problem Solving*. Reading, MA: Addison-Wesley, 1984.

Peat, F. D. *Artificial Intelligence: How Machines Think*. New York: Baen, 1985.

Politakis, P. *Empirical Analysis for Expert Systems*. Los Altos, CA: Morgan Kaufmann (Pitman), 1985.

Pylyshyn, Z. W. *Computation and Cognition: Toward a Foundation for Cognitive Science*. Cambridge, MA: MIT Press, 1984.

Quine, W. V. O. *Word and Object*. Cambridge, MA: MIT Press, 1960.

Rose, F. *Into the Heart of the Mind: An American Quest for Artificial Intelligence*. New York: Harper & Row, 1984.

Rosenberg, J. M. *Dictionary of Artificial Intelligence and Robotics*. New York: Wiley, 1986.

Rosenblatt, F. *Principles of Neurodynamics*. New York: Spartan Books, 1962.

Rumelhart, D. E. & J. L. McClelland. *Parallel Distributed Processing: Explorations in the Microstructures of Cognition*, in 2 volumes. Cambridge, MA: MIT Press, 1986.

Sager, N. *Natural Language Information Processing*. New York: Addison-Wesley, 1981.

Sawyer, B. & D. Foster. *Programming Expert Systems in Modula-2*. New York: Wiley, 1986.

Sawyer, B. & D. Foster. *Programming Expert Systems in Pascal.* New York: Wiley, 1986.

Schank, R. C. & R. P. Abelson. *Scripts, Plans, Goals, and Understanding.* Hillsdale, NJ: Lawrence Erlbaum Associates, 1977.

Schank, R. C. *Dynamic Memory: A Theory of Learning in Computers and People.* Cambridge, UK: Cambridge University Press, 1982.

Schank, R. C. *Explanation Patterns: Understanding Mechanically and Creatively.* Hillsdale, NJ: Lawrence Erlbaum Associates, 1986.

Schank, R. C. with P. Childers. *The Cognitive Computer: On Language, Learning, and Artificial Intelligence.* Reading, MA: Addison Wesley, 1984.

Schildt, H. *Artificial Intelligence Using C: The C Programmer's Guide to AI Techniques.* Berkeley, CA: Osborne McGraw-Hill, 1987.

Searle, J. R. *Intentionality: An Essay in the Philosophy of Mind.* Cambridge, UK: Cambridge University Press, 1983.

Sell, P. S. *Expert Systems: A Practical Introduction.* New York: Wiley, 1985.

Shafer, D. *Artificial Intelligence Programming on the Macintosh.* Indianapolis, IN: Howard W. Sams, 1986.

Shapiro, S. C. *Techniques of Artificial Intelligence.* New York: Van Nostrand, 1979.

Shirai, Y. & J-I. Tsujii. *Artificial Intelligence: Concepts, Techniques, and Applications.* New York: Wiley, 1985.

Shortliffe, E. H. & B. G. Buchanan. *Computer-based Medical Consultations: MYCIN.* New York: American Elsevier, 1976.

Simon, H. A. *The Sciences of the Artificial,* 2nd edition. Cambridge, MA: MIT Press, 1982.

Simons, G. L. *Expert Systems and Micros.* New York: Wiley, 1986.

Simons, G. L. *Is Man a Robot?* New York: Wiley, 1986.

Springer, S. P. & G. Deutsch. *Left Brain, Right Brain,* revised edition. New York: W. H. Freeman, 1985.

Steels, L. & J. A. Campbell. *Progress in Artificial Intelligence.* New York: Wiley, 1985.

Stevens, L. *Artificial Intelligence, the Search for the Perfect Machine.* Hasbrouck Heights, NJ: Hayden, 1985.

Thompson, B. & W. Thompson. *Designing and Implementing Your Own Expert System*. New York: McGraw-Hill, 1985.

Tomita, M. *Efficient Parsing for Natural Language: A Fast Algorithm for Practical Systems*. Boston: Kluwer, 1986.

Torrance, S. *The Mind and the Machine: Philosophical Aspects of Artificial Intelligence*. New York: Wiley, 1984.

Touretzky, D. *The Mathematics of Inheritance Systems*. Los Altos, CA: Morgan Kaufmann (Pitman), 1986.

Townsend, C. & D. Foucht. *Designing and Programming Personal Expert Systems*. New York: Tab, 1986.

Uhr, L. *Parallel Multi-Computers and Artificial Intelligence*. New York: Wiley, 1986.

Van Horn, M. *Understanding Expert Systems*. New York: Bantam, 1986.

Von Neumann, J. *The Computer and the Brain*. New Haven, CT: Yale University Press, 1958.

Wallace, M. *Communicating with Databases in Natural Language*. New York: Wiley, 1984.

Weiss, S. M. & C. A. Kulikowski. *A Practical Guide to Designing Expert Systems*. New York: Rowman & Allanheld, 1984.

Weizenbaum, J. *Computer Power and Human Reason*. San Francisco: W. H. Freeman, 1976.

Wenger, E. *Artificial Intelligence and Tutoring Systems: Computational Approaches to the Communication of Knowledge*. Los Altos, CA: Morgan Kaufmann, 1987.

Wertz, H. *Automatic Correction & Improvement of Programs*. New York: Wiley, 1986.

Whitehead, A. N. & B. Russell. *Principia Mathematica*, in 2 volumes. Cambridge, UK: Cambridge University Press, 1925.

Wilensky, R. *Planning and Understanding*. Reading, MA: Addison-Wesley, 1983.

Williamson, M. *Artificial Intelligence for Microcomputers: The Guide for Business Decisionmakers*. New York: Brady, 1985.

Winograd, T. & F. Flores. *Understanding Computers and Cognition*. Norwood, NJ: Ablex, 1985.

Articles, Papers, and Technical Reports

Aho, A. V. "Indexed Grammars: An Extension of the Context-free Grammars," in *J. ACM*, vol. 15, 1968, pp. 647-671.

Aikings, J. S., J. C. Kunz, & E. H. Shortliffe. "PUFF: An Expert System for Interpretation of Pulmonary Function Data," in *Computers and Biomedical Research*, vol. 16, 1983, pp. 199-208.

Allen, J. F. "Toward a General Theory of Action and Time," in *Artificial Intelligence*, vol. 23, 1984, pp. 123-154.

Alvarado, S., M. Dyer, & M. Flowers. "Editorial Comprehension in OpEd Through Argument Units," in *Proc. AAAI*, 1986, pp. 250-256.

Anderson, J. R. "Knowledge Compilation: The General Learning Mechanism" (in Michalski, Carbonell, & Mitchell, *II*, 1986, pp. 289-310).

Anderson, J. R. & B. J. Reiser. "The LISP Tutor," in *BYTE*, vol. 10, no. 4, 1985, pp. 159-175.

Apte, C. & S. J. Hong. "Using Qualitative Reasoning to Understand Financial Arithmetic," in *Proc. AAAI*, 1986, pp. 942-948.

Baas, L. & J. R. Bourne. "A Rule-Based Microcomputer System for Electroencephalogram Evaluation," in *IEEE Trans. on Biomedical Engineering*, vol. BME-31, no. 10, 1984.

Bachant, J. & J. McDermott. "R1 Revisited: Four Years in the Trenches," in *AI Magazine*, vol. 5, no. 3, 1984.

Ballard, B. W. "The *-Minimax Search Procedure for Trees Containing Chance Nodes," in *Artificial Intelligence*, vol. 21, 1983, pp. 327-350.

Ballard, D. H. "Vision," in *BYTE*, vol. 10, no. 4, 1985, pp. 245-261.

Bar-Hillel, Y. "A Demonstration of the Nonfeasibility of Fully Automatic High Quality Translation" (in Alt, 1960, pp. 158-163).

Barber, G. R. "Lisp vs. C for Implementing Expert Systems," in *AI Expert*, vol. 2, no. 2, 1987, pp. 28-31.

Barton Jr., G. E. *Toward a Principle-Based Parser*. AI Memo no. AIM-788, MIT, 1984.

Baudet, G. M. "On the Branching Factor of the Alpha-Beta Pruning Algorithm," in *Artificial Intelligence*, vol. 10, 1978.

Berliner, H. "The 1985 Fredkin Competition" and "Hitech Wins North America Computer Chess Championship," in *ACM SIGART Newsletter*, no. 96, 1986, pp. 22-28.

Berliner, H. "The B* Tree Search Algorithm: A Best-First Proof Procedure," in *Artificial Intelligence*, vol. 12, 1979, pp. 23-40 (reprinted in Pearl, 1983).

Berliner, H. & C. Ebeling. "The SUPREM Architecture: A New Intelligent Paradigm," in *Artificial Intelligence*, vol. 28, 1986, pp. 3-8.

Berliner, H. & M. Campbell. "Using Chunking to Solve Chess Pawn Endgames," in *Artificial Intelligence*, vol. 23, 1984, pp. 97-120.

Bernstein, A., et al. "A Chess-Playing Program for the IBM 704 Computer," in *Proc. West. Joint Computer Conf.*, 1958, pp. 157-159.

Bhattacharya, S. & A. Bagchi. "Making Best Use of Available Memory When Searching Game Trees," in *Proc. AAAI*, 1986, pp. 163-167.

Blank, D. M. *Creativity : Built by Bisociation or Variations on a Theme*. Unpublished paper, 1986.

Bobrow, D. G. "Natural Language Input for a Computer Problem-Solving System" (in Minsky, 1968, pp. 135-215).

Bobrow, D. G. & T. Winograd. "An Overview of KRL, a Knowledge Representation Language," in *Cognitive Science*, vol. 1, 1977, pp. 3-46 (reprinted in Brachman & Levesque, 1985, pp. 263-286).

Bock, P. "The Emergence of Artificial Intelligence: Learning to Learn," in *AI Magazine*, vol. 6, no. 3, 1985, pp. 180-190.

Boley, H. "Artificial Intelligence Languages and Machines," in *Technology and Science of Informatics*, vol. 2, no. 3, 1983.

Bourne, D. A. "CML: A Meta-Interpreter for Manufacturing," in *AI Magazine*, vol. 7, no. 4, 1986, pp. 86-96.

Brachman, R. J. "'I Lied About the Trees' (or, Defaults and Definitions in Knowledge Representation)," in *AI Magazine*, vol. 6, no. 3, 1985.

Brachman, R. J. "On the Epistemological Status of Semantic Networks" (in Brachman & Levesque, 1985, pp. 191-216).

Brachman, R. J. "What IS-A Is and Isn't: An Analysis of Taxonomic Links in Semantic Networks," in *IEEE Computer*, vol. 16, no. 10, 1983, pp. 30-36.

Brachman, R. J. "What's in a Concept: Structural Foundations for Semantic Networks," in *Int'l. J. of Man-Machine Studies*, vol. 9, no. 2, 1977, pp. 127-152.

Brady, M. "Artificial Intelligence and Robotics," in *Artificial Intelligence*, vol. 26, 1985, pp. 79-121.

Bratko, I. & M. Gams. "Error Analysis of the Minimax Principle" (in Clarke, 1982, pp. 1-15).

Buchanan, B. G. & E. Feigenbaum. "DENDRAL and Meta-DENDRAL: Their Applications Dimension," in *Artificial Intelligence*, vol. 11, 1978.

Buchanan, B. G. & R. O. Duda. "Principles of Rule-Based Expert Systems," in *Advances In Computers*, vol. 22, 1983.

Burton, R. R. & W. A. Woods. "A Compiling System for Augmented Transition Networks," in *Proc. 6th Int'l. Conf. on Comp. Ling*, 1976.

Burton, R. R. *Semantic Grammar: An Engineering Technique for Constructing Natural Language Understanding Systems*. BBN Report no. 3453 (ICAI no. 3), Bolt, Beranek, and Newman, 1976.

Bylander, T. & S. Mittal. "CRSL: A Language for Classificatory Problem Solving and Uncertainty Handling," in *AI Magazine*, vol. 7, no. 3, 1986, pp. 66-77.

Campbell, A. N., V. F. Hollister, R. O. Duda, & P. E. Hart. "Recognition of a Hidden Mineral Deposit by an Artificial Intelligence Program," in *Science*, vol. 217, no. 3, 1982, pp. 927-929.

Carroll, J. M. & J. McKendree. "Interface Design Issues for Advice-Giving Expert Systems," in *Commun. ACM*, vol.30, no. 1, 1987, pp. 14-31.

Chabris, C. F. "Computer Chess," in *START*, vol. 2, no. 2, 1987 (in press).

Chabris, C. F. "How to Design a Knowledge Base," appendix to *Expert Opinion* user manual. San Francisco: Antic Publishing, 1986.

Chabris, C. F. "The AI Apprentice: Explore Expert Systems with XLisp," in *START*, vol. 1, no. 2, 1986, pp. 22-31.

Chabris, C. F. *A Framework for Solving Problems*. Unpublished paper, 1986.

Chabris, C. F. *Approaches to Expertise*. Unpublished paper, 1987.

Chakrabarti, P. P., S. Ghose, & S. C. Desarkar. "Heuristic Search Through Islands," in *Artificial Intelligence*, vol. 29, 1986, pp. 339-347.

Charniak, E. "A Common Representation for Problem-Solving and Language-Comprehension Information," in *Artificial Intelligence*, vol. 16, 1981, pp. 225-255.

Charniak, E. "On the Use of Framed Knowledge in Language Comprehension," in *Artificial Intelligence*, vol. 11, 1978, pp. 225-265.

Charniak, E. "The Bayesian Basis of Common Sense Medical Diagnosis," in *Proc. AAAI*, 1983, pp. 70-73.

Chen, J. *A Computer Model of the Lateralization Process in Humans: An Examination from an Artificial Intelligence Perspective.* Unpublished paper, 1987.

Chen, J. *NETL and the Connection Machine: New Wave Parallel Processing.* Unpublished paper, 1986.

Chomsky, N. "Three Models for the Description of Language," in *IEEE Trans. on Information Theory*, vol. 2, 1956, pp. 113-124.

Christensen, J. & R. Korf. "A Unified Theory of Heuristic Evaluation Functions and its Application to Learning," in *Proc. AAAI*, 1986, pp. 148-152.

Clancey, W. J. "From Guidon to Neomycin and Heracles in Twenty Short Lessons," in *AI Magazine*, vol. 7, no. 3, 1986, pp. 40-60.

Clancey, W. J. "Heuristic Classification," in *Artificial Intelligence*, vol. 27, 1985, pp. 289-350.

Clancey, W. J. "The Epistemology of a Rule-Based Expert System -- A Framework for Explanation," in *Artificial Intelligence*, vol. 20, 1983.

Cohen, D. "Automatic Compilation of Logical Specifications into Efficient Programs," in *Proc. AAAI*, 1986, pp. 21-25.

Cohen, P., A. Davis, D. Day, M. Greenberg, R. Kjeldsen, S. Lander, & C. Loiselle. "Representativeness and Uncertainty in Classification Systems," in *AI Magazine*, vol. 6, no. 3, 1985, pp. 136-149.

Collins, A. & E. F. Loftus. "A Spreading-Activation Theory of Semantic Processing," in *Psychological Review*, vol. 82, no. 6, 1975, pp. 407-428.

Cooke, S., C. Hafner, T. McCarty, M. Meldman, M. Peterson, J. Sprowl, N. Sridharan, & D. A. Waterman. "The Applications of Artificial Intelligence to Law: A Survey of Six Current Projects," in *Proc. AFIPS*, vol. 50, 1981.

Cullingford, R. E. *Script Application: Computer Understanding of Newspaper Stories.* Computer Science Research Report no. 116, Yale University, 1978.

Darwish, N. M. "A Quantitative Analysis of the Alpha-Beta Pruning Algorithm," in *Artificial Intelligence*, vol. 21, 1983, pp. 405-433.

Davis, R. "Diagnostic Reasoning Based on Structure and Behavior," in *Artificial Intelligence*, vol. 24, 1984 (reprinted in Bobrow, 1985, pp. 347-410).

Davis, R. "Meta-rules: Reasoning About Control," in *Artificial Intelligence*, vol. 15, 1980, pp. 179-222.

Davis, R. "Teiresias: Applications of Meta-level Knowledge" (in Davis & Lenat, 1982).

Davis, R. & B. Buchanan. "Meta-Level Knowledge: Overview and Applications," in *Proc. IJCAI*, 1977, pp. 920-927 (reprinted in Brachman & Levesque, 1985, pp. 389-397).

Davis, R. & R. G. Smith. "Negotiation as a Metaphor for Distributed Problem Solving," in *Artificial Intelligence*, vol. 20, 1983, pp. 63-109.

Davis, R., B. Buchanan, & E. Shortliffe. "Production Rules as a Representation for a Knowledge-Based Consultation Program," in *Artificial Intelligence*, vol. 8, 1977, pp. 15-45 (reprinted in Brachman & Levesque, 1985, pp. 371-388).

Davis, R., H. Austin, I. Carlbom, B. Frawley, P. Pruchnik, R. Sneiderman, & J. A. Gilreath. "The Dipmeter Advisor: Interpretation of Geologic Signals," in *Proc. IJCAI*, 1981, pp. 846-849.

Davis. R. "Expert Systems: Where are we? And where do we go from here?" in *AI Magazine*, vol. 3, no. 1, 1982, pp. 3-22.

Deering, M. F. "Architectures for AI," in *BYTE*, vol. 10, no. 4, 1985, pp. 193-206.

DeKleer, J. "Reasoning About Multiple Faults," in *Proc. AAAI*, 1986, pp. 132-139.

Dell, S. "Positive Feedback in Hierarchical Connectionist Models: Applications to Language Production," in *Cognitive Science*, vol. 9, 1985, pp. 3-23.

Doyle, J. "A Glimpse of Truth-Maintenance" (in Winston & Brown, 1979, pp. 119-135).

Doyle, J. "The Ins and Outs of Reason Maintenance," in *Proc. IJCAI*, 1983, pp. 349-351.

Dreyfus, H. *Alchemy and Artificial Intelligence*. Rand Corporation Paper P3244 (AD 625 179), 1965.

Dreyfus, H. L. "From Micro-Worlds to Knowledge Representation: AI at an Impasse" (in Haugeland, 1981, pp. 161-204).

Dreyfus, H. L. & S. E. Dreyfus. "From Socrates to Expert Sytstems: The Limits of Calculative Rationality," in *Technology In Society*, vol. 6, 1984, pp. 217-233.

Duda, R. O., J. G. Gaschnig, & P. E. Hart. "Model Design in the Prospector Consultant System for Mineral Exploration" (in Michie, 1980).

Duda, R. O., P. E. Hart, & G. L. Sutherland. "Semantic Network Representations in Rule-based Inference Systems" (in Hayes-Roth & Waterman, 1978).

Dym, C. L. & S. Mittal. "Knowledge Acquisition from Multiple Experts," in *AI Magazine*, vol. 6, no. 2, 1985, pp. 32-36.

Earley, J. "An Efficient Context-Free Parsing Algorithm," in *Commun. ACM*, vol. 13, 1970, pp. 94-102 (reprinted in Grosz, Sparck Jones, & Webber, 1986, pp. 25-34).

Edelson, T. "Can a System be Intelligent if it Never Gives a Damn," in *Proc. AAAI*, 1986, pp. 298-302.

Edwards, D. & T. Hart. *The α–β Heuristic*. AI Memo no. 30, MIT, 1963.

Elliot, R. J. & M. E. Lesk. "Route Finding in Street Maps by Computers and People," in *Proc. AAAI*, 1980, pp. 258-261.

Engelmore, R. & T. Allan. "Structure and Function of the Crysalis System," in *Proc. IJCAI*, 1979.

Epstein, S. A. "RiTSE: The Reactor Trip Simulation Environment," in *ACM SIGART Newsletter*, no. 97, 1986, pp. 23-24.

Ernst, G. "Sufficient Conditions for the Success of GPS," in *J. ACM*, vol. 16, no. 4, 1969, pp. 517-533.

Fain, J., F. Hayes-Roth, H. Sowizral, & D. Waterman. *Programming Examples in ROSIE*, Technical Report N-1646-ARPA, Rand Corporation, 1981.

Feigenbaum, E. A. "The Art of Artificial Intelligence: Themes and Case Studies of Knowledge Engineering," in *Proc. IJCAI*, 1977, pp. 1014-1029.

Feldman, J. A. "Connections," in *BYTE*, vol. 10, no. 4, 1985, pp. 277-284.

Fenanzo Jr., A. J. "Darwinian Evolution as a Paradigm for AI Research," in *ACM SIGART Newsletter*, no. 97, 1986, pp. 22-23.

Findler, N. V. "Air-Traffic Control: A Challenge for Artificial Intelligence," in *AI Expert*, vol. 2, no. 1, 1987, pp. 59-66.

Firdman, H. E. "Components of AI Systems," in *AI Expert*, vol. 1, no. 1, 1986, pp. 81-85.

Fischler, M. A. & O. Firschein. "Intelligence & The Computer: The Central Role of Representation," in *AI Expert*, vol. 1, no. 4, 1986, pp. 43-49.

Fisher, E. L. "An AI-based Methodology for Factory Design," in *AI Magazine*, vol. 7, no. 4, 1986, pp. 72-85.

Forgy, C. L. "Rete: A Fast Algorithm for the Many Pattern/Many Object Pattern Match Problem," in *Artificial Intelligence*, vol. 19, 1982.

Forgy, C. L. & S. J. Shepard. "Rete: A Fast Match Algorithm," in *AI Expert*, vol. 2, no. 1, 1987, pp. 34-40.

Freiling, M., J. Alexander, S. Messick, S. Rehfuss, & S. Shulman. "Starting a Knowledge Engineering Project: A Step-by-Step Approach," in *AI Magazine*, vol. 6, no. 3, 1985, pp. 150-164.

Freedman, R. S. & R. P. Frail. "OPGEN: The Evolution of an Expert System for Process Planning," in *AI Magazine*, vol. 7, no. 5, 1986, pp. 58-70.

Frey, P. W. "A Bit-Mapped Classifier," in *BYTE*, vol. 11, no. 12, 1986, pp. 161-172.

Gazdar, G. *Applicability of Indexed Grammars to Natural Languages*. Center for the Study of Language and Information Report no. CSLI-85-34, Stanford University, 1985.

Gelertner, H. "Empirical Explorations of SYNCHEM," in *Science*, vol. 197, 1977, pp. 1041-1049.

Genesereth, M. R. "An Overview of Meta-level Architecture," in *Proc. AAAI*, 1983, pp. 119-124.

Gillogly, J. L. "The Technology Chess Program," in *Artificial Intelligence*, vol. 3, 1972.

Gordon, J. & E. H. Shortliffe. "A Method for Managing Evidential Reasoning in a Hierarchical Hypothesis Space," in *Artificial Intelligence*, vol. 26, 1985, pp. 323-357.

Gray, N. A. B. "Applications of Artificial Intelligence for Organic Chemistry: Analysis of C-13 Spectra," in *Artificial Intelligence*, vol. 22, 1984, pp. 1-21.

Greenblatt, R., et al. "The Greenblatt Chess Program," in *Proc. AFIPS Fall Joint Computer Conf.*, 1967, pp 801-810.

Griesmer, J. H., S. J. Hong, M. Karnaugh, J. K. Kastner, M. I. Schor, R. L. Ennis, D. A. Klein, K. R. Milliken, & H. M. Van Woerkom. "YES/MVS: A Continuous Real Time Expert System," in *Proc. AAAI*, 1984.

Grosz, B. & C. L. Sidner. *The Structures of Discourse Structure*. Center for the Study of Language and Information Report no. CSLI-85-39, Stanford University, 1985.

Haas, N. & G. G. Hendrix. "Learning by Being Told: Acquiring Knowledge for Information Management" (in Michalski, Carbonell, & Mitchell, 1983, pp. 405-427).

Hall, R. "Learning by Failing to Explain," in *Proc. AAAI*, 1986, pp. 568-572.

Hall, R. P. & D. F. Kibler. "Differing Methodological Perspectives in Artificial Intelligence Research," in *AI Magazine*, vol. 6, no 3, 1985, pp. 166-178.

Hammond, K. "CHEF: A Model of Case-Based Planning," in *Proc. AAAI*, 1986, pp. 267-271.

Harris, L. R. "A High Performance Natural Language Processor for Data Base Query," in *ACM SIGART Newsletter*, no. 61, 1977.

Harris, L. R. "Experience with INTELLECT: Artificial Intelligence Technology Transfer," in *AI Magazine*, vol. 5, no. 2, 1984.

Harris, L. R. "The Heuristic Search Under Conditions of Error," in *Artificial Intelligence*, vol. 5, 1974, pp. 217-234.

Hart, P. E., A. Barzilay, & R. O. Duda. "Qualitative Reasoning for Financial Assessments," in *AI Magazine*, vol. 7, no. 1, 1986, pp. 62-68.

Hart, P. E., R. O. Duda, & M. T. Einaudi. "PROSPECTOR -- A Computer-based Consultation System for Mineral Exploration," in *Mathematical Geology*, vol. 10, no. 5, 1978.

Hayes, D. G. "Dependency Theory: A Formalism and Some Observations," in *Language*, vol. 40, 1964, pp. 511-525.

Hayes, P. J. "The Frame Problem and Related Problems in Artificial Intelligence" (in Elithorn & Jones, 1973).

Hayes, P. J. *Mapping Input Onto Schemas.* Computer Science Report TR-29, University of Rochester, 1978.

Hayes-Roth, B. "A Blackboard Architecture for Control," in *Artificial Intelligence*, vol. 26, 1985, pp. 251-321.

Hendrix, G. G. "Expanding the Utility of Semantic Networks Through Partitioning," in *Proc. IJCAI*, 1975, pp. 115-121.

Hewitt, C. "Concurrency in Intelligent Systems," in *AI Expert*, vol. 1, no. 1, 1986, pp. 43-50.

Hewitt, C. "How to Use What You Know," in *Proc. IJCAI*, 1975, pp. 189-198.

Hewitt, C. "The Challenge of Open Systems," in *BYTE*, vol. 10, no. 4, 1985, pp. 223-242.

Hewitt, C. *PLANNER: A Language for Manipulating Models and Proving Theorems in a Robot.* AI Research Report no. 168, MIT, 1970.

Hildreth, E. C. "Computations Underlying the Measurement of Visual Motion," in *Artificial Intelligence*, vol. 23, 1984, pp. 309-354.

Hinton, G. E. "Learning in Parallel Networks," in *BYTE*, vol. 10, no. 4, 1985, pp. 265-273.

Hofstadter, D. R., G. Clossman, & M. J. Meredith. *Shakespeare's Plays Were'nt Written by him, but by Someone Else of the Same Name.* Computer Science Technical Report no. 96, Indiana Unversity, 1980.

Hofstadter, D. R., M. Mitchell, & R. M. French. *Fluid Concepts and Creative Analogies: A Theory and its Computer Implementation.* FARG Document 87-1, University of Michigan, 1987.

Hood, G. "Neural Modeling As One Approach to Machine Learning" (in Michalski, Carbonell, & Mitchell, *Guide*, 1986, pp. 103-108).

Huyn, N., R. Dechter, & J. Pearl. "Probabilistic Analysis of the Complexity of A*," in *Artificial Intelligence*, vol. 15, 1980, pp. 241-254.

Ibaraki, T. "Generalization of Alpha-Beta and SSS* Search Procedures," in *Artificial Intelligence*, vol. 29, 1986, pp. 73-117.

Johnson, P. & W. Lehnert. "Beyond Explanatory Programming: A Methodology and Environment for Conceptual Natural Language Processing," in *Proc. AAAI*, 1986, pp. 594-600.

Johnson, P. E. "What Kind of Expert Should a System Be?" in *J. Medicine and Philosophy*, vol. 8, 1983, pp. 77-97.

Johnson, W. L. & E. Soloway. "Proust," in *BYTE*, vol. 10, no. 4, 1985, pp. 179-190.

Jorgensen, C. & C. Matheus. "Catching Knowledge in Neural Nets," in *AI Expert*, vol. 1, no. 4, 1986, pp. 30-41.

Kahn, G. S. "Knowledge Acquisition: Investigations and General Principles" (in Michalski, Carbonell, & Mitchell, *Guide*, 1986, pp. 119-122).

Karp, R. M. & J. Pearl. "Searching for an Optimal Path in a Tree with Random Costs," in *Artificial Intelligence*, vol. 21, 1983, pp. 99-116.

Kastner, J., C. Apté, J. Griesmer, S. J. Hong, M. Karnaugh, E. Mays, & Y. Tozawa, "A Knowledge-based Consultant for Financial Marketing," *AI Magazine*, vol. 7, no. 5, 1986, pp. 71-79.

Kibler, D. & R. P. Hall. "A Model of Acquiring Problem Solving Expertise" (in Michalski, Carbonell, & Mitchell, *Guide*, 1986, pp. 137-141).

Kline, P. & S. Dolins. "Problem Features that Influence the Design of Expert Systems," in *Proc. AAAI*, 1986, pp. 956-962.

Knuth, D. E. & R. W. Moore. "An Analysis of Alpha-Beta Pruning," in *Artificial Intelligence*, vol. 6, 1975.

Korf, R. E. "A Program that Learns to Solve Rubik's Cube," in *Proc. AAAI*, 1982, pp. 164-167.

Korf, R. E. "Depth-first Iterative Deepening: An Optimal Admissable Tree Search," in *Artificial Intelligence*, vol. 27, 1985, pp. 97-109.

Kosslyn, S. M., J. Brunn, K. R. Cave, & R. W. Wallach. "Individual Differences in Mental Imagery Ability: A Computational Analysis" (in Pinker, 1985, pp. 195-242).

Kumar, V. & L. Kanal. "A General Branch and Bound Formulation for Understanding and Synthesizing And/Or Tree Search Procedures," in *Artificial Intelligence*, vol. 21, 1983, pp. 179-198.

Kuno, S. & A. G. Oettinger. "Multiple-Path Syntactic Analyzer" (in Grosz, Sparck Jones, & Webber, 1986, pp. 17-23).

Kyle, T. G. "Using AI as a Research Tool," in *ACM SIGART Newsletter*, no. 97, pp. 29-31.

Laird, J. E. & A. Newell. "A Universal Weak Method: Summary of Results," in *Proc. IJCAI*, 1983.

Laird, J. E., P. S. Rosenbloom, & A. Newell. "Towards Chunking as a General Learning Mechanism," in *Proc. AAAI*, 1984.

Laird, J., P. Rosenbloom, & A. Newell. "Chunking in Soar: The Anatomy of a General Learning Mechanism," in *Machine Learning*, vol. 1, 1986, pp. 11-46.

Langley, P., G. L. Bradshaw, & H. A. Simon. "Rediscovering Chemistry with the BACON System" (in Michalski, Carbonell, & Mitchell, 1983, pp. 307-329).

Lebowitz, M. "Memory-based Parsing," in *Artificial Intelligence*, vol. 21, 1983, pp. 363-404.

Lecot, K. & D. S. Parker. "Control Over Inexact Reasoning," in *AI Expert*, vol. 1, no. 1, 1986, pp. 32-43.

Lehnert, W. "A Conceptual Theory of Question Answering," in *Proc. IJCAI*, 1977, pp. 158-164.

Lenat, D. B. "AM: Discovery in Mathematics as Heuristic Search" (in Davis & Lenat, 1982).

Lenat, D. B. "EURISKO: A Program that Learns New Heuristics and Domain Concepts," in *Artificial Intelligence*, vol. 21, 1983, pp. 31-59.

Lenat, D. B. & J. S. Brown. "Why AM and Eurisko Appear to Work," in *Proc. AAAI*, 1983, pp. 236-240.

Lenat, D. B., M. Prajash, &. M. Shepherd. "CYC: Using Commonsense Knowledge to Overcome Brittleness and Knowledge Acquisition Bottlenecks," in *AI Magazine*, vol. 6, no. 9, 1986, pp. 65-85.

Levesque, H. J. "Foundations of a Functional Approach to Knowledge Representation," in *Artificial Intelligence*, vol. 23, 1984, pp. 155-212.

Levesque, H. J. "Making Believers out of Computers (1985 Computers and Thought Award Lecture)," in *Artificial Intelligence*, vol. 30, 1986, pp. 81-108.

Levesque, H. J. & R. Brachman. "A Fundamental Tradeoff in Knowledge Representation and Reasoning (Revised Version)" (in Brachman & Levesque, 1985, pp. 41-70).

Looney, C. G. & A. R. Alfize. "Toward Expert Systems on a Chip," in *ACM SIGART Newsletter*, no. 98, 1986, pp. 26-28.

Luckhart, C. & K. Irani. "An Algorithmic Solution of N-Person Games," in *Proc. AAAI*, 1986, pp. 158-162.

Lytinen, S. "Dynamically Combining Syntax and Semantics in Natural Language Processing," in *Proc. AAAI*, 1986, pp. 574-578.

Maida, A. S. & S. C. Shapiro. "Intensional Concepts in Propositional Semantic Networks," in *Cognitive Science*, vol. 6, 1982, pp. 291-330 (in Brachman & Levesque, 1985, pp. 170-189).

Marr, D. "An Essay on the Primate Retina," in *Vision Research*, vol. 14, 1974, pp. 1377-1388.

Marr, D. "Artificial Intelligence: A Personal View," in *Artificial Intelligence*, vol. 9, 1977, pp. 37-48 (reprinted in Haugeland, 1981, pp. 129-142).

Marr, D. "Representing Visual Knowledge," in *A.M.S. Lectures in the Life Sciences*, vol. 10, 1978, pp. 101-180.

Martelli, A. "On the Complexity of Admissable Search Algorithms," in *Artificial Intelligence*, vol. 8, 1977, pp. 1-13.

Martin, J. & D. Neiman. "Rule-Based Programming in OPS83," in *AI Expert*, vol. 1, no. 1, 1986, pp. 54-63.

McCarthy, J. "Epistemological Problems in Artificial Intelligence," in *Proc. IJCAI*, 1977, pp. 1038-1044 (reprinted in Brachman & Levesque, 1985, pp. 23-30).

McCarthy, J. "First Order Theories of Individual Concepts and Propositions" (in Brachman & Levesque, 1985, pp. 524-533; also in *Machine Intelligence*, 9).

McCarthy, J. "Programs wth Common Sense" (in Brachman & Levesque, 1985, pp. 300-307; also in Minsky, 1968).

McCarthy, J. "Recursive Functions of Symbolic Expressions and their Computation by Machine," *Commun. ACM*, vol. 7, 1960, pp. 184-195.

McCulloch, W. S. & W. Pitts. "A Logical Calculus of the Ideas Immanent in Neural Nets," in *Bull. Math. Biophys.*, vol. 5, 1943, pp. 115-137.

McDermott, D. "Artificial Intelligence Meets Natural Stupidity," in *ACM SIGART Newsletter*, no. 57, 1976 (reprinted in Haugeland, 1981, pp. 143-160).

McDermott, D. & E. Davis. "Planning Routes Through Uncertain Territory," in *Artificial Intelligence*, vol. 22, 1984, pp. 107-156.

McDermott, D., M. M. Waldrop, R. Schank, B. Chandrasekaran, & J. McDermott. "The Dark Ages of AI: A Panel Discussion at AAAI-84," in *AI Magazine*, vol 6, no. 3, 1985, pp. 122-134.

McDermott, J. "R1's Formative Years," in *AI Magazine*, vol. 2, no. 2, 1981, pp. 21-29.

McDermott, J. "R1: A Rule-Based Configurer of Computer Systems," in *Artificial Intelligence*, vol. 19, 1982.

McDermott, J. "XSEL: A Computer Sales Person's Assistant" (in *Machine Intelligence 10*, 1982, pp. 325-337).

McDermott, J. & C. Forgy. "Production System Conflict Resolution Strategies" (in Waterman & Hayes-Roth, 1978, pp. 177-199).

McDermott, J., A. Newell, & J. Moore. "The Efficienty of Certain Production System Implementations" (in Waterman & Hayes-Roth, 1978, pp. 155-176).

McKeown, K. R. "Discourse Strategies for Generating Natural-Language Text," in *Artificial Intelligence*, vol. 27, 1985, pp. 1-41.

Mérõ, L. "A Heuristic Search Algorithm with Modifiable Estimate," in *Artificial Intelligence*, vol. 23, 1984, pp. 13-27.

Michaelsen, R. H., D. Michie, & A. Boulanger. "The Technology of Expert Systems," in *BYTE*, vol. 10, no. 4, 1985, pp. 303-312.

Michalski, R., S. Amarel, D. B. Lenat, D. Michie, & P. H. Winston. "Machine Learning: Challenges of the Eighties" (in Michalski, Carbonell, & Mitchell, *II*, 1986, pp. 27-41).

Miller, R., H. Pople, & J. Myers. "Internist-1, an Experimental Computer-based Diagnostic Consultant for General Internal Medicine," in *New England Journal of Medicine*, vol. 307, 1982, pp. 468-476.

Minsky, M. "A Framework for Representing Knowledge" (in Brachman & Levesque, 1985, pp. 245-262).

Minsky, M. "Communicating with Alien Intelligence," in *BYTE*, vol. 10, no. 4, 1985, pp. 127-138.

Minsky, M. "Steps Towards Artificial Intelligence," in *Proc. IRE*, 1961, pp. 8-30 (reprinted in Feigenbaum & Feldman, 1963, pp. 406-450).

Minsky, M. "Why People Think Computers Can't," in *AI Magazine*, vol. 3, no. 3, 1982, pp. 3-15.

Moore, R. "A Serial Scheme for the Inheritance of Properties," in *ACM SIGART Newsletter*, no. 53, 1975, pp. 8-9.

Moore, R. C. *The Role of Logic in Artificial Intelligence.* Technical Note 335, SRI International, 1984.

Moses, J. "Symbolic Integration: The Stormy Decade," in *Commun. ACM*, vol. 14, 1971, pp. 548-560.

Moses. J. *Symbolic Integration.* Research Report MAC-TR-47, MIT, 1967.

Moskowitz, L. "Rule-Based Programming," in *BYTE*, vol. 11, no. 12, 1986, pp. 217-224.

Nau, D. S. "Pathology on Game Trees Revisited and an Alternative to Minimaxing," in *Artificial Intelligence*, vol. 21, 1983, 221-244.

Nau, D. S., V. Kumar, & L. Kanal. "General Branch and Bound, and Its Relation to A* ad AO*," in *Artificial Intelligence*, vol. 23, 1984, pp. 29-58.

Newborn, M. M. "The Efficiency of the Alpha-Beta Search on Trees with Branch-Dependent Terminal Node Scores," in *Artificial Intelligence*, vol. 8, 1977.

Newell, A. "Production Systems: Models of Control Structures" (in Chase, 1972).

Newell, A. "SOAR: An Architecture for General Intelligence," in *Artificial Intelligence*, 1987 (in press).

Newell, A. "The Knowledge Level," in *Artificial Intelligence*, vol. 18, 1982, pp. 87-127.

Newell, A. & H. A. Simon. "Computer Science as Empirical Inquiry: Symbols and Search (1975 Turing Award Lecture)," in *Commun. ACM*, vol. 19, no. 3, 1976, pp. 113-126 (reprinted in Haugeland, 1981, pp. 35-66).

Newell, A. *Unified Theories of Cognition.* William James Lectures, Harvard University, February-April 1987.

Newell, A., J. Shaw, & H. A. Simon. "Empirical Explorations of the Logic Theory Machine," in *Proc. West. Joint Computer Conf.*, 1957, pp. 218-239 (reprinted in Feigenbaum & Feldman, 1963, pp. 109-133).

Newell, A., J. Shaw, & H. Simon. "Chess-Playing Programs and the Problem of Complexity," in *IBM J. Res. Develop.*, vol. 2, 1958, pp. 320-335 (reprinted in Feigenbaum & Feldman, 1963, pp. 39-70).

Nizuma, S. & T. Kitahashi. "A Problem-Decomposition Method Using Differences or Equivalence Relations Betweed States," in *Artificial Intelligence*, vol. 25, 1985, pp. 117-151.

Osborne, R. L. "Online, Artificial-Intelligence-Based Turbine Generator Diagnostics," in *AI Magazine*, vol. 7, no. 4, 1986, pp. 97-103.

Palay, A. J. "The B* Tree Search Algorithm: New Results," in *Artificial Intelligence*, vol. 19, 1982.

Pan, J. Y-C. & J. M. Tenenbaum. "PIES: An Engineer's Do-It-Yourself Knowledge System for Interpretation of Parametric Test Data," in *AI Magazine*, vol. 7, no. 4, 1986, pp. 62-69.

Papert, S. *The Artificial Intelligence of Hubert L. Dreyfus: A Budget of Fallacies.* AI Memo no. 54, MIT, 1968.

Patel-Schneider, P. F. "Small Can be Beautiful in Knowledge Representation," in *Proc. IEEE Workshop on Principles of Knowledge-Based Systems*, 1984, pp. 11-16.

Pearl, J. "Asymptotic Properties of Minimax Trees and Game-Searching Procedures," in *Artificial Intelligence*, vol. 14, 1980, pp. 113-138.

Pearl, J. "The Solution for the Branching Factor of the Alpha-Beta Pruning Algorithm and its Optimality," in *Commun. ACM*, vol. 25, 1982, pp. 559-564.

Pentland, A. P. "Perceptual Organization and the Representation of Natural Form," in *Artificial Intelligence*, vol. 28, 1986, pp. 293-331.

Pentland, A. P. "Shading into Texture," in *Artificial Intelligence*, vol. 29, 1986, pp. 147-170.

Pereira, F. & D. Warren. "Definite Clause Grammar for Language Analysis -- A Survey of the Formalism and a Comparison with Augmented Transition Networks," in *Artificial Intelligence*, vol. 13, 1980, pp. 231-278.

Perrault, C. R. "On the Mathematical Properties of Linguistic Theories," in *Comp. Ling.*, vol. 10, 1984, pp. 165-176 (reprinted in Grosz, Sparck Jones, & Webber, 1986, pp. 5-16).

Perrault, C. R. & B. J. Grosz. "Natural Language Interfaces," in *Annual Review of Computer Science*, vol. 1, 1986 (also Technical Note 393, SRI International, 1986).

Perry, J. *Language, Mind, and Information*. Center for the Study of Language and Information Report no. CSLI-85-44, Stanford University, 1985.

Pitrat, J. "A Chess Combination Program that Uses Plans," in *Artificial Intelligence*, vol. 8, 1977.

Politakis, P. & S. M. Weiss. "Using Empirical Analysis to Refine Expert System Knowledge Bases," in *Artificial Intelligence*, vol. 22, 1984, pp. 23-48.

Prerau, D. S. "Selection of an Appropriate Domain," in *AI Magazine*, vol. 6, no. 2, 1985, pp. 26-30.

Purves, W. K. "A Biologist Looks at Cognitive AI," in *AI Magazine*, vol. 6, no. 2, 1985, pp. 38-42.

Quillian, M. R. "Semantic Memory" (in Minsky, 1968).

Quillian, M. R. "The Teachable Language Comprehender: A Simulation Program and Theory of Language," in *Commun. ACM*, vol. 12, 1969, pp. 459-476.

Quillian, M. R. "Word Concepts: A Theory and Simulation of Some Basic Semantic Capabilities," in *Behavioral Science*, vol. 12, 1967, pp. 410-430 (reprinted in Brachman & Levesque, 1985, pp. 97-118).

Quinlan, J. R. "Learning Efficient Classification Procedures and Their Application to Chess End Games" (in Michalski, Carbonell, & Mitchell, 1983, pp. 463-482).

Rabin, M. O. & D. Scott. "Finite Automata and their Decision Problems," in *IBM J. Res. Develop.*, vol. 3, 1959, pp. 114-125.

Raphael, B. "SIR: A Computer Program for Semantic Information Retrieval" (in Minsky, 1968, pp. 33-145).

Ratner, D. & M. Warmuth. "Finding a Shortest Solution for the NxN Extension of the 15-PUZZLE is Intractable," in *Proc. AAAI*, 1986, pp. 168-172.

Reece, P. "Perceptrons & Neural Nets," in *AI Expert*, vol. 2, no. 1, 1987, pp. 50-57.

Reichman-Adar, R. "Extended Person-Machine Interface," in *Artificial Intelligence*, vol. 22, 1984, pp. 157-218.

Reitman, W. & B. Wilcox. "Pattern Recognition and Pattern-Directed Inference in a Program for Playing Go" (in Hayes-Roth & Waterman, 1978).

Rieger, C. "An Organization of Knowledge for Problem Solving and Language Comprehension," in *Artificial Intelligence*, vol. 7, 1976, pp. 89-127 (reprinted in Brachman & Levesque, 1985, pp. 487-507).

Ritchie, G. D. & F. K. Hanna. "AM: A Case Study in AI Methodology," in *Artificial Intelligence*, vol. 23, 1984, pp. 249-268.

Robinson, J. "DIAGRAM: A Grammar for Dialogues," in *Commun. ACM*, vol. 25, 1982, pp. 27-47 (reprinted in Grosz, Sparck-Jones, & Webber, 1986, pp. 139-159).

Roizen, I. & J. Pearl. "A Minimax Algorithm Better than Alpha-Beta? Yes and No," in *Artificial Intelligence*, vol. 21, 1983, pp. 199-220.

Rolandi, W. G. "Knowledge Engineering in Practice," in *AI Expert*, vol. 1, no. 4, 1986, pp. 58-62.

Rosenbloom, P. S. "A World-Championship-Level Othello Program," in *Artificial Intelligence*, vol. 19, 1982.

Rosenbloom, P. S. & A. Newell. "The Chunking of Goal-Hierarchies: A Generalized Model of Practice" (in Michalski, Carbonell, & Mitchell, *II*, 1986, pp. 247-288).

Rosenbloom, P. S., J. E. Laird, J. McDermott, A. Newell, & E. Orciuch. "R1-SOAR, An Experiment in Knowledge-Intensive Programming in a Problem-Solving Architecture," in *Proc. IEEE Workshop on Principles of Knowledge-Based Systems*, 1984.

Samuel, A. "Some Studies in Machine Learning Using the Game of Checkers II," in *IBM J. Res. Develop.*, vol. 11, no. 6, 1967, pp. 601-617.

Samuel, A. "Some Studies in Machine Learning Using the Game of Checkers," in *IBM J. Res. Develop.*, vol. 3, no. 3, 1959, pp. 211-229 (reprinted in Feigenbaum & Feldman, 1963, pp. 71-105).

Sathi, A., T. E. Morton, & S. F. Roth. "Callisto: An Intelligent Project Management System," in *AI Magazine*, vol. 7, no. 5, 1986, pp. 34-52.

Saund, E. "Abstraction and Representation of Continuous Variables in Connectionist Networks," in *Proc. AAAI*, 1986, pp. 638-644.

Scarl, E., J. Jamieson, & C. Delaune. "Knowledge-Based Fault Monitoring and Diagnosis in Space Shuttle Propellant Loading," in *Proc. National Aeronautics and Electronics Conf.*, 1984.

Schaefer, P., I. Bozma, & R. Beer. "Knowledge-Based Validity Maintenance for Production Systems," in *Proc. AAAI*, 1986, pp. 918-922.

Schank, R. C. "Conceptual Dependency: A Theory of Natural Language Understanding," in *Cognitive Psychology*, vol. 3, no. 4, 1972.

Schank, R. C. & C. J. Rieger III. "Inference and the Computer Understanding of Natural Language," in *Artificial Intelligence*, vol. 5, 1974, pp. 373-412 (reprinted in Brachman & Levesque, 1985, pp. 119-140).

Schank, R. C. & L. Hunter. "The Quest to Understand Thinking," in *BYTE*, vol. 10, no. 4, 1985, pp. 143-155.

Schank, R. C. & W. G. Lehnert. *The Conceptual Content of Conversations*. Computer Science Research Report no. 160, Yale University, 1979.

Schooley, P. A. "Learning Evaluation Functions" (in Michalski, Carbonell, & Mitchell, *Guide*, 1986, pp. 295-298).

Schrodt, P. A. "Predicting International Events," in *BYTE*, vol. 11, no. 12, 1986, pp. 177-192.

Schubert, L. "Extending the Expressive Power of Semantic Networks," in *Artificial Intelligence*, vol. 7, 1978, pp. 163-198.

Searle, J. R. "Minds, Brains, and Programs," in *Behavioral and Brain Sciences*, vol. 3, 1980, pp. 417-424 (reprinted in Haugeland, 1981, pp. 282-306).

Searle, J. R. "What is an Intentional State?" in *Mind*, vol. 88, 1979, pp. 72-94.

Searle, J. R. *Minds and Brains Without Programs*. Unpublished paper, 1983.

Selfridge, M. "A Computer Model of Child Language Learning," in *Artificial Intelligence*, vol. 29, 1986, pp. 171-216.

Selfridge, O. "Pandemonium: A Paradigm for Learning," in *Proc. Symposium on Mechanisation of Thought Processes*, 1959.

Shannon, C. "Automatic Chess Player," in *Scientific American*, vol. 182, no. 48, 1950.

Shannon, C. "Programming a Digital Computer for Playing Chess," in *Philosophical Magazine*, vol. 41, 1950, pp. 356-375.

Shieber, S. M. "Evidence Against the Context-freeness of Natural Language," in *Language and Philosophy*, vol. 8, 1985, pp. 333-343.

Simmons, R. "'Commonsense' Arithmetic Reasoning," *Proc AAAI*, 1986, pp. 118-124.

Simon, H. A. "Optimal Problem-Solving Search: All-or-None Solutions," in *Artificial Intelligence*, vol. 6, 1975, pp. 235-247.

Simon, H. A. "Search and Reasoning in Problem Solving," in *Artificial Intelligence*, vol. 21, 1983, pp. 7-29.

Simon, H. A. "The Structure of Ill-structured Problems," in *Artificial Intelligence*, vol. 4, 1974, pp. 181-201.

Simon, H. A. "Why Should Machines Learn?" (in Michalski, Carbonell, & Mitchell, 1983, pp. 25-37).

Simon, H. A. & K. Gilmartin. "A Simulation of Memory for Chess Positions," in *Cognitive Psychology*, vol. 5, 1973, pp. 29-46.

Slagle, J. "A Heuristic Program that Solves Symbolic Integration Problems in Freshman Calculus," in *J. ACM*, vol.10, no. 4, 1963, pp. 507-520 (reprinted in Feigenbaum & Feldman, 1963, pp. 191-203).

Slagle, J. & J. Dixon. "Experiments with Some Programs that Search Game Trees," in *J. ACM*, vol. 16, no. 2, 1969, pp. 189-207.

Slagle, J. & J. Dixon. "Experiments with the M & N Tree Searching Program," in *Commun. ACM*, vol. 13, no. 3, 1970, p. 147.

Slagle, J. *Game Trees, M & N Minimaxing, and the M & N Alpha-Beta Procedure*. AI Group Report no. 3, UCRL-4671, University of California Lawrence Radiation Laboratory, 1963.

Smith, B. C. *Reflection and Semantics in a Procedural Language*. Research Report LCS-TR-272, MIT, 1982 (Prologue reprinted in Brachman & Levesque, 1985, pp. 31-40).

Smith, S. F., M. S. Fox, & P. S. Ow. "Construction and Maintaining Detailed Production Plans: Investigations into the Development of Knowledge-based Factory Scheduling Systems," in *AI Magazine*, vol. 7, no. 4, 1986, pp. 45-61.

Stanfill, C. & D. Waltz. "Toward memory-based reasoning," in *Commun. ACM*, vol. 29, no. 12, 1986, pp. 1213-1228.

Stefik, M. & D. Bobrow. "Object-Oriented Programming: Themes and Variations," in *AI Magazine*, vol. 6, no. 4, 1985, pp. 40-62.

Stockman, G. C. "A Minimax Algorithm Better than Alpha-Beta?" in *Artificial Intelligence*, vol. 12, 1979, pp. 179-196.

Sussman, G. J. & G. L. Steele Jr. "Constraints: A Language for Expressing Almost-Hierarchical Descriptions," in *Artificial Intelligence*, vol. 14, 1980, pp. 1-39.

Swartout, W. R. "XPLAIN: A System for Creating and Explaining Expert Consulting Programs," in *Artificial Intelligence*, vol. 21, 1983, pp. 285-325.

Tarsi, M. "Optimal Search on Some Game Trees," in *J. ACM*, vol. 30, 1983, pp. 389-396.

Thinking Machines Corporation. *Introduction to Data Level Parallelism.* Technical Report 86.14, Thinking Machines, 1986.

Thompson, B. A. & W. A. Thompson. "Finding Rules in Data," in *BYTE*, vol. 11, no. 12, 1986, pp. 149-158.

Thompson, B. A. & W. A. Thompson. "Inside an Expert System," in *BYTE*, vol. 10, no. 4, 1985, pp. 315-330.

Turing, A. M. "Computing Machinery and Intelligence," in *Mind*, vol. 59, 1950, pp. 433-460 (reprinted in Feigenbaum & Feldman, 1963, pp. 11-35).

Valiant, L. G. "General Context-free Recognition in Less than Cubic Time," in *J. Comp. and Sys. Sc.*, vol. 10, 1975, pp. 308-315.

Valiant, L. G. "What Can Be Learned?" (in Michalski, Carbonell, & Mitchell, *Guide*, 1986, pp. 349-352).

Waltz, D. L. "Artificial Intelligence," in *Scientific American*, vol. 247, no. 10, 1982, pp. 118-133.

Waltz, D. L. "Understanding Line Drawings of Scenes with Shadows" (in Winston, 1975).

Waltz, D. L. *Connectionist Models: Not Just a Notational Variant, Not a Panacea.* Unpublished paper, 1986.

Waltz, D. L. & J. B. Pollack. "Massively Parallel Parsing: A Strongly Interactive Model of Natural Language Interpretation," in *Cognitive Science*, vol. 9, 1985, pp. 51-74.

Waterman, D. A. & M. Peterson. "Rule-based Models of Legal Expertise," in *Proc. AAAI*, 1980.

Weizenbaum, J. "ELIZA: A Computer Program for the Study of Natural Language Communication Between Man and Machine," in *Commun. ACM*, vol. 9, 1965, pp. 36-45.

Wilensky, R. *Understanding Goal-Based Stories.* Computer Science Research Report no. 140, Yale University, 1978.

Wilkins, D. E. "Domain-independent Planning: Representation and Plan Generation," in *Artificial Intelligence*, vol. 22, 1984, pp. 269-301.

Wilkins, D. E. "Using Patterns and Plans in Chess" (in Frey, 1983).

Wilks, Y. "An Intelligent Analyzer and Understander of English," in *Commun. ACM*, vol. 18, no. 5, 1975, pp. 264-274.

Williams, B. C. "Doing Time: Putting Qualitative Reasoning on Firmer Ground," in *Proc. AAAI*, 1986, pp. 105-112.

Winograd, T. "Frame Representations and the Declarative/Procedural Controversy" (in Brachman & Levesque, 1985, pp. 357-370).

Winston, P. H. "Learning and Reasoning by Analogy: The Details," in *Commun. ACM*, vol. 23, no. 12, 1980.

Winston, P. H. "Learning Structural Descriptions from Examples" (in Winston, 1975, pp. 157-209).

Winston, P. H. *Learning New Principles from Precedents and Exercises: The Details.* AI Memo no. AIM-632, MIT, 1981.

Woods, W. A. "Optimal Search Strategies for Speech Understanding Control" (in Webber & Nilsson, 1981).

Woods, W. A. "Procedural Semantics for a Question-Answering Machine," in *Proc. AFIPS Fall Joint Computer Conf.*, 1968, pp. 457-471.

Woods, W. A. "Transition Network Grammars for Natural Language Analysis," in *Commun. ACM*, vol. 13, no. 10, 1970, pp. 591-606 (reprinted in Grosz, Spark Jones, & Webber, 1986, pp. 71-87).

Woods, W. A. "What's in a Link? Foundations for Semantic Networks" (in Brachman & Levesque, 1985, pp. 217-241).

Yan, J. "Model-Driven Reasoning for Diagnosis," in *ACM SIGART Newsletter*, no. 98, 1986, page 25.

Anthologies

Alt, F. L. *Advances in Computers.* New York: Academic Press, 1960.

Androiole, S. J. *Applications in Artificial Intelligence.* New York: Petrocelli, 1985.

Beal, D. F. *Advances in Computer Chess 4.* Oxford: Pergamon, 1986.

Bobrow, D. G. *Qualitative Reasoning About Physical Systems.* Cambridge, MA: MIT Press, 1985 (reprinted from *Artificial Intelligence*, vol. 24, 1984).

Booth, A. D. *Machine Translation.* Amsterdam: North Holland, 1967.

Brachman, R. J. & H. J. Levesque. *Readings in Knowledge Representation.* Los Altos, CA: Morgan Kaufmann, 1985.

Brady, J. M. & R. C. Berwick. *Computational Models of Discourse*. Cambridge, MA: MIT Press, 1983.

Brady, J. M. *Computer Vision*. Amsterdam: North Holland, 1981.

Brady, J. M., J. M. Hollerbach, T. L. Johnson, T. Loranzo-Pérez, & M. T. Mason. *Robot Motion: Planning and Control*. Cambridge, MA: MIT Press, 1982.

Bramer, M. A. *Computer Game Playing: Theory and Practice*. Chichester: Ellis Horwood, 1983.

Brown, F. M. *The Frame Problem in Artificial Intelligence: Proceedings of the 1987 Workshop*. Los Altos, CA: Morgan Kaufmann, 1987.

Bundy, A. *Catalogue of Artificial Intelligence Tools*, 2nd revised edition. Berlin: Springer-Verlag, 1986.

Chase, W. G. *Visual Information Processing*. New York: Academic Press, 1973.

Cimbala, S. *Artificial Intelligence and National Security*. Lexington, MA: Lexington, 1986.

Clancey, W. & E. Shortliffe. *Readings in Medical Artificial Intelligence: The First Decade*. Reading, MA: Addison-Wesley, 1984.

Clarke, M. R. B. *Advances in Computer Chess 1*. Edinburgh: Edinburgh University Press, 1977.

Clarke, M. R. B. *Advances in Computer Chess 2*. Edinburgh: Edinburgh University Press, 1980.

Clarke, M. R. B. *Advances in Computer Chess 3*. Oxford: Pergamon, 1982.

Cohn, A. G. & J. R. Thomas. *Artificial Intelligence and its Applications*. New York: Wiley, 1986.

Coombs, M. *Developments in Expert Systems*. Orlando, FL: Academic Press, 1984.

Davies, R. *Intelligent Information Systems: Progress and Prospects*. New York: Wiley, 1986.

Davis, R. & D. B. Lenat. *Knowledge-Based Systems in Artificial Intelligence*. New York: McGraw-Hill, 1982.

Elithorn, A. & D. Jones. *Artificial and Human Thinking*. San Francisco: Jossey-Bass, 1973.

Ellis Horwood (publisher). *Machine Intelligence*, 12-volume series. Chichester, UK: Ellis Horwood.

Feigenbaum, E., & J. Feldman. *Computers and Thought.* New York: McGraw-Hill, 1963.

Fischler, M. & O. Firschein. *Readings in Computer Vision: Issues, Problems, Principles, and Paradigms.* Los Altos, CA: Morgan Kaufmann, 1987.

Frey, P. W. *Chess Skill in Man and Machine*, 2nd edition. New York: Springer-Verlag, 1983.

Galambos, J. A. *Knowledge Structures.* Hillsdale, NJ: Lawrence Erlbaum Associates, 1986.

Gale, W. A. *Artificial Intelligence and Statistics.* Reading, MA: Addison-Wesley, 1986.

Georgeff, M. P. & A. L. Lansky. *Reasoning About Actions and Plans: Proceedings of the 1986 Workshop.* Los Altos, CA: Morgan Kaufmann, 1987.

Gill, K. S. *Artificial Intelligence for Society.* New York: Wiley, 1986.

Grishman, R. & R. Kittredge. *Analyzing Language in Restricted Domains.* Hillsdale, NJ: Lawrence Erlbaum Associates, 1986.

Grosz, B. J., K. Sparck Jones, & B. L. Webber. *Readings in Natural Language Processing.* Los Altos, CA: Morgan Kaufman, 1986.

Halpern, J. Y. *Theoretical Aspects of Reasoning About Knowledge: Proceedings of the 1986 Conference.* Los Altos, CA: Morgan Kaufmann, 1986.

Haugeland, J. *Mind Design.* Cambridge, MA: MIT Press, 1981.

Hayes, J. E. & D. Michie. *Intelligent Systems: The Unprecedented Opportunity.* New York: Wiley, 1984.

Hayes-Roth, F. & D. A. Waterman. *Pattern Directed Inference Systems.* New York: Academic Press, 1978.

Hayes-Roth, F., D. A. Waterman, & D. B. Lenat. *Building Expert Systems.* Reading, MA: Addison-Wesley, 1983.

Hinton, G. E. & J. A. Anderson. *Parallel Models of Associative Memory.* Hillsdale, NJ: Lawrence Erlbaum Associates, 1981.

Klahr, P. & D. A. Waterman. *Expert Systems: Techniques, Tools, and Applications.* Reading, MA: Addison-Wesley, 1986.

Kolodner, J. L. & C. K. Riesbeck. *Experience, Memory, and Reasoning.* Hillsdale, NJ: Lawrence Erlbaum Associates, 1986.

Kowalik, J. S. *Knowledge Based Problem Solving.* Englewood Cliffs, NJ: Prentice-Hall, 1986.

Lehnert, W. G. & M. H. Ringle. *Strategies for Natural Language Processing.* Hillsdale, NJ: Lawrence Erlbaum Associates, 1982.

Michalski, R. S., J. G. Carbonell, & T. M. Mitchell. *Machine Learning: A Guide to Current Research.* Boston: Kluwer, 1986.

Michalski, R. S., J. G. Carbonell, & T. M. Mitchell. *Machine Learning: An Artificial Intelligence Approach, Volume II.* Palo Alto, CA: Morgan Kaufmann, 1986.

Michalski, R. S., J. G. Carbonell, & T. M. Mitchell. *Machine Learning: An Artificial Intelligence Approach.* Palo Alto, CA: Tioga, 1983.

Michie, D. *Expert Systems in the Microelectronic Age.* Edinburgh, UK: Edinburgh University Press, 1980.

Michie, D. *Introductory Readings in Expert Systems.* New York: Gordon and Breach, 1982.

Minsky, M. *Semantic Information Processing.* Cambridge, MA: MIT Press, 1968.

O'Shea, T. & M. Eisenstadt. *Artificial Intelligence: Tools, Techniques, and Applications.* New York: Harper and Row, 1984.

Pearl, J. *Search and Heuristics.* Amsterdam: North Holland, 1983 (reprinted from *Artificial Intelligence,* vol. 20, 1983).

Pinker, S. *Visual Cognition.* Cambridge, MA: MIT Press, 1985 (reprinted from *Cognition,* vol. 18, 1984).

Reitman, W. *Artificial Intelligence Applications for Business.* Norwood, NJ: Ablex, 1984.

Rich, C. & R. C. Waters. *Readings in Artificial Intelligence and Software Engineering.* Los Altos, CA: Morgan Kaufmann, 1986.

Schank, R. C. & K. M. Colby. *Computer Models of Thought and Language.* San Francisco: W. H. Freeman, 1973.

Schank, R. C. *Conceptual Information Processing.* Amsterdam: North Holland, 1975.

Schwab, E. C. & J. C. Nusbaum. *Pattern Recognition by Humans and Machines,* in 2 volumes. Orlando, FL: Academic Press, 1986.

Sparck-Jones, K. & Y. Wilks. *Automatic Natural Language Parsing.* New York: Wiley, 1985.

Sternberg, R. J. *The Handbook of Human Intelligence.* Cambridge, UK: Cambridge University Press, 1982.

Webber, B. L. & N. J. Nilsson. *Readings in Artificial Intelligence*. Los Altos, CA: Morgan Kaufmann, 1981.

Winston, P. H. & K. A. Prendergast. *The AI Business: The Commercial Uses of Artificial Intelligence*. Cambridge, MA: MIT Press, 1984.

Winston, P. H. & R. H. Brown. *Artificial Intelligence: An MIT Perspective*, in 2 volumes. Cambridge, MA: MIT Press, 1979.

Winston, P. H. *The Psychology of Computer Vision*. New York: McGraw-Hill, 1975.

Yadzani, M. *Artificial Intelligence: Principles and Applications*. London: Chapman & Hall, 1986.

Yazdani, M. & N. Narayanan. *Artificial Intelligence: Human Effects*. New York: Wiley, 1985.

AI Languages

Bratko, I. *Prolog Programming for Artificial Intelligence*. Reading, MA: Addison-Wesley, 1986.

Bromley, H. *Lisp Lore: A Guide to Programming the Lisp Machine*. Boston: Kluwer, 1986.

Brooks, R. A. *Programming in Common Lisp*. New York: Wiley, 1985.

Brownston, L., R. Farrell, E. Kant, & N. Martin. *Programming Expert Systems in OPS5: An Introduction to Rule-Based Programming*. Reading, MA: Addison-Wesley, 1985.

Burnham, W. D. & A. R. Hall. *Prolog Proramming and Applications*. New York: Wiley, 1985.

Clocksin, W. F. & Mellish, C. S. *Programming in Prolog*, 2nd edition. New York: Springer-Verlag, 1984.

Hassemer, T. *Looking at Lisp*. Reading, MA: Addison-Wesley, 1984.

Hogger, C. J. *Introduction to Logic Programming*. New York: Academic Press, 1984.

Kluzniak, F. & S. Szpakowicz, with J. S. Bien. *Prolog for Programmers*. New York: Academic Press, 1985.

Marcus, C. *Prolog Programming*. Reading, MA: Addison-Wesley, 1986.

Rogers, J. B. *A Prolog Primer*. Reading, MA: Addison-Wesley, 1986.

Steele Jr., G. L. *Common Lisp: The Language.* Burlington, MA: Digital Press, 1984.

Sterling, L. & E. Shapiro. *The Art of Prolog.* Cambridge, MA: MIT Press, 1986.

Tatar, D. *A Programmer's Guide to Common Lisp.* Burlington, MA: Digital Press, 1987.

Touretzky, D. *Lisp: A Gentle Introduction to Symbolic Computation.* New York: Harper & Row, 1984.

Wilensky, R. *Common LispCraft.* New York: W. W. Norton, 1986.

Wilensky, R. *LispCraft.* New York: W. W. Norton, 1984.

Winston, P. H. & B. K. P. Horn. *Lisp*, 2nd edition. Reading, MA: Addison-Wesley, 1984.

Pascal and Programming

Aho, A. V., Hopcroft, J. E., & J. D. Ullman. *Data Structures and Algorithms.* Reading, MA: Addison-Wesley, 1983.

Carroll, D. W. *Programming with Turbo Pascal.* New York: McGraw-Hill/Micro Text, 1985.

Jensen, K. & N. Wirth. *Pascal User Manual and Report: ISO Pascal Standard*, 3rd edition (prepared by A. B. Mickel & J. F. Miner). New York: Springer-Verlag, 1985.

Lewis, H. R. & C. H. Papadimitriou. *Elements of the Theory of Computation.* Englewood Cliffs, NJ: Prentice-Hall, 1981.

Reingold, E. M. & W. J. Hansen. *Data Structures.* Boston: Little, Brown, 1983.

Rohl, J. S. *Recursion via Pascal.* Cambridge, UK: Cambridge University Press, 1984.

Tarjan, R. E. *Data Structures and Network Algorithms.* Philadelphia, PA: Society for Industrial and Applied Mathematics, 1983.

Wirth, N. *Programming in Modula-2*, 3rd edition. New York: Springer-Verlag, 1985.

APPENDIX 2: SOURCES OF AI INFORMATION

This appendix discusses some of the resources to which you can turn for information of all sorts on all aspects of artificial intelligence. Included are organizations, periodical publications, and online/telecommunications services.

Organizations

American Association for Artificial Intelligence, 445 Burgess Drive, Menlo Park, CA, 94025-3496, (415) 328-3123. AAAI is the principal society supporting AI in the United States, with about 10,000 members as of this writing. AAAI sponsors the National Conference on Artificial Intelligence and participates in the International Joint Conference on Artificial Intelligence (IJCAI), which awards the Computers and Thought Award. AAAI members receive the *AI Magazine*, as well as reduced rate subscriptions to other journals and registration for conferences.

Association for Computing Machinery, 11 West 42nd Street, New York, NY, 10036. ACM, the oldest organization of computer professionals, sponsors Special Interest Groups on Artificial Intelligence (SIGART) and Symbolic and Algebraic Manipulation (SIGSAM). It also publishes the Communications *of the ACM* and the *Journal of the ACM*, which often include AI-related articles.

Institute of Electrical and Electronics Engineers, Computer Society, 10662 Los Vaqueros Circle, Los Alamitos, CA, 90720-2578. The IEEE Computer Society sponsors an annual AI conference and publishes *IEEE Expert*, *Transactions on Pattern Analysis and Machine Intelligence*, and *Journal of Robotics and Automation*.

Boston Computer Society, One Center Plaza, Boston, MA, 02108. The BCS, the largest computer user group, sponsors an Artificial Intelligence Interest Group that publishes a newsletter, distributes public-domain AI software, and holds a meeting and tutorials each month.

261

Capital PC User Group. The CPCUG sponsors an AI Special Interest Group that publishes the CPCUG AI Newsletter, 1417 N. Scott Street #201, Arlington, VA, 22209.

Delaware Valley AI Society, c/o Bob Cimprich, The MATRIX Organization, P.O. Box 613, Elmer, NJ, 08318, (215) 293-1980.

Fifth Generation Computing Group, P.O. Box 390622, Mountain View, CA, 94039.

Arizona Artificial Intelligence, c/o Greg Gotcher, Hewlett-Packard, 8080 Pointe Parkway, Phoenix, AZ, 85044, (602) 272-8037.

IQLISP Users' Group, P.O. Box 457, Riverside, CT, 06878.

Canadian Artificial Intelligence Society, 243 College Street, Toronto, M5T 2Y1, Canada. Holds an annual conference and publishes a newsletter.

Magazines

AI Expert. Published monthly by CL Publications Inc., 650 Fifth Street, Suite 311, San Francisco, CA, 94107, (415) 957-9353. Subscriptions are $39/year.

AI Magazine. Published 5 times per year by the American Association for Artificial Intelligence.

Canadian AI Newsletter. Published by the Canadian Artificial Intelligence Society.

Expert System User Magazine. Published by Cromwell House, 20 Bride Lane, London, EC48DX, England.

Intelligence. Published by Intelligence, P.O. Box 20008, New York, NY, 10025.

Knowledge Engineering. Published by Richmond Research, P.O. Box 366, Village Station, 201 Varick Street, New York, NY, 10014.

BYTE. Published 13 times per year by McGraw-Hill Inc., One Phoenix Mill Lane, Peterborough, NH, 03458, (603) 924-9281. Subscriptions are $21/year from BYTE Subscriptions, P.O. Box 590, Martinsville, NJ, 08836. BYTE often publishes special issues on AI-related topics, including AI in general (April 1985), Declarative Languages (August 1985), and Knowledge Representation (November 1986).

Journals

Artificial Intelligence. Published 9 times per year by Elsevier Science Publishers B.V., Journals Department, P.O. Box 211, 1000 AE Amsterdam, The Netherlands. Subscriptions are approximately $200/year (special discounts are available) from Elsevier Science Publishers Inc., Journal Information Center, 52 Vanderbilt Avenue, New York, NY, 10017, (212) 867-9040.

Applied Artificial Intelligence. Published quarterly by Hemisphere Publishing Corporation, Journals Department, 79 Madison Avenue, New York, NY, 10016., (212) 725-1999. Subscriptions are $55/year.

AISB Quarterly. The Newsletter of the Society for the Study of Artificial Intelligence and Simulation of Behavior, published by the Institute of Educational Technology, The Open University, Walton Hall, Milton Keynes, MK7 6AA, England.

Data and Knowledge Engineering. Published 9 times per year by Elsevier Science Publishers B.V., Journals Department, P.O. Box 211, 1000 AE Amsterdam, The Netherlands. Subscriptions are approximately $100/year (special discounts available) from Elsevier Science Publishers Inc., Journal Information Center, 52 Vanderbilt Avenue, New York, NY, 10017, (212) 867-9040.

Expertise: The Journal of Expert Systems. Published monthly by the Expert Systems Developers Association, P.O. Box 262052, Tampa, FL, 33685, (415) 391-4846. Subscriptions are $25/year, $35/year outside U.S.

Expert Systems. Published quarterly by Learned Information Ltd., Besselsleigh Road, Oxford, OX13 6LG, England. Subscriptions are $49/year from Learned Information Inc., Medford, NJ, 08055, (609) 654-6266.

Expert Systems: Research & Applications. Published by JAI Press, 36 Sherwood Place, P.O. Box 1678, Greenwich, CT, 06838-1678.

Intelligent Systems. Published by John Wiley & Sons, Inc., 605 Third Avenue, New York, NY, 10158, (800) 526-5368. Subscriptions are $120/year.

Automated Reasoning. Published quarterly by Kluwer Academic Publishers Inc., 101 Phillip Drive, Assinippi Park, Norwell, MA, 02061, (617) 749-5262. Subscriptions are $36/year.

Machine Learning. Published quarterly by Kluwer Academic Publishers Inc., 101 Phillip Drive, Assinippi Park, Norwell, MA, 02061, (617) 749-5262. Subscriptions are $35/year.

Logic Programming. Published quarterly by Elsevier Science Pulishers B.V., P.O. Box 211, 1000 AE Amsterdam, The Netherlands. Subscriptions from Elsevier Science Publishers Inc., Journal Information Center, 52 Vanderbilt Avenue, New York, NY, 10017, (212) 867-9040.

Cognitive Science. Published quarterly by Ablex Publishing Corporation, 355 Chestnut Street, Norwood, NJ, 07648.

Computer Vision. Published by Kluwer Academic Publishers Inc., 101 Phillip Drive, Assinippi Park, Norwell, MA, 02061, (617) 749-5262.

Future Generation Computer Systems. Published 6 times per year by Elsevier Science Publishers B.V., P.O. Box 211, 1000 AE Amsterdam, The Netherlands. Subscriptions are approximately Dfl. 421.00/year.

New Generation Computing. Published quarterly by Springer-Verlag, 175 Fifth Avenue, New York, NY, 10010, (212) 460-1500. Subscriptions are $96/year.

Communications of the ACM. Published monthly by the Association for Computing Machinery.

Journal of the ACM. Published quarterly by the Association for Computing Machinery.

SIGART Newsletter. Published by the Special Interest Group on Artificial Intelligence of the Association for Computing Machinery. Editorial address: Keith Price, Institute for Robotics and Intelligent Systems, Powell Hall 234-MC-0273, University of Southern California, Los Angeles, CA, 90089-0273, (213) 743-5526, sigart%dworkin@USC-ECL.ARPA.

SIGSAM Bulletin. Published by the Special Interest Group on Symbolic and Algebraic Manipulation of the Association for Computing Machinery. Editorial address: Franz Winkler, Institut für Mathematik, Johannes Kepler Universität, A-4040 Linz, Austria, (732) 231381-9229, K310270@AEARN.BITNET.

IEEE Expert. Published quarterly by the IEEE Computer Society. The Fall 1987 issue covers AI applications in financial expert systems.

Transactions on Pattern Analysis and Machine Intelligence. Published bimonthly by the IEEE Computer Society.

Industry Newsletters

AInteractions. Published in the United States by Texas Instruments Inc. Distributed free of charge by AInteractions, Texas Instruments Inc., 12501 Research Boulevard, Mail Station 2244, Austin, TX, 78759. (Individual requests only.)

AI Trends Newsletter. Published by DM Data Inc., 6900 East Camelback Road, Scottsdale, AZ, 85251.

Applied Artificial Intelligence Reporter. Published monthly by the University of Miami, Intelligent Computer Systems Research Institute, P.O. Box 248235, Coral Gables, FL, 33124, (304) 284-5195. Subscriptions are $49/year from ICS Research Institute, P.O. Box 1309-EP, Fort Lee, NJ, 07024.

Artificial Intelligence Markets Newsletter. Published monthly by AIM Publications Inc., P.O. Box 156, Natick, MA, 01760, (617) 653-1622. Subscriptions are $255/year.

Artificial Intelligence Report. Published monthly by Artificial Intelligence Publications, 3600 West Bayshore Road, Suite 3, Palo Alto, CA, 94303, (415) 424-1447. Subscriptions are $200/year.

Expert Systems Strategies. Published monthly by Cutter Information, 1100 Massachusets Avenue, Arlington, MA, 02174, (617) 648-8700. Subscriptions are $247/year.

inTellIgence. Published in Europe by Texas Instruments Corporate Market Communications. Distributed free of charge by Keith Goldup, MS 36, Texas Instruments Ltd., Manton Lane, Bedford, MK41 7PA, England. (Individual requests only.)

Machine Intelligence News. Published monthly by Oyez IBC Ltd., Bath House, 3rd floor, 56 Holborn Viaduct, London, ECIA 2EX, England, 01-236 4080. Subscriptions are £110/year.

The AI Software Market Report. Published by Intelli Research Inc., 12900 Atherton Ct., Los Altos Hills, CA, 94022, (415) 949-1290. Subscriptions are $395/year.

The Spang Robinson Report. Published monthly by The Spang Robinson Report, 3600 West Bayshore Road, Palo Alto, CA, 94303. Subscriptions are $295/year.

Online/Telecommunications Services

Compuserve Information Service. CIS and AI Expert magazine sponsor the AI Forum, which includes a message section and several libraries of AI-related articles, AI Expert programs, and public-domain software (including demonstration versions of commercial products).

Electronic Mailing Lists and Newsgroups. If you have access to the ARPAnet, usually via a mini- or mainframe computer, you can request to subscribe to the following AI-related electronic publications by sending electronic mail requests to the associated addresses:

- Artificial Intelligence   AILIST-REQUEST@SRI-STRIPE
- Natural Language &
  Knowledge Representation   NL-KR REQUEST@ROCHESTER
- Vision   VISION-LIST-REQUEST@ADS
- Neural Networks   NEURON-REQUEST%TI-CSL.CSNET
                                        @CSNET-RELAY
- Parallel Symbolic Computing PARSYM-REQUEST@TI-CSL.CSNET
                                        @CSNET-RELAY
- Logic Programming &
  Theorem Proving   PROLOG-DIGEST-REQUEST@SU-SCORE
- AI in Education   AI-ED-REQUEST@SUMEX-AIM
- Common Lisp   COMMON-LISP-REQUEST@SU-AI
- Scheme (a dialect of Lisp)   SCHEME-REQUEST@MC.LSC.MIT
- XLisp   INFO-XLISP-REQUEST@SPICE.CS.CMU

If you use a computer running the Unix operating system that is connected via UUCP to the Usenet system, you may be able to read the following relevant newsgroups with *rn*, *readnews*, *vnews*, or similar software: comp.ai, mod.ai (AILIST messages), comp.cog-eng, comp.lang.lisp, comp.lang.prolog, comp.lang.pascal, comp.sources, mod.sources (AI Expert programs).

BYTE Information Exchange. BIX, which is operated by the publishers of BYTE, sponsors ongoing conferences on Artificial Intelligence and related topics.

Arity Corporation. Arity maintains a bulletin board service for Prolog messages and programs: (617) 369-5622, 300/1200/2400 baud.

Boston Computer Society. The BCS AI Interest Group sponsors a Common Lisp and XLisp bulletin board service that also carries AI Expert programs: (617) 492-2399, 8 data bits, 1 stop bit, no parity, full duplex, 300/1200 baud.

Electronic AI Expert. Information and programs relating to articles published in AI Expert can be downloaded from the following bulletin board services, 8 data bits, 1 stop bit, no parity, 300/1200 baud:

Chicago, IL	(309) 342-5302	Seattle, WA	(206) 848-9232
East Lansing, MI	(517) 355-3276	Woodbury, CT	(203) 263-5783

Miscellaneous Resources

AI Masters. A series of videotaped lectures on various aspects of AI, including vision, knowledge acquisition, planning and implementing expert systems, and logic programming, delivered by well-known AI researchers. Published by Addison-Wesley Training Systems, Route 128, Reading, MA, 01867, (617) 944-3700 x2714.

The Minerva Group, P.O. Box 835, Amherst, MA, 01004, (802) 387-4034. Minerva publishes a series of videotaped university-level courses on AI, Expert Systems, and Lisp.

APPENDIX 3: AI PRODUCTS AND MANUFACTURERS

Artificial intelligence has spawned a large industry, with many hardware and software vendors developing products designed specifically for the research, development, and delivery of AI-based applications. This appendix simply divides a list of those manufacturers and their products into the categories of programming languages, software tools and applications, hardware systems, and consulting and research organizations. Bundy's *Catalogue of Artificial Intelligence Tools*, Appendices A-C of Frenzel's *Crash Course in Artificial Intelligence and Expert Systems*, and Waterman's *Guide to Expert Systems* were among the sources consulted to compile this information. For more information on any of the items mentioned here, please contact the individual companies.

Programming Languages

ACT Informatique
12 Rue de la Montagne-Ste Genevieve
75005 Paris, France
46 33 72 60
Le_Lisp

Advanced AI Systems Inc.
P.O. Box 39-0360
Mountain View, CA, 94039-0360
(415) 961-1121
AAIS Prolog

Advanced Computer Tutoring Inc.
701 Amberson Avenue
Pittsburgh, PA, 15232
(412) 621-5111
LISP-ITS

AI WARE Inc.
11000 Cedar Avenue, Suite 212
Cleveland, OH, 44106
(216) 421-2380
AI Flavors

Applied Logic Systems Inc.
P.O. Box 90, University Station
Syracuse, NY, 13210-0090
(315) 471-3900
ALS Prolog

Arity Corporation
30 Domino Drive
Concord, MA, 01742
(617) 371-1243
Arity/Prolog

268

Artelligence
1402 Preston Road
Dallas, TX, 75240
(214) 437-0361
OPS5+

Automata Design Associates
1570 Dresher Street
Philadelphia, PA, 19025
(215) 355-5400
UNXLISP, VML PROLOG

Borland International
4585 Scotts Valley Drive
Scotts Valley, CA, 95066
(800) 255-8008
Turbo C, Turbo Pascal, Turbo Prolog,
Turbo Prolog Toolbox

Chalcedony Software
5580 La Jolla Boulevard, Suite 126
La Jolla, CA, 92037
(619) 483-8513
PROLOG/i, PROLOG/m

C-LAMBDA
1559 Rockville Pike
Rockville, MD, 20852
(301) 230-0749
Lisp-to-C Translator

Cognitive Systems Inc.
234 Church Street
New Haven, CT, 06510
(203) 773-0726
CSI LISP

Computer Thought Corporation
840 Avenue F, Suite 104
Plano, TX, 75074
(214) 424-3511
OPS5+

Computing Insights
P.O. Box 4033
Madison, WI, 53700
iLISP

Coral Software
P.O. Box 307
Cambridge, MA, 02142
(617) 547-2662
Common Lisp

Crosfield Composition Systems Inc.
570 Taxter Road
Elmsford, NY, 10523
CSI Lisp Toolkit

Data Directions Inc.
37 Jerome Avenue
Bloomfield, CT, 06002
(203) 242-8551
DDI-OPS

Digital Equipment Corporation
200 Baker Avenue
West Concord, MA, 01742
Vax Lisp, Vax OPS5

Digitalk Inc.
5200 West Century Boulevard
Los Angeles, CA, 90045
(213) 645-1082
Methods, Smalltalk/V

Drasch Computer Software
RFD #1 Box 202
Ashford, CT, 06278
(203) 429-3817
Clisp

Dynamic Master Systems Inc.
P.O. Box 566456
Atlanta, GA, 30356
(404) 565-0771
TOPSI

ExperTelligence Inc.
559 San Ysidro Road
Santa Barbara, CA, 93108
(805) 969-7871
ExperLisp, ExperCommonLisp,
ExperInterface Builder, ExperProlog II,
ExperOPS5 Plus

Expert Systems International
1700 Walnut Street
Philadelphia, PA, 19103
(215) 735-8510
ESP Frame-Engine, PROLOG-2

Franz Inc.
1141 Harbor Bay Parkway
Alameda, CA, 94501
(415) 769-5656
Franz Lisp, Extended Common Lisp

Gnosis
4005 Chestnut Street
Philadelphia, PA, 19104
(215) 387-1500
P-LISP

Gold Hill Computers Inc.
163 Harvard Street
Cambridge, MA, 02139
(617) 492-2071
*Golden Common Lisp, GCLISP 286
Developer, GCLISP 386 Developer*

IBUKI
399 Main Street
Los Altos, CA, 94022
Kyoto Common Lisp

Integral Quality Inc.
P.O. Box 31970
Seattle, WA, 98103
(206) 527-2918
IQCLISP, IQLISP

Interface Computer GmbH
Oberfohringen Strasse 24a+b
D-8000 Munchen 81, Germany
IF/PROLOG

Intermetrics Inc.
733 Concord Avenue
Cambridge, MA, 02138
Intermetrics Common Lisp

Levien Instruments Company
P.O. Box 31
McDowell, VA, 24458
(703) 396-3345
BYSO LISP

Logiciel Avenue Software
C.P. 2085, Terminus
Quebec, G1K 7M9, Canada
(418) 641-0441
PROLOG II

LogicWare Inc.
1100 Finch Avenue West, Suite 600
Downsview, Ontario, M3J 2V5, Canada
(416) 665-0022, (617) 547-2393
MPROLOG, Prolog Primer

Lucid Inc.
707 Laurel Street
Menlo Park, CA, 94025
(800) 843-4204
Lucid Common Lisp

Metacomco
5353 Scotts Valley Drive
Scotts Valley, CA, 95066
(408) 375-5012
Cambridge Lisp, QL-Lisp

MicroProducts Inc.
370 West Camino Gardens Boulevard
Boca Raton, FL, 33432
(305) 392-9800
PowerLisp

Microsoft Inc.
10700 Northrup Way, P.O. Box 97200
Bellevue, WA, 98009
(800) 426-9400
Microsoft LISP

Norell Data Systems
3400 Wilshire Boulevard, P.O. Box 70127
Los Angeles, CA, 90070
(213) 748-5978
LISP/88

Northwest Computer Algorithms
P.O. Box 1747
Novato, CA, 94948
(415) 897-1302
AMPERE, LEARN LISP, LISPTEX,
OPS-5, RLISP, REDUCE, VOLTA

Optimized Systems Software Inc.
1221B Kentwood Avenue
San Jose, CA, 95129
(408) 446-3099
Personal Prolog

PPI
Glen Road
Sandy Hook, CT, 06482
(203) 426-1875
Objective-C, Vici

Pro Code International
15930 SW Colony Place
Portland, OR, 97224
(503) 684-3000
Waltz Lisp

Production Systems Technologies Inc.
642 Gettysburg Street
Pittsburgh, PA, 15206
(412) 362-3117
OPS83

Programming Logic Systems Inc.
31 Crescent Drive
Milford, CT, 06460
(203) 877-7988
apes, microPROLOG, microPROLOG
Professional, macPROLOG, sigmaPROLOG

Quintus
2345 Yale Street
Palo Alto, CA, 94306
(415) 494-3612
Quintus Prolog

r/1 Group
7623 Leviston Street
El Cerrito, CA, 94530
(415) 527-1438
UniLISP

Rational Visions
7111 West Indian School Road, Suite 131
Phoenix, AZ, 85033
XPRO: Extended Prolog

Sapiens Software Corporation
236 Mora Street
Santa Cruz, CA, 95060
(408) 458-1990
Sapiens Star Sapphire

Science Applications International
Corporation
1710 Goodridge Drive, P.O. Box 1303
McLean, VA, 22102
SAIC OPS5

Semantic Microsystems
4470 S.W. Hall Street, Suite 340
Beaverton, OR, 97005
(503) 643-4539
MacScheme

Softsmarts Inc.
4 Skyline Road
Woodside, CA, 94062
(415) 327-8100
Smalltalk AT

Solution Systems Inc.
335 Washington Street
Norwell, MA, 02061
(617) 659-1571
TransLISP, TransLISP Plus, PROLOG-86

Systems Designers Software Inc.
444 Washington Street, Suite 407
Woburn, MA, 01801
(617) 935-8009
POPLOG

Texas Instruments
P.O. Box 809063
Dallas, TX, 75380-3345
(800) 527-3500
PC-Scheme, TI PROLOG

The LISP Company
430 Monterrey Avenue, #4
Los Gatos, CA, 95030
(408) 354-3668
TLC-LISP

The Programmer's Shop
128 Rockland Street
Hanover, MA, 02339
(617) 826-7531
Prolog-86

The Soft Warehouse Inc.
3615 Harding Avenue, Suite 505
Honolulu, HI, 96816
(808) 734-5801
muLISP

The Software Toolworks
15233 Ventura Boulevard, Suite 1118
Sherman Oaks, CA, 91403
(818) 986-4885
LISP-80

The Whitewater Group
Technology Innovation Center
906 University Place
Evanston, IL, 60201
(312) 491-2370
ACTOR

University of Utah
Computer Science Department
Salt Lake City, UT, 84112
Portable Standard Lisp

VERAC Incorporated
9605 Scranton Road, Suite 500
San Diego, CA, 92121
(619) 457-5550
GeoFlavors

Westcomp Software Engineering Group
517 North Mountain Avenue
Upland, CA, 91786-5016
(714) 982-1738
CLISP

ZETA-SOFT Limited
55 Wheeler Street
Cambridge, MA, 02134
(617) 868-4634
ZETA-C

Software Tools and Applications

Antic Publishing
544 Second Street
San Francisco, CA, 94107
Expert Opinion

Apocalypse Systems
1556 Halford Avenue, Suite 115A
Santa Clara, CA, 95051
Tax Genius

Applied Expert Systems
Five Cambridge Center
Cambridge, MA, 02142
(617) 492-7322
PlanPower

Arity Corporation
(see Programming Languages)
Arity/Expert System, Arity/SQL

The Athena Group
575 Madison Avenue, Suite 1006
New York, NY, 10022
(212) 605-0224
Portfolio Manager Advisor

Austrian Research Institute for Artificial
Intelligence
Schottengasse 3
A-1010 Vienna, Austria
+43-222-6632810
VIE-PCX, VIE-KET

Automated Reasoning Corporation
290 West 12th Street, Suite 1D
New York, NY, 10014-1933
IN-ATE, LISP IN-ATE, Micro IN-ATE,
Micro IN-ATE Workstation

Avalanche Development Company
947 Walnut Street
Boulder, CO, 80302
Intelligent Markup System

BBN Laboratories
10 Moulton Street
Cambridge, MA, 02238
KL-ONE, KL-TWO

Brattle Research Corporation
215 First Street
Cambridge, MA, 02142
ArtiFact

California Intelligence
912 Powell Street, #8
San Francisco, CA, 94108
(415) 391-4846
XSYS-II

Conception et Realisation
Industrielles de Logiciel
12 bis Rue Jean Jaures
92807 Puteaux, France
1-776-34-37, 4-776-34-37
MO-LRO

Decision Support Software Inc.
1300 Vincent Place
McLean, VA, 22101
(703) 442-7900
Expert Choice

DecisionWare Inc.
2033 Wood Street, Suite 218
Sarasota, FL, 33577
RightWriter

ExperTelligence Inc.
(see Programming Languages)
ExperFacts

Expert Systems International
(see Programming Languages)
ESP Advisor

EXSYS Inc.
P.O. Box 75158, Contract Station 14
Albequerque, NM, 87194
(505) 836-6676
EXSYS

General Research Corporation
7655 Old Springhouse Road
McLean, VA, 22102
(703) 893-5915
TIMM-PC

Georgia Tech Research Institute
Artificial Intelligence Branch
Atlanta, GA, 30332
(404) 894-3419
GEST

Gilmore Aerospace
1800 Century Boulevard, Suite 1230
Atlanta, GA, 30345
(404) 728-0312
ABEST, DIPS

Gold Hill Computers Inc.
(see Programming Languages)
ACORN, GoldWorks

Grandmaster Inc.
P.O. Box 2567
Spokane, WA, 99220
(509) 747-6773
Office Automation Toolkit

Hewlett-Packard Corporation
3000 Hanover Street
Palo Alto, CA, 94304
HPRL

Human Edge Software Corporation
2445 Faber Place
Palo Alto, CA, 94303
(800) 624-5227
Expert Ease

Inference Corporation
5300 West Century Boulevard, 5th Floor
Los Angeles, CA, 90045
ART, *SMP*

Intellicorp
1975 El Camino Real West
Mountain View, CA, 94040
(415) 965-5650
KEE, *SimKit*

IntelligenceWare
9800 S. Sepulveda Boulevard, Suite 730
Los Angeles, CA, 90045
(213) 417-8896
Auto-Intelligence, *Intelligence/Compiler*,
Experteach-II

Intelligent Machine Company
3813 North 14th Street
Arlington, VA, 22201
(703) 528-9136
KNOWOL, *KNOWOL+*

KDS Corp.
934 Hunter Road
Willmette, IL, 60091
(312) 251-2621
KDS2

Kemp-Carraway Heart Institute
Birmingham, AL, 35234
(205) 252-6697
FLOPS

Level Five Research Inc.
503 Fifth Avenue
Indialantic, FL, 32903
(305) 729-9046
Insight, Insight 2+

Lightwave Consultants
P.O. Box 290539
Tampa, FL, 33617
(813) 988-5033
ESIE

Lisp Machine Inc.
6 Tech Drive, Building #4
Andover, MA, 01810
(617) 682-0500
Integrated Knowledge Environment

LITHP Systems B.V.
Meervalweg 72
1121 JP Landsmeer, The Netherlands
Acquaint

LogicWare Inc.
(see Programming Languages)
TWAICE, *The AI Edge Program*

Machine Intelligence Corporation
1593 Locust Avenue
Bohemia, NY, 11716
(516) 589-1676
MICE

McGraw-Hill Books
P.O. Box 400
Hightstown, NJ, 08520
Micro Expert, *Pro Expert*

Micro Data Base Systems
P.O. Box 248
Lafayette, IN, 47902
(317) 463-2581
GURU

Mountain View Press
P.O. Box 4656
Mountain View, CA, 94040
Expert-2

Neuron Data Inc.
444 High Street
Palo Alto, CA, 94301
(415) 321-4488
Nexpert, Nexpert Object

Palladian Software Inc.
Four Cambridge Center, 11th Floor
Cambridge, MA, 02142
(617) 661-7171
Financial Advisor, Operations Advisor

Paperback Software International
2830 Ninth Street
Berkeley, CA, 94710
(415) 644-2116
VP-Expert

Personal Computer Engineers
6033 West Century Boulevard, Suite 400
Los Angeles, CA, 90045
(213) 757-7537
KOPS

Programs in Motion Inc.
10 Sycamore Road
Wayland, MA, 01778
(617) 653-5093
1st-CLASS

Radian Corporation
8501 Mo-Pac Boulevard, P.O. Box 9948
Austin, TX, 78766
RuleMaster

Science Applications International
Corporation
(see Programming Languages)
GESBT

Scientific Analysis Inc.
36 East Baltimore Pike, Suite 106A
Media, PA, 19063
(215) 566-0801
Small-X

Silogic Inc.
9841 Airport Boulevard, #600
Los Angeles, CA, 90045
(213) 337-7477
The Knowledge WorkBench

Smart Systems Technology
6870 Elm Street, Suite 300
McLean, VA, 22101
(703) 448-8562
ARBY

Software Architecture and Engineering Inc.
Artificial Intelligence Center
1600 Wilson Boulevard
Arlington, VA, 22209
(703) 276-7910
KES

Software Intelligence Laboratory Inc.
1593 Locust Avenue
Bohemia, NY, 11716
(516) 589-1676
WIZDOM PX, WIZDOM PXS,
WIZDOM XS

Software Plus Limited
1652 Albemarle Drive
Crofton, MD, 21114
(301) 261-0264
CxPERT

Symbolics Inc.
4 New England Tech Center
555 Virginia Road
Concord, MA, 01742
MACSYMA

Syntelligence
1000 Hamlin Court, P.O. Box 3620
Sunnyvale, CA, 94088
SYNTEL

Teknowledge
525 University Avenue
Palo Alto, CA, 94301
M.1a, M.1, S.1

Texas Instruments
(see Programming Languages)
Arborist, Personal Consultant Easy,
Personal Consultant Plus

TExpert Systems Inc.
12607 Aste
Houston, TX, 77065
(713) 469-4068
CLASS

The Carnegie Group Inc.
650 Commerce Court, Station Square
Pittsburgh, PA, 15219
(412) 642-6900
Knowledge Craft, Language Craft

The Soft Warehouse Inc.
(see Programming Languages)
muMATH

Thinking Software Inc.
46-16 65th Place
Woodside, NY, 11377
(718) 429-4922
Turbo Expert

Thunderstone
P.O. Box 839
Chesterland, OH, 44026
(216) 449-6104
Assimilation, Comprehension, Logic-Line

UMECORP
275 Magnolia Avenue
Larkspur, CA, 94939
(415) 924-3644
Advisor Expert System Designer, Think!

Xerox Special Information Systems
250 North Halstead Street, P.O. Box 5608
Pasadena, CA, 91107
(818) 351-2351
HUMBLE

Hardware Systems

Apollo
330 Billerica Road, MS 47
Chelmsford, MA, 01824
(617) 256-6600 x4889

Digital Equipment Corporation
(see Programming Languages)

Hewlett-Packard Corporation
(see Software Tools and Applications)

Lisp Machine Inc.
(see Software Tools and Applications)

Symbolics Inc.
(see Programming Languages)

Tektronix Inc.
AI Marketing
P.O. Box 1000, MS 63-635
Wilsonville, OR, 97070

Texas Instruments
Data Systems Group
P.O. Box 2909, MS 2068
Austin, TX, 78769

UMECORP
(see Software Tools and Applications)

Xerox Special Information Systems
(see Software Tools and Applications)

Consulting and Research Organizations

Advanced Decision Systems
201 San Antonio Circle, Suite 286
Mountain View, CA, 94040

Aldo Ventures
525 University Avenue, Suite 1206
Palo Alto, CA, 94301

Amoco Production Company
Research Center
4502 East 41st Street, P.O. Box 591
Tulsa, OK, 74102

Arthur D. Little Inc.
25 Acorn Park
Cambridge, MA, 02140

Artificial Intelligence Corporation
100 Fifth Avenue
Waltham, MA, 02254

Automated Reasoning Corporation
290 West 12th Street, Suite 1-D
New York, NY, 10014

Bolt, Beranek and Newman Inc.
Computer Science Division
50 Moulton Street
Cambridge, MA, 02238

Booz, Allen & Hamilton Inc.
4330 East West Highway
Bethesda, MD, 20814

Computer Thought Corporation
1721 Plano Parkway, Suite 125
Plano, TX, 75075

Desktop AI
1720 Post Road East
Westport, CT, 06880

Digital Equipment Corporation
Intelligent Systems Group
77 Reed Road
Hudson, MA, 01749

EG&G Idaho Inc.
P.O. Box 1625
Idaho Falls, ID, 83415

ESL Inc.
495 Java Drive
P.O. Box 3510
Sunnyvale, CA, 94088

Expert-Knowledge Systems Inc.
6313 Old Chesterbrook Road
McLean, VA, 22101

Fairchild Laboratory for
Artificial Intelligence Research
Fairchild Advanced Research
and Development
4001 Miranda Avenue
Palo Alto, CA, 94304

FMC Central Engineering Laboratories
Artificial Intelligence Center
1185 Coleman Avenue, Box 580
Santa Clara, CA, 95052

Ford Aerospace & Communications
Corporation
Artificial Intelligence Laboratory
P.O. Box 58487
1150 Gemini Avenue
Houston, TX, 77258

General Dynamics
Electronics Division
P.O. Box 85227, Drawer 544
San Diego, CA, 92138-5227

General Electric Company
Research & Development Center
1 River Road
Schenectady, NY, 12345

General Motors Research Laboratories
Computer Science Department
Warren, MI, 48090-9057

Gould Intelligent Systems Laboratory
10340 Democracy Lane, Suite 200
Fairfax, VA, 22030

Grumman Data Systems
1355 Beverly Road, Suite 200
McLean, VA, 22101

GTE Laboratories
40 Sylvan Road
Waltham, MA, 02254

Hewlett-Packard Computer Research Center
Applied Technology Laboratory
1501 Page Mill Road
Palo Alto, CA, 94304

Hughes Aircraft Company
Artificial Intelligence Center
23901 Calabasas Road
Calabasas, CA, 91302

Information Sciences Institute
4676 Admiralty Way
Marina del Rey, CA, 90292

Intellicorp
(see Software Tools and Applications)

International Business Machines Corporation
Palo Alto Scienfitic Center
1530 Page Mill Road
Palo Alto, CA, 94303

International Business Machines Corporation
Thomas J. Watson Research Center
P.O. Box 218
Yorktown Heights, NY, 10598

Interstate Electronics Corporation
708 East Vermont Avenue
Anaheim, CA, 92803

Jet Propulsion Laboratory
California Institute of Technology
4800 Oak Grove Drive
Pasadena, CA, 91109

Kestrel Institute
Research Laboratory
1801 Page Mill Road
Palo Alto, CA, 94304

KLA Instruments Corporation
3901 Burton Drive
P.O. Box 58016
Santa Clara, CA, 95052

Lockheed Advanced Marine Systems
P.O. Box 4000
Santa Clara, CA, 95054

Lockheed Missiles and Space Company Inc.
Lockheed Palo Alto Research Laboratory
3251 Hanover Street
Palo Alto, CA, 94304

Los Alamos National Laboratory
Group NSP/AWT MS F668
Los Alamos, NM, 87545

Martin Marietta
103 Chesapeake Park Plaze
Baltimore, MD, 21220

McDonnell Douglas Corporation
16441 Space Center Boulevard
Houston, TX

Microelectronics and Computer Technology
Corporation
9430 Research Boulevard
Echelon Building 1, Suite 200
Austin, TX, 78759

Naval Personnel Research
and Development Center
San Diego, CA, 92152

Navy Center for Applied Research
in Artificial Intelligence
Naval Research Laboratory
4555 Overlook Avenue, S.W.
Washington, DC, 20375

Northrop Aircraft Division
P.O. Box 2282
Hawthorne, CA, 90251-2282

Olivetti Advanced Technology Center
10430 South DeAnza Boulevard
Cupertino, CA, 95014

PAR Technology Corporation
Seneca Plaza, Route 5
New Hartford, NY, 13413

Planning Research Corporation
Government Information Systems
1500 Planning Research Drive
McLean, VA, 22102

Rockwell International Science Center
1049 Camino Dos Rios
Thousand Oaks, CA, 91360

Schlumberger Limited
Artificial Intelligence Laboratory
3340 Hillview Avenue
Palo Alto, CA, 94304

Southwest Research Institute
6220 Culebra Road
San Antonio, TX, 78284

Sperry Corporation
12010 Sunrise Valley Drive
Reston, VA, 22091

SRI International
333 Ravenswood Avenue
Menlo Park, CA, 94025

Symbolics Inc.
Research and Development
Four Cambridge Center
Cambridge, MA, 02142

Systems Control Technology Inc.
1801 Page Mill Road
Palo Alto, CA, 94303

Teknowledge Inc.
(see Software Tools and Applications)

Tektronix Inc.
Computer Research Laboratory
Knowledge-Based Systems Group
P.O. Box 500, MS 50-662
Beaverton, OR, 97077

Texas Instruments
Computer Science Laboratory
P.O. Box 226015, MS 238
Dallas, TX, 75266

The MITRE Corporation
Burlington Road
Bedford, MA, 01730

The Rand Corporation
1700 Main Street
Santa Monica, CA, 90406

The Standard Oil Company
P.O. Box 94694
Cleveland, OH, 44101-4694

TRW Defense Systems
One Space Park
Redondo Beach, CA, 90278

United Technologies Research Center
MS 35, Silver Lane
East Hartford, CT, 06108

Wang Laboratories Inc.
One Industrial Avenue, MS 014-02A
Lowell, MA, 01851

Westinghouse Research and Development
Center
1310 Beulah Road
Pittsburgh, PA, 15235

Xerox Palo Alto Research Center
Intelligent Systems Laboratory
3333 Coyote Hill Road
Palo Alto, CA, 94304

APPENDIX 4:   GLOSSARY OF AI TERMINOLOGY

The colorful terminology of AI includes unique definitions for familiar words like *abduction*, *British Museum*, *children*, *extension*, and *inheritance*. The terms explained in this alphabetical listing are those specific to artificial intelligence and some of its related fields that you are likely to encounter elsewhere in this book or in other publications about AI. For each concept, I have tried to provide in familiar terms the generally agreed upon definition; however, the volatile nature of AI and the wide range of applications to which it is put ensure that several interpretations or uses are possible.

Longer definitions may be found in Bundy's *Catalogue of Artificial Intelligence Tools*, Appendix D of Frenzel's *Crash Course in Artificial Intelligence and Expert Systems*, in AI textbooks, and in *The Handbook of AI*. Glossaries for specific AI subfields are included in Laird, Rosenbloom, and Newell's *Universal Subgoaling and Chunking*, Michalski, Carbonell, and Mitchell's *Machine Learning II*, Marr's *Vision*, and Waterman's *Guide to Expert Systems*.

2 1/2 Dimensional Sketch is an intermediate level of representation in Marr's framework of early visual processing that describes the surfaces in the image and their orientations from a viewer-centered reference frame.

A* is an optimal algorithm that uses a cost function and an underestimating heuristic evaluation function to find optimal solutions to state-space search problems by expanding the partial path that minimizes their sum; when the heuristic is always 0, the search degrades to uniform-cost.

Abduction is a rule of logical inference that states if we know that A implies B, and if we find B to be true, we can say A is true. Although this is an unsound form of reasoning, it enables diagnostic reasoning with "educated guesses" about causation from symptoms.

Action is a consequent element in the right-hand side of a production rule that is performed when the rule fires; it can be one or more facts that become true, procedures that are executed, or messages that are printed, for example.

Actor is (1) an entity or individual performing a primitive action in conceptual dependency theory, or (2) a new object-oriented programming language, similar to SmallTalk, and used for AI applications.

Admissibility is a constraint on the heuristic evaluation function used in the A* state-space search algorithm, whose satisfaction ensures that the procedure will always terminate with the optimal solution to the problem; it requires that all estimates of remaining distance to the goal state be underestimates of the true distance.

Algorithm is a step-by-step procedure that specifies exactly how a problem is to be solved.

Alpha-Beta Pruning (α–β) is the most popular algorithm for searching game trees; it stems from the realization that once a move has been effectively refuted, there is no need to search for a better refutation; under optimal conditions; it can search twice as deep as standard MINIMAX with the same number of static evaluations.

Analogy is a method of learning and reasoning, in which a new problem is solved by matching its structure with similar, previously solved problems.

Antecedent — see *premise*.

Arc is a pointer connecting two nodes in a graph, such as an operator in state-space search or a move in game playing.

Architecture is the basic underlying structure of a processing system (intelligent or otherwise), representing the level of primitive operations that cannot be changed and form the building blocks for all other operations executed by the system; in most computers, the hardware organization is the architectural level.

Artificial Intelligence (AI) is a science that studies primarily techniques for making computers exhibit intelligent behavior, ways of illuminating human cognitive processes, and the construction of an autonomous, generally intelligent, artificial system.

Associative Memory — see *content-addressable memory*.

Attribute — see *feature*.

Augmented Transition Network (ATN) is a device for processing and a formalism for representing the syntactic structure of complex languages, especially natural languages; it is a recursive transition network with the addition of registers and conditional tests.

Automatic Programming is a subfield of AI and software engineering that studies systems that can themselves either write new computer programs or modify existing ones.

B* is an iterative search algorithm mainly used for game trees; it is similar to alpha-beta pruning, differing in its maintenance of separate "optimistic" and "pessimistic" evaluations for positions.

Backtracking (Chronological/Dependency-directed) is a control strategy that retracts decisions when they lead to unsatisfactory consequences; chronological backtracking goes in the order the choices were made, whereas dependency-directed backtracking identifies the choices that the failure resulted from and goes directly back to them.

Backward Chaining is an inference algorithm for production systems that starts with a fact to be proved and finds all the rules with that fact in their action parts; it then tries recursively to satisfy the conditions of those rules, working backwards from a hypothesis through a proof that it is correct.

Bayesian Inference is a means by which a reasoning system can use Bayes's Theorem to handle uncertain information using conditional and prior probabilities, either alone or in combination with a rule-based system; it is a more formal technique than the certainty factors used in MYCIN and its derivatives.

Best-First Search is a state-space search technique that uses heuristic information about the desirability of states—their distance from the goal state—to order them for exploration as the search tree is generated; not guaranteed to find optimal solutions.

Bitmap is a low-level representation in image understanding that indicates the gray-scale intensity of each pixel in a two-dimensional array representing the input image.

Blind Search is any type of non-heuristic, uninformed search strategy.

Blocks World is a microworld—an unrealistic toy problem domain—used by many AI systems in lieu of a real-world situation; it has many of the superficial characteristics of more general domains but is difficult to expand without enormous complications.

Bottom-up (Parsing/Processing) is a data-driven problem-solving strategy that proceeds from the data input to a procedure up a hierarchy—a grammar in parsing, a tree-structured knowledge base in expert systems, or a representation system in vision—to the solution of the problem. (See also *Top-down*.)

Branch-and-Bound Search — see *uniform-cost search*.

Branching Factor is the average number of children per node in a tree, and measures the "bushiness" of the tree and the rate at which it grows in size.

Breadth-First Search is a search technique that explores the search tree one level at a time, expanding all states on a level before moving on to the next; it is guaranteed to terminate in an optimal solution, measured only in the number of states expanded.

British Museum Procedure is a horribly inefficient search algorithm that generates moves or operators at random until it arrives at the desired problem solution.

Candidate Elimination is a version-space learning procedure for single concept descriptions that removes from the set of possible concepts all candidates that do not cover a new positive example or that do cover a new negative example.

Candidate Generation is a procedure used in diagnostic reasoning systems to reduce the set of possibly faulty components by generating suspects and then either proving or disproving that they could be faulty.

Certainty Factor (CF) is a numeric value, often ranging from -1.0 to +1.0, with 0.0 indicating no knowledge, that represents the degree of certainty attached to a fact or conclusion; certain inference rules can compute the certainty of inferences based on the certainties of their premises.

Children are the successors of a node in a tree, represented in pictures as nodes below their common parent node.

Chinese Room is a metaphor used by John Searle to describe a computer that is programmed to display intelligent behavior; a non-Chinese can learn the Chinese language well enough to fool people without any knowledge of what he is saying, but he is not really understanding the language, just as a computer cannot really understand the world.

Chunking is a mechanism for rote learning and skill acquisition that generally involves abstracting information from previous problem-solving experiences to create new rules that lessen the amount of search required by skipping over intermediate states.

Cognition is the process of producing intelligent behavior by computing and/or thinking; the basic tenet of AI and cognitive science is that all cognitive phenomena arise from some form of computation.

Cognitive Modelling is an approach to creating intelligent behavior by directly simulating processes known or believed to occur in the human brain, as opposed to creating procedures that seem to "do the right thing" regardless of their mental authenticity.

Cognitive Science is the study of human intelligence (one of the goals of AI) using the techniques and knowledge of experimental psychology, computer science, neurobiology, linguistics, philosophy, and anthropology.

Combinatorial Explosion is the fundamental problem in any search-based system that limits its practical usefulness with large problem spaces, in which the number of alternatives to explore increases very fast as the search progresses; for example, a search tree with branching factor 5 can only be explored one level deeper by a computer 5 times faster.

Commonsense Knowledge is the everyday knowledge about the world and its contents that underlies most other, domain-specific knowledge; it is the kind of declarative knowledge we usually want to represent with semantic networks and frame systems.

Computer Vision — see *image understanding*.

Conceptual Dependency (CD) is a theory of semantics developed for representing all knowledge in natural language understanding applications that is based on a system of eleven primitive acts into which all others can be decomposed. (See also *scripts*.)

Condition is an element in the premise part of a production rule; often, the conditions are conjoined, so that all must be satisfied for the rule to trigger.

Confidence Value — see *certainty factor*.

Conflict Set is a structure that collects all the rules in a production system that can fire in any given cycle of the system; that is, all productions whose antecedent conditions are satisfied by the current contents of working memory.

Conflict-Resolution Strategy is a predefined method for deciding which rule in a production system should fire in a cycle when more than one are triggered (the conflict set contains more than one rule); examples would include selecting the rule with the highest certainty factor, the one highest in a pre-established order, or the first one to enter the conflict set.

Connection Machine is a massively parallel computer with tens of thousands of highly interconnected, tiny 1-bit processors; it is suitable for connectionist simulations and other large-input tasks requiring high speed.

Connectionism is a framework and methodology for cognitive modelling that represents information processing at a fundamentally lower level than traditional symbol manipulation, a level whose primitive units resemble neurons and their connections rather than symbols and higher level structures built out of them.

Consequent — see *action*.

Constraint Satisfaction is a powerful problem-solving method in AI that views the problem space as a set of constraints on the solution that can be applied at intermediate points to drastically curtail search; in connectionist networks, local constraints represented by lateral inhibition can be satisfied by a relaxation process. (See also *Waltz's algorithm*.)

Constraint Suspension is a new algorithm for candidate generation that represents the system being diagnosed as a network of constraints and then selectively suspends those constraints one-by-one; a component whose behavior becomes globally consistent when the rules governing its operation are suspended is a likely candidate.

Context-Free Grammar (CFG) is a grammar whose constituents are terminal symbols, nonterminal symbols, and rewrite rules that have a single nonterminal on their left-hand sides and a string of any symbols on their right-hand sides; therefore, the legal rewritings of a nonterminal symbol do not depend on the other symbols near it.

Context-Sensitive Grammar (CSG) is a grammar identical to a context-free grammar but whose rewrite rules may contain both terminal and nonterminal symbols in their left-hand sides.

Control Strategy is an overall method to control the flow of processing in problem solving algorithms; examples include depth-first or breadth-first for search and forward or backward chaining for production systems.

Convolution — see *filtering*.

Cost Function is a procedure, modelled as a mathematical function mapping states onto numbers, that computes the expense of getting to a state (that has already been reached) in a state-space from the start state.

Credit-assignment Problem in learning is that of determining which procedures in the preformance element contributed to a correct solution and which did not, so that the learning element can modify the appropriate portions of the system.

Data-Driven — see *bottom-up*.

Decision Procedure is a precise algorithm that takes as input a string of symbols and decides whether or not it is a member of a language; therefore, a particular decision procedure is taken to define a non-finite language.

Declarative Knowledge is ordinary knowledge about concepts and the relationships between them, independent of any procedures to manipulate them.

Deduction is a sound process of logical inference that uses the following rule: given A implies B, if we know A to be true, we can conclude that B is also true; it is this sound rule, called *modus ponens*, which underlies virtually all logical arguments and proofs.

Default Value in a frame system is a value that a property of a new concept automatically receives, normally through inheritance, until it gets its own value directly.

Depth-First Search is a search technique that pursues paths in the state-space as far down as possible before backing up and choosing different alternatives; in infinite state spaces it will never terminate, but it often finds solutions quicker than breadth-first search.

Discourse Analysis is a level of natural language processing that tries to understand a sentence and resolve its ambiguities by placing it in the framework of the overall conversation; it involves considerations of intention, motivation, prejudice, and so on.

Discrimination Network is a tree-structured device that classifies objects into categories by branching through tests on their features until it reaches a leaf that names the proper class.

Domain is an area or field of expertise and knowledge, either of a human being or computer program, that delimits the class of problems to which the system can be applied.

Edge is a boundary between two surfaces in a visual scene, the detection of which is the major problem for early low-level vision. (See also *arc*.)

EPAM (Elementary Perceiver And Memorizer) is a system developed by Feigenbaum and Simon for learning simple concepts and categories based on a discrimination network that grows as new positive training examples are presented.

Evaluation Function is a procedure, modelled as a mathematical function mapping states onto numbers, that computes the desirability of a state in a state-space by estimating its distance to a goal state, or the cost of solving the problem from that starting point.

Expert System (ES) is a knowledge-based system capable of performance in some restricted problem domain comparable to or better than that of human experts; it often has the ability to explain its conclusions and interactively acquire new knowledge.

Expert Systems Shell is an "empty" expert system with all the components but the domain-specific knowledge base, which can be created by a human expert without AI experience; it usually provides interactive guidance to simplify the initial knowledge acquisition process.

Explanation Facility is the capability of an expert system's inference engine to explain to its users how it reaches its conclusions by describing which rules (in the case of a production system knowledge base) were fired, when, and why or why not.

Extension is the definition of a concept according to the examples of it in the world; extensionally, the "morning star" is the same as the "evening star" because the two terms denote the same physical object.

Facet — see *slot*.

Feature is an attribute or distinguishing aspect of a concept or object.

Feature Vector is a representation for concepts in learning systems that simply lists an object's feature names and their values; it is similar to a frame but strictly specifies only intensional features and not extensional properties like class membership.

Filler is a value that occupies a slot in a frame, often represented as a pointer to another frame in a frame system.

Filtering is a process used by perception systems to modify its input, in content but not in format, in order to remove noise and highlight its important features and regularities; in vision, this consists of applying various mathematical functions to each point in a bitmap.

Finite Automaton (FA) is the simplest interesting computational device; it can model the decision procedure for any regular language but cannot handle all context-free languages.

Fire is for a rule that has already been triggered to be selected for application and have its action part executed.

Forward Chaining is an inference algorithm for production systems that operates in cycles, each time collecting all the rules that trigger, choosing one (conflict resolution), firing it, and repeating the process until no productions trigger.

Frame is a data structure, similar to a record in a relational database, which represents a concept with a name and various properties arranged in slot/filler pairs.

Frame Problem is a notorious representation and reasoning problem that asks how a system can know which elements of its knowledge become invalid as time passes, as when a robot moves into a new room and must somehow "unlearn" that it was at its previous location.

Frame System is an inheritance hierarchy of frames, including default values and procedure attachment, to make a complete system for representing declarative knowledge.

Fuzzy Reasoning — see *reasoning under uncertainty*.

Game Tree is a search tree used in adversarial game playing situations, in which the states are board positions and the operators legal moves.

Generalization is the act of converting a specific concept into a new concept that covers, or subsumes, both the original concept as well as one or more additional concepts; it is an unsound form of logical reasoning, but an essential operation in learning from examples.

Generalized Cones/Cylinders are the primitive elements in a structural representation of three-dimensional objects in which any element is composed of several connected axes, as in the stick figure of a man, with closed figures of varying size surrounding them.

Generate-and-Test is a problem solving strategy that hypothesizes entire solutions at once and then checks them for correctness, rather than building up a solution that is known to be correct the first time, as in optimal heuristic search.

Genetic Algorithms are adaptive search techniques based on principles derived from natural population genetics, and are currently being applied to various problems in science, engineering, and AI.

Goal-Directed (Behavior/Reasoning) describes a system that makes its decisions in problem solving on the basis of explicitly represented goal conditions it is trying to establish, as in means-ends analysis or the proof metaphor of backward chaining inference.

Goals/Subgoals are objective states set up for or by a problem solver to guide its search.

Grammar is any formal framework that describes the syntactic structure of a language, usually by establishing various categories for words and sequences, as well as rules that restrict how those sequences may be combined in sentences in the language.

Graph is a structure consisting of nodes and arcs arranged with arbitrary connections, either directed or undirected, that can model the structure of AI concepts such as state-spaces or production systems used in backward chaining.

Heuristic is a rule of thumb, a piece of information that can provide useful guidance to a problem solver but which is not guaranteed to be applicable or beneficial in all situations; it contrasts with an algorithm, which by design specifies a procedure that will always work.

Heuristic Search is search using heuristic knowledge to focus the exploration of the state space on more promising paths, avoiding dead ends, cycles, and blind alleys.

Hill Climbing is a search technique that is similar to best-first search in that it always tries to minimize the distance remaining to the goal (regardless of accumulated cost), but it only retains one node at a time in its OPEN queue; the effect is to have the search get stuck on local "hills," or maxima in the curve of negative remaining distance.

Image Analysis/Understanding is the principal problem for computer vision systems, and consists of processing a perceived image of the external world to extract the important and relevant conceptual information and relationships that describe the contents of the world. (See also *vision*.)

Induction is the process of learning and formulating new concepts given only examples (positive and/or negative) of them.

Inference Engine is the component of an expert system that lies between the knowledge base and the user interface and does the work of making deductions to solve problems; with production systems, it typically uses either a forward or backward chaining algorithm.

Information Processing is an abstraction of the functionings of the brain, mind, and computer to a high enough level to make them identical, not in detail but in input and output conditions; it views processes as "black boxes" whose inner workings need not be precisely understood as long as their input-output mappings can be simulated.

Inheritance enables a concept, such as "dog," in a semantic network or frame system to automatically acquire the properties of its superclass(es), such as "animal" and "mammal," without having them explicitly attached to the concept itself; it works by scanning up the instance and subclass links to find ancestor concepts in the hierarchy.

Intelligence — see Figure 2-1 for attempted definitions.

Intension is the definition of a concept according to its innate properties; intensionally, the "morning star" is different from the "evening star" because the two appear at different characteristic times even though they are the same physical object.

Intentionality is a property, claimed by John Searle to be necessary for true intelligence but impossible to realize in a nonhuman system, that enables concepts to be directed at objects in the real world and underlies mental states like beliefs, desires, goals, and intentions.

Keyword Analysis is a primitive technique of natural language processing, whereby input sentences are scanned for certain special words and patterns that signal actions for the program to take.

Knowledge is any information that is useful for the task being performed.

Knowledge Acquisition is a learning problem for expert systems that involves augmenting the knowledge of a running system, either by receiving it from human experts or by creating it automatically, as in chunking.

Knowledge Base is the store of domain-specific knowledge of an AI program; in a rule-based expert system it is the production system being used by the inference engine.

Knowledge Engineering is the practice of building expert systems by extracting from experts their domain and problem-specific knowledge and representing it in a suitable form for computer implementation.

Knowledge Representation is the science of encoding real-world knowledge in an efficient format that makes it easy for programs to use it and generally satisfies the desiderata listed in Figure 3-1.

Knowledge-Based Approach (to intelligence) says that intelligence arises from vast bodies of knowledge rather than any particularly clever algorithms, and that the right way to design intelligent programs is to build-in large quantities of domain-specific knowledge.

Knowledge-Based System (KBS) is a system that achieves intelligent behavior by using fairly simple algorithms with a large body of specific and commonsense knowledge, rather than by applying powerful but complex algorithms with little domain-specific information.

Language is, formally, a set of strings; if the set is finite, it can be simply enumerated, but if it is infinite it must be represented as a finite decision procedure.

Lateral Inhibition in connectionist networks is the existence of bidirectional, negatively weighted links between mutually inconsistent, competing features at the same level in a recognition hierarchy.

Leaf (Node) is a node in a tree with no children.

Learning is the improvement of performance with experience over time, and includes becoming more efficient, rote learning, category induction, knowledge acquisition, and scientific discovery.

Learning Element is the portion of a learning AI system that decides how to modify the performance element and implements those modifications; it normally includes any learning algorithms employed by the system.

Lisp (List Processing), developed by John McCarthy in the late 1950s, is the dominant programming language for AI research and development because of its built-in facilities for manipulating symbols and lists in sophisticated structures.

Logic is any precisely defined formal reasoning system that includes well-formed-formulae, axioms, and rules of inference that allow new theorems to be deduced from the axioms and other existing theorems; it is used explicitly as a representation and reasoning tool by many, and implicitly in the operation of most, AI systems.

Logic Programming (LP) is the use of logic as a programming language, in which programs consist of axioms and control is exercised by a theorem-proving algorithm.

Machine Learning is the study of making computer systems exhibit learning behavior.

Means-Ends Analysis is a problem-solving strategy that works by analyzing the difference between the current state and the desired goal state and choosing the operator that is thought to be best at reducing that difference; it was pioneered in the GPS system.

Metalevel Knowledge is knowledge about knowledge, or higher-order information in a knowledge base about its organization, structure, and usage.

Metarule is a rule in a knowledge base whose conditions and actions mention both elements in working memory and other rules in the system; it is most commonly used to control the search conducted by the inference engine in ways the standard algorithms cannot.

MINIMAX is a method for searching game trees that deals with an adversary by assuming that he will always choose moves to minimize the result or static evaluation (towards $-\infty$) at his turn; if the player on move always tries to maximize, the line of best play can be found.

Morpheme is a combination of phonemes that is a valid word in the language being used.

Natural Language Interface (NLI) is a program used as a front-end to an application program, such as a database manager or expert system, that enables the user to communicate with the application in a subset of a natural language like English instead of the special language and commands of the software.

Natural Language Processing (NLP) is the problem of constructing internal representations of input in a human language like English or a subset of it, to convert information from a language convenient for the user into one convenient for the computer system.

Network — see *graph*.

Neural Network in biology is a interconnected web of nerve cells; in AI it denotes a parallel distributed processing network modelled closely on the properties of real neurons.

Nonmonotonic Logic is any system of logic in which the set of axioms and theorems is permitted to decrease in size as time goes on, and is one way to attack the frame problem.

Nonterminal Symbol in a grammar does not appear in the sentences of the language generated by the grammar, but rather represents a category or legal combination of symbols in the rewrite rules of the grammar, such as NP for "noun phrase" in English.

Object-Oriented Programming (OOP) is a metaphor for computation, often used in AI systems, that considers programs as collections of semi-autonomous objects that get work done by sending messages back and forth, executing instructions received from other objects, and returning results.

Operationalization is the process of implementing in the performance element improvements discovered by the learning element in an AI system; it can sometimes be circumvented by the single-representation trick, which ensures that the knowledge used by the PE and LE is in a consistent, interchangeable format.

Operators are procedures, modelled as mathematical functions, that can be applied to problem states in state-spaces to transform them into other legal states; solving a problem consists of applying a sequence of operators to transform the start into a goal state.

OPS5 is the most popular language for rule-based programming with production systems; it uses forward chaining control with a fast conflict-resolution algorithm.

Parallel Distributed Processing (PDP) — see *connectionism*.

Parsing is the lowest level of natural language processing, and is concerned with deciding whether and how a sentence is a member of a language by examining its syntactic structure.

Path in state-space search is a sequence of operators in a search tree.

Pattern Matching takes a specific structure and a more general model structure (the pattern) and determines whether one is a specific instance of the other, and if so, how the variable elements in the pattern are instantiated in the example.

Perception is the process of receiving continuous stimulation from the environment, in forms like light for vision or sound for speech understanding, and deriving its relevant semantic contents by constructing a conceptual representation of it.

Pixel (Picture Element) is a single cell in an image, usually represented as a bitmap of intensity values.

Phenomonology is a philosophical theory of intelligence, proposed as an alternative to the "rationality" represented by information processing, which stresses environmental factors and the contribution of social context and expectations to perception and cognitive acts.

Phonemes are elementary units of speech that compose spoken utterances, such as vowel and diphthong sounds in English.

Planning is the process of preparing in advance of an action a procedure or set of guidelines for performing it; search can be viewed as inefficient, primitive planning that does not allow for contingencies.

Pragmatics is the area of linguistics that studies the interactions between sentences to understand ambiguities like pronoun reference and intended meanings; also, a level of dialogue analysis in natural language processing that seeks to solve the problems developed by such ambiguities.

Preference Semantics is a system of semantic primitives that uses about 75 basic objects and relations in various combinations to represent more complex concepts.

Premise is the antecedent IF-part on the left-hand side of a production rule that lists the conditions under which the rule is applicable and whose satisfaction is necessary before the rule can be used.

Prepare/Deliberate Tradeoff is the fundamental constraint of knowledge-based systems, which states that the amount of search (deliberation) required to solve problems at a given level of performance will decline as the amount of knowledge (preparation) increases.

Primal Sketch is an intermediate representation in visual processing between the low-level bitmap and the high-level conceptual model of the image to be understood; it segregates the image into regions like lines and blobs, and indicates the two-dimensional orientation of each grouping.

Problem Space — see *state space*.

Procedural Knowledge is knowledge about how to perform various tasks, usually represented by procedures that do them.

Procedure Attachment is the augmentation of a slot in a frame with an entire procedure to compute its filler whenever its value is needed, such as a function to calculate densities from masses and volumes.

Production Rule is an IF-THEN, premise-action association used to represent both declarative and procedural knowledge needed to solve problems.

Production System is an organized collection of production rules that work together to solve one or more problems under an appropriate inference algorithm.

Program Synthesis/Transformation — see *automatic programming*.

Prolog (Programming in Logic) is the most popular logic programming language used for AI applications, especially natural language processing with its built-in definite clause grammar facility and expert systems with its backward-chaining theorem prover.

Qualitative Reasoning is understanding and reasoning about real-world physical processes, such as those operating in a digital computer or nuclear reactor, in non-numeric terms.

Reason Maintenance System (RMS) is an extended truth maintenance system capable of handling inferences in nonmonotonic logic.

Reasoning Under Uncertainty is the problem of making inferences and solving problems when some of the input data or stored knowledge is not known to be true; it often involves assigning certainties or probabilities to pieces of information and developing procedures that can calculate the certainty of their conclusions from the certainties of their inputs.

Recursion occurs when a procedure causes itself to be executed, either by calling it directly or by calling another procedure that in turn calls the original, before it has completed its computations; it is contrasted with iteration, when a procedure loops within itself.

Recursive Transition Network (RTN) is a device that parses sentences with context-free grammars by representing the set of rules for rewriting each nonterminal symbol as a separate finite automaton that can make recursive jumps to other automata as the condition for branching to a new state.

Regular Expression (RE) is a simple formalism for representing regular languages.

Regular Grammar (RG) is a restricted context-free grammar, allowing only rules with a single nonterminal symbol on the right-hand side, that is just powerful enough to represent regular languages.

Regular Language is the simplest type of language, and includes all finite languages as well as those infinite languages which follow simple linear patterns; natural languages are most definitely not regular.

Relaxation is a method of constraint satisfaction and computation in connectionist networks that repeatedly updates the contents of a network until it reaches quiescence, indicating that it has stabilized in a solution that satisfies all the local constraints.

Rewrite Rule is a rule in a grammar that allows the replacement of a combination of symbols by another combination of symbols so as either to generate sentences of the language (top-down) or reduce a given sentence to the root symbol S (bottom-up).

Robotics is a research program that studies the construction of artificial autonomous agents, fully intelligent and able to perceive their environment and move about in it just like a human being.

Root (Node) is the node at the top of a tree, from which all other nodes in the tree ultimately stem; in search trees it represents the start state, in game trees it represents the starting position, and in backward chaining it represents the initial fact to be proved.

Rote Learning is learning by memorization, free of any real understanding of what is being learned or why.

Rule — see *production rule*.

Rule-Based (Programming/System) describes a methodology that views programs declaratively, as production systems or sets of logical axioms, rather than as collections of interactive procedures; it embodies the knowledge-based approach used in applied AI.

Scene Analysis/Understanding — see *image analysis/understanding*.

Script is a structure that represents stories and plans as sequences of primitive actions represented in conceptual dependency theory; together with information about time, location, etc. it can be used in language understanding for filling in missing details, answering questions about narrative texts, and other purposes.

Search is the process of exploring alternative courses of action in order to solve problems or make plans for their later solution.

Search Space — see *state space*.

Search Tree is a model of state-space search processes in which the start state is the root node, the children of a node are those states which can be reached from it by the application of a single operator, and the goal states are leaves in the fully constructed tree.

Semantic Grammar is a type of grammar used in natural language interfaces in which the semantic analysis of input sentences is collapsed into the syntactic parsing process.

Semantic Network is a knowledge representation formalism that presents each concept as a node in a graph and the relations between concepts as labelled arcs between nodes; the meaning of a concept is derived from its relationships to all other concepts in the network.

Semantic Primitives are elementary units of meaning out of which all other concepts are composed, and are used to provide a base level of representation which, if it can be reasoned with soundly, allows us to manipulate all other concepts that can be represented.

Semantics is the level of analysis in natural language processing that is concerned with the meaning of sentences, which is derived from the meanings of component words and phrases and from the surrounding context.

Single-Representation Trick — see under *operationalization*.

Slot is an element in a frame that represents a property or feature of the object, whose value is contained in the filler for the slot.

Smalltalk is an object-oriented programming language and graphics-based development environment that is often used for AI applications.

Sombrero Filtering is a filtering process for images that applies a function shaped like a Mexican hat to each neighborhood in the bitmap and has the effect of highlighting edges by transforming them into zero-crossings.

Speech Recognition/Understanding is the perceptual problem of transducing some auditory input, represented as a two-dimensional graph of intensity over time, into a representation of the language it encodes, when the problem becomes one of natural language processing.

State Space is a representation of a problem domain as a set of states, or configurations of the problem elements, and operators, or manipulations that convert one state into another, that can be drawn as a directed graph in which nodes are states and arcs are operators.

Store/Compute Tradeoff — see *prepare/deliberate tradeoff*.

Stored-Program Digital Computer is a device, essentially equivalent in computational power to a Turing Machine, which gets its instructions from its own writable memory rather than a separate control store; therefore, its programs can modify themselves and be replaced without building a whole new machine.

Strong AI is the name given by John Searle to a research program whose goal is the creation of a complete artificial mind that will actually understand and experience cognitive states in the same way the human mind does. (See also *robotics*, *weak AI*.)

Symbol is the elementary object in a traditional information processing AI theory, in which intelligent behavior is believed to arise from the manipulation of discrete symbols that refer to real-world concepts or combinations of them; in natural language processing, a symbol is any element in the alphabet of the language under consideration.

Syntax is the level of analysis in language processing that decides whether a sentence is in a language and how its structural features make it a member of the language; it interacts strongly with the levels of semantics and pragmatics.

Terminal Symbol is a character in the alphabet for a particular language which can appear in strings that are sentences of that language, such as "a" or "b" for English.

Top-down (Parsing/Processing) is the characteristic approach of an analytic system that starts with a high-level description of the input to be recognized, such as an expectation of what it might be, and attempts to fit the data to that hypothesis (if possible); if it fails, it can try different hypotheses, possibly derived from preliminary bottom-up processes.

Transformational Grammar is a syntactic theory that extends context-free grammar by allowing various surface-level transformations that maintain the "deep structure" of a parse tree for a sentence while changing aspects like interrogative or declarative case; it therefore represents different forms of the same sentence essentially identically.

Tree is a directed acyclic graph with unique parents, a structure consisting of nodes and arcs between them arranged in a tree shape with the single root node at the top. (See also *node, arc, children, root, leaf.*)

Trigger is for a rule's premise to be satisfied by data in working memory, thus making it ready to fire.

Truth Maintenance System (TMS) is a device for recording the justifications of conclusions so that if a once-proved theorem should become invalid, those theorems whose proof relied on it can be retracted or rejustified without disturbing others that are still valid.

Turing Machine (TM) is a formal model of computation that is maximally general in that any possible computational process can be executed by an appropriately constructed TM.

Turing Test (TT) is an empirical test that decrees a computer system intelligent if a human examiner cannot distinguish (at better than chance level) between in an a human witness in anonymous conversation.

Type/Token Distinction is the problem in knowledge representation of determining which of a concept's properties apply only to the instances of the concept (the tokens) and which apply only to the concept itself (the type).

Uniform-cost Search is a state-space search algorithm which uses a cost function to compute the expense of paths in the search tree and always expands the partial path of minimum cost; it degrades to breadth-first search when all operators have equal cost.

Units in connectionist, parallel distributed processing networks, are highly interconnected, tiny processors that compute simple functions of their input signals from other units to produce a similar output result.

Version Space is a structure used by the candidate-elimination algorithm for single concept learning; using feature-vector representations, it evolves separate necessary and sufficient conditions for category membership.

Vertex is a point at the junction of two edges in a visual scene; when scenes are constrained to come from the blocks world, there are a limited number of legal vertex types, which can be identified using Waltz's Algorithm. (See also *node*.)

Vision is the process of receiving, transducing, and understanding images represented initially as light and finally as an appropriate and useful conceptual structure. (See also *computer vision*.)

Von Neumann Bottleneck is a problem that arises in serial, stored-program digital computers when the channel between memory and central processor is not "wide enough" to accommodate the enormous traffic and competition for resources; it has led to the development of "non-Von Neumann" parallel architectures, as in the Connection Machine.

Waltz's Algorithm is an extension and fundamental improvement on work by Huffman and Clowes on determining the orientation of vertices in three-dimensional blocks world images; it introduced the techniques of real-world constraints and their propagation through networks to solve problems.

Weak AI is the name given by John Searle to a research program that views AI as a tool for exploring human behavior and cognitive processes and for producing useful computer applications. (See also *strong AI*.)

Weak Methods are techniques for problem solving in AI that are largely independent of any special knowledge or specific problem; heuristic search algorithms are the most common weak methods.

Working Memory (WM) in a production system holds transient data about the problem currently being solved, such as facts given or deduced about the problem; in psychology, this is called short-term memory, whereas long-term memory stores the system's actual production rules and the procedures they use.

Zero-crossing is a point or line in a filtered image between two pixel groups, one of which is all positive and the other all negative, that can be used to determine edges in the original image when the filtering procedure is appropriate.

APPENDIX 5: TURBO PASCAL SUMMARY

This appendix provides brief instructions on compiling and running the programs presented in Chapters 3 through 7, as well as summary reference information on Turbo Pascal 3.0 for the MS-DOS environment. If you have a CP/M or non-Turbo Pascal system, consult its reference manual and other documentation. If you want to use the Modula-2 language, you will have to convert the programs first; we recommend Wirth's *Programming in Modula-2*, 3rd edition and Jensen and Wirth's *Pascal User Manual and Report*, 3rd edition as the standard works to consult.

If you have a hard disk, put all the programs in your Turbo Pascal directory; if you have only floppy disks, you should be able to fit the Turbo Pascal 3.0 files *TURBO.COM*, *TURBO.MSG*, and all the programs on one single-sided double-density disk (360K). We strongly encourage you to make backup copies of all programs before trying to compile and run them. When you are ready to experiment, enter the Turbo Pascal environment. The following menu screen will be displayed:

```
Logged drive: A

Work file:
Main file:

Edit      Compile   Run    Save
Dir       Quit compiler    Options

Text:     0 bytes
Free: 62903 bytes

>
```

From here you can press **W** to load the source code for one of the programs into Turbo Pascal's workspace, or **E** to modify or type in a program. Always be sure to

302

save your work with **S**. Testing a program is as simple as pressing **C** and **R**. For more information on the main menu, see the Turbo Pascal Reference Manual.

Compiler Directives

Enclose in comments, precede by $, as in {$B-}.

A	Absolute code (no recursion)	default A+	(CP/M-80 only)
B	I/O mode selection	default B+	
C	Control-S and -C	default C+	
D	Device Checking	default D+	(MS-DOS, PC-DOS only)
F	Number of open files	default F16	(MS-DOS, PC-DOS only)
G	Input file buffer	default G0	(MS-DOS, PC-DOS only)
I	I/O error handling	default I+	
I	Include files		
K	Stack checking	default K+	(not available under CP/M-80)
P	Output file buffer	default P0	(MS-DOS, PC-DOS only)
R	Index range checking	default R-	
U	User interrupt	default U-	
V	**var**-parameter type checking	default V+	
W	Nesting of **with** statements	default W2	(CP/M-80 only)
X	Array optimization	default X+	(CP/M-80 only)

Compiler Error Messages

01	; expected
02	: expected
03	, expected
04	(expected
05	) expected
06	= expected
07	:= expected
08	[expected
09	] expected
10	. expected
11	.. expected
12	**begin** expected

13   **do** expected
14   **end** expected
15   **of** expected
17   **then** expected
18   **to** or **downto** expected
20   Boolean expression expected
21   File variable expected
22   Integer constant expected
23   Integer expression expected
24   Integer variable expected
25   Integer or real constant expected
26   Integer or real expression expected
27   Integer or real variable expected
28   Pointer variable expected
29   Record variable expected
30   Simple type expected
31   Simple expression expected
32   String constant expected
33   String expression expected
34   String variable expected
35   Textfile expected
36   Type identifier expected
37   Untyped file expected
40   Undefined label
41   Unknown identifier or syntax error
42   Undefined pointer type in preceding type definitions
43   Duplicate identifier or label
44   Type mismatch
45   Constant out of range
46   Constant and **case** selector type do not match
47   Operand type(s) does not match operator
48   Invalid result type
49   Invalid string length
50   String constant length does not match type
51   Invalid subrange base type
52   Lower bound greater than upper bound
53   Reserved word
54   Illegal assignment
55   String constant exceeds line

56	Error in integer constant
57	Error in real constant
58	Illegal character in identifier
60	Constants are not allowed here
61	Files and pointers are not allowed here
62	Structured variables are not allowed here
63	Textfiles are not allowed here
64	Textfiles and untyped files are not allowed here
65	Untyped files are not allowed here
66	I/O not allowed here
67	Files must be **var** parameters
68	File components may not be files
69	Invalid ordering of fields
70	Set base type out of range
71	Invalid **goto**
72	Label not within current block
73	Unidentified **forward** procedure(s)
74	**inline** error
75	Illegal use of **absolute**
90	File not found
91	Unexpected end of source
97	Too many nested **with** blocks
98	Memory overflow
99	Compiler overflow

Editor Commands

^ means hold down the Control key.

^S	Move cursor left one character
^D	Move cursor right one character
^I	Move cursor right to next tab or back to left margin (also TAB)
^E	Move cursor up one line
^X	Move cursor down one line
^A	Move cursor left one word
^F	Move cursor right one word
^W	Scroll screen up one line
^Z	Scroll screen down one line

^R	Move cursor up one screen page of text
^C	Move cursor down one screen page of text
^Q,S	Move cursor to beginning of line
^Q,D	Move cursor to end of line
^Q,E	Move cursor to top of screen
^Q,X	Move cursor to bottom of screen
^Q,R	Move cursor to beginning of file
^Q,C	Move cursor to end of file
^Q,B	Move cursor to beginning of marked block
^Q,K	Move cursor to end of marked block
^Q,P	Move cursor to previous cursor position
^G	Delete character at cursor position
^T	Delete word to the right of cursor
^Y	Delete line containing cursor
^Q,Y	Delete from cursor position to end of line
^N	Insert line break at cursor position
^P	Insert special control character
^K,B	Mark beginning of block
^K,K	Mark end of block
^K,T	Mark single word
^K,Y	Delete marked block
^K,H	Hide marked block
^K,C	Copy marked block to cursor position
^K,V	Move marked block to cursor position
^K,W	Write marked block to disk file
^K,R	Insert from disk file at cursor position
^Q,F	Find a given string:

       B: Backwards from cursor position to beginning of text
       G: Global search using entire text regardless of cursor position
       n: Skip the first n-1 occurrences of the search string
       U: Ignore upper/lower case when matching
       W: Find whole words only
       ?: Show command options

^Q,A   Find a given string and replace it with a different string:

       B: Backwards from cursor position to beginning of text
       G: Global search using entire text regardless of cursor position
       n: Skip the first n-1 occurrences of the search string
       N: Replace without asking for confirmation
       U: Ignore upper/lower case when matching

           W: Find whole words only
           ?: Show command options
^L   Repeat the previous find or find/replace operation
^U   Abort command currently in progress
^V   Toggle insert mode on/off
^Q,I   Toggle autoindentation mode on/off
^Q,L   Undo, restoring line to previous contents
^K,D   Exit editor and return to Turbo Menu

I/O Error Messages

01   File does not exist
02   File not open for input
03   File not open for output
04   File not open
10   Error in numeric format
20   Operation not allowed on a logical device
21   Not allowed in direct mode
22   Assign to std files not allowed
90   Record length mismatch
91   Seek beyond end-of-file
99   Unexpected end-of-file
F0   Disk write error
F1   Directory is full
F2   File size overflow
F3   Too many open files
FF   File disappeared

Runtime Error Messages

01   Floating point overflow
02   Division by zero attempted
03   **sqrt** argument error
04   **ln** argument error
10   String length error
11   Invalid string index
90   Index out of range

91   Scalar or subrange out of range
F0   Overlay file not found
FF   Heap-stack collision

Standard Identifiers

Italicized entries are reserved and cannot be redefined.

absolute	exp	mark	sqrt
and	*external*	maxavail	str
arctan	false	maxint	*string*
array	*file*	mem	succ
assign	filepos	memavail	swap
aux	filesize	memw	text
auxinptr	fillchar	*mod*	textbackground
auxoutptr	flush	move	textcolor
begin	*for*	new	textmode
black	*forward*	*nil*	*then*
blue	frac	normvideo	*to*
blockread	freemem	nosound	trm
blockwrite	*function*	*not*	true
boolean	getmem	odd	trunc
brown	*goto*	*of*	*type*
buflen	gotoxy	*or*	*until*
byte	graphbackground	ord	upcase
case	graphcolormode	output	usr
chain	graphmode	overlay	usrinptr
char	graphwindow	*packed*	usroutptr
chr	green	palette	val
close	halt	pi	*var*
clreol	heapptr	plot	wherex
clrscr	hi	port	wherey
con	hires	pos	*while*
concat	hirescolor	pred	white
coninptr	*if*	*procedure*	window
conoutptr	*in*	*program*	*with*
const	*inline*	ptr	write
constptr	input	random	writeln

copy	insert	randomize	*xor*
cos	insline	read	yellow
crtexit	int	readln	
crtinit	integer	real	
cyan	iresult	*record*	
darkgray	kbd	red	
delay	keypressed	release	
delete	*label*	rename	
delline	length	*repeat*	
dispose	lightblue	reset	
div	lightcyan	rewrite	
do	lightgray	round	
downto	lightgreen	seek	
draw	lightmagenta	*set*	
else	lightred	*shl*	
end	ln	*shr*	
eof	lo	sin	
eoln	lowvideo	sizeof	
erase	lst	sound	
execute	lstoutptr	sqr	
exit	magenta	sqrt	

INDEX

A*algorithm, 160-161
A*algorithm in Pascal, 169
    behavior of, 161-162
    measuring search, 163
    new search example, 162-163
alpha-beta algorithm, 184
    alternatives to, 185-186
    analysis of, 184, 186
    enhancements to, 186
alpha-beta pruning, 180-184
alpha-cutoff, 182
artificial intelligence, 1-2
    applications, 2-3
    critics of, 30
    history, 6-8
    important events, 7-8
    term first used, 11
associative memory, 47
augmented transition networks
    (ATN), 90-95
automatic theorem-proving, 6

backtracking, 82
backward chaining, 116-117
BASIC, 105
basic search algorithms, 141
Berliner, Hans, 5, 12, 185
Bernstein, Alex, 5
best-first search, 158-160
beta-cutoff, 182
bitcomp, 197
Block, Ned, 23

Boole, George, 6
bottom-up parsing, 82
Brachman, 70
branch-and-bound search, 147-151
breadth-first algorithms, 48
breadth-first search, 147-151
British Museum procedure, 141-142

candidate generation by
    constraint suspension, 125
candidate-elimination concept
    learning algorithm, 212
certainty factor, 113-114
Charniak, 19, 70
Chinese Room, 34
choice of search algorithm, 167-168
choice-point, 82
Chomsky, Noam, 84
chunking, 205-206
cognitive economy, 53
cognitive modelling, 15
cognitive science, 2
Colby, Kenneth, 23
computer and brain, 14-16
computer vision, 195
concept learning, 207
conceptions, 6
conceptual dependency, 58-59
connectionism, 214-216

constraint network, 125
content-addressable memory, 47
context file, 132
context-free languages, 77
context-free subsets, 84-89
context-sensitive, 90
credit-assignment problem, 206

Davis, Randall, 107, 124-125
decision procedure, 73
declarative knowledge, 29-30
deep structure, 93
defaults and cancellations, 56
deliberation, 28-29
Dell, Gary, 217
DENDRAL, 12
dependency record, 125
depth-first-search, 143-147
derivation, 80
design heuristics, 166-167
diagnosis, 109-112
dictionary network, 50
differentiation program, 25
digital electronics
    troubleshooting, 124-127
Digital Equipment Corp., 106
discrimination, 207-208
distributed representations, 217
domain expert, 127
Dreyfus, Hubert, 30-32, 36

edge detection, 199-202
effective branching factor, 163
eight-puzzle, 162-163, 167
ELIZA, 4, 13, 32
empiricism, 6
EPAM models, 207-211
episodic memory, 57-58
error propagation learning, 216
event hierarchy, 61

expert systems, 4-5, 104-105
    applications of, 105-108
    capabilities of, 108-109
    case study: medical
        diagnosis, 109-112
    components of, 108-109
    performance of, 130-131
extensional meaning, 65

feedback, 217
feedforward network, 216
Feigenbaum, Edward, 207
Feldman, Jerome, 221
filler, 52
first order logic, 66
Forgy, Charles, 106
forward chaining, 116-117
frame systems, 52-53
    database in Pascal, 67-68
    general value inheritance
        procedure, 56
    inheritance in, 55
    problem, 66-67
    structure of, 54

game playing, 5-6
game playing in Pascal, 189-191
game tree, 174-177
Gaussian convolution, 199
general grammars, 90-95
general languages, 77
General Problem Solver, 12
generalist school, 16
Godel's First Incompleteness
    Theorem, 6
Greenblatt, Richard, 5, 12

Harnad, Steven, 23
heuristic evaluation function,
    159

heuristic search, 5, 137
Hillis, W. Daniel, 224
HiTech, 5, 13
Hofstadter, Douglas, 35
horizon effect, 186-187
Human Access Language
    (HAL), 3

if-needed demon, 57
inference engine, 108
information processing, 14, 15
intelligence, 21-23
    attempted definitions of, 22
    detecting and measuring, 23-
        24
    theories of, 21
intelligent searching, 158
intelligent software, 2
intension vs. extension, 65-66
intensional meaning, 65
intentionality, 34
Intersection Search, 49
iterative deepening, 188

keyword analysis, 4
killer move heuristic, 188-189
knowledge base, 108
knowledge engineering, 5, 105,
    127-130
Knowledge Representation
    Hypothesis, 27
knowledge representation, 13,
    27-28, 38-39
    problems in, 62
knowledge-based approach, 26

language, 72-73
    context-free, 79-83, 89-90
    definition, 73-74
    parsing, 76-77

regular, 76-79
larger semantic network, 44
lateral inhibition, 218
laws, 6
learning element, 203
learning rule, 216
left recursion, 82
Leibnitz, Gottfried, 6
lexical bias, 217
links, 40, 47
Lisp, 19, 93
local representations, 217
Lotus, 3

MacHack, 5, 12
machine learning, 203-204
machine translation, 72
MACSYMA, 12
Maida, Anthony, 65, 69
Marcus, Mitchell, 77
Marr, David, 197
maximizing player, 180
McCarthy, John, 11,70
McDermott, John, 19, 70, 106
measurable performance, 23
metalevel knowledge, 118-119
metarules, 118
microscripts, 61
microworld, 13
MINIMAX, 174-176
    algorithm, 176
    refining, 177
minimizing player, 180
Minsky, Marvin, 11, 36, 61
MYCIN, 109-124
    backward-chaining inference
        procedure, 116
    certainty factors, 114-115
    consultation with, 110-111
    forward-chaining inference

procedure, 117
goal-oriented reasoning, 115-
118
production rules, 112-113

name, 52
natural language interface
(Pascal), 98-100
natural language interfaces, 95-
97
natural language processing, 3-4
Necker Cube, 220-221
Newell, Allen, 11
Nilsson, Nils, 168, 172
nodes, 40, 47

operators, 152-154

PADVISOR, 132-134
Palay, Andrew, 186
Papert, Seymour, 31
parallel distributed processing
(PDP), 214
PARRY, 23
parse tree, 81
penetrance, 163
perceiving in parallel, 218-221
perception, 16
performance element, 203
phenomenological theory, 31
phoneme repetition, 217
phonemes, 215
phrase structure trees, 89
pixel, 199
planning, 6
Pollack, Jordan, 220
pragmatics, 74-76
predicate calculus, 66
preparation, 28, 29
prepare/deliberate tradeoff, 28

primacy of knowledge, 28
Principia Mathematica, 7
problem domain, 105, 138
problem-reduction formalism,
138
procedural knowledge, 29-30
procedure attachment, 57
production rules, 5
production system in Pascal,
132-133
programming connectionist
systems, 224
programming exercises, 68-69,
100-101, 133-134, 192-193
programs and exercises, 18
Pylyshyn, Zenon, 34

qualitative reasoning, 124
query language (QL), 96
Quicksort program, 24
quiescence search, 186-188
Quillian, Ross, 40, 70

reasoning under uncertainty, 114
reasoning, 38
recursive transition network
(RTN), 83, 86, 87
recursive-descent parser, 98
references, 19-20, 36-37, 70-71,
102-103, 135-136, 172, 194,
225-226
Reflection Hypothesis, 27
register, 92
representation in vision, 197-199
rewrite rules, 80
robotics, 2
rote learning, 204-207
Rubik's Cube, 168
rule-based expert system, 112
Russell, Bertrand, 7

Schank, Roger, 58, 61, 62
Script Applier Mechanism, 62
scripts for understanding, 59-62
search, 137-140
search applications, 141
search comparison, 151-152
search strategy, 142-143
Searle, John, 33-35
Sejnowski, Terrence, 216
semantic grammar, 96, 97
semantic memory, 49
semantic networks, 40, 41, 49
    architecture of, 40-43
    design of, 43-45
    manipulation of, 46-48
    problems with, 50-52
    Quillian's, 49-50
    simple, 42
    with property relations, 45
semantic primitives, 57
SEMANTIC.PAS, 67-68
semantics, 74-76
sensations, 6
sequential process, 222
Shannon, Claude, 10
Shapiro, Stuart, 65,69
shells, 5
SHRDLU, 12, 13, 32, 59
Simon, Herbert, 11, 14, 31
simulation rules, 125
single-representation trick, 204
Smith, Brian, 27
sombrero filtering edge
    highlighting algorithm, 201
speech production, 215-218
spreading activation, 49
state space search, 137-139
static evaluation function, 177-178
static evaluations, 177-180

strong AI, 33
subway script, 61
supplemental material, 19
symbolic knowledge
    representation, 39
symbolic mathematics, 6
syntax, 74-76

TEIRESIAS, 119-124
terminal symbols, 80
top-down parsing, 82
Total Turing Test,(TTT), 23
Turing Test, 9-13
Turing, Alan, 8, 23
type/token distinction, 62-65

uniform-cost search, 155-158
unstructured domain, 105

Value Inheritance Procedure
    (VIP), 48, 55
value inheritance, 53-56
version space models, 211-214

vision problem, 196-197
von Neumann, John, 35-36, 37

Waltz, David, 220
weak AI, 33
weighted links, 214
Weizenbaum, Joseph, 32-33, 36
Whitehead, Alfred North, 7
Wilks, Yorick, 58
Winograd, Terry, 12, 32, 37
Woods, William, 51, 102
working memory, 108

zero-crossings, 201